HOLY TRINITY: HOLY PEOPLE

The Didsbury Lectures
Series Preface

The Didsbury Lectures, delivered annually at Nazarene Theological College, Manchester, are now a well-established feature on the theological calendar in Britain. The lectures are planned primarily for the academic and church community in Manchester but through their publication have reached a global readership.

The name "Didsbury Lectures" was chosen for its double significance. Didsbury is the location of Nazarene Theological College, but it was also the location of Didsbury College (sometimes known as Didsbury Wesleyan College), established in 1842 for training Wesleyan Methodist ministers.

The Didsbury Lectures were inaugurated in 1979 by Professor F. F. Bruce. He was followed annually by highly regarded scholars who established the series' standard. All have been notable for making high calibre scholarship accessible to interested and informed listeners.

The lectures give a platform for leading thinkers within the historic Christian faith to address topics of current relevance. While each lecturer is given freedom in choice of topic, the series is intended to address topics that traditionally would fall into the category of "Divinity." Beyond that, the college does not set parameters. Didsbury lecturers, in turn, have relished the privilege of engaging in the dialogue between church and academy.

Most Didsbury lecturers have been well-known scholars in the United Kingdom. From the start, the college envisaged the series as a means by which it could contribute to theological discourse between the church and the academic community more widely in Britain and abroad. The publication is an important part of fulfilling that goal. It remains the hope and prayer of the College that each volume will have a lasting and positive impact on the life of the church, and in the service of the gospel of Christ.

** not yet published

† deceased

Holy Trinity: Holy People

The Theology of Christian Perfecting

T. A. NOBLE

CASCADE *Books* · Eugene, Oregon

HOLY TRINITY: HOLY PEOPLE
The Theology of Christian Perfecting

The Didsbury Lectures Series

Cascade Books
A Division of Wipf and Stock Publishers
199 W. 8th Ave., Suite 3
Eugene, OR 97401

www.wipfandstock.com

ISBN 13: 978-1-62032-720-3

Cataloging-in-Publication data:

Noble, Thomas A.

Holy Trinity: holy people : the theology of Christian perfecting / T. A. Noble.

The Didsbury Lectures Series

xvi + 242 p. ; 23 cm. Includes bibliographical references and index.

ISBN 13: 978-1-62032-720-3

1. Sanctification—Biblical teaching. 2. Sanctification—Christianity. 3. Doctrine of sanctification. 4. Holiness. I. Series. II. Title.

BT765 N635 2013

Manufactured in the U.S.A.

In Memoriam

Hugh Rae (1921–2009)
College Principal
whose cheerful wit, perceptive wisdom, and warm humanity
reflected the perfect love of God

Contents

Preface

To be invited to give the thirty-fourth series of Didsbury Lectures at Nazarene Theological College, Manchester in October 2012 was for me a great privilege and delight. The institution of the lecture series in 1979 was at the suggestion of my colleague, Dr Kent Brower, with the advice of his mentor, Prof. F. F. Bruce, who gave the first series. It was then my duty as dean of the college to invite and host the first ten lecturers, including my own former professor, T. F. Torrance. Later teachers of mine included in the series were Prof. J. B. Torrance and Prof. David F. Wright.

Our original intention was to call the series the Frame Lectures, to commemorate the founder of the college, Dr George Frame, but he refused to have any memorials. Had we waited a short time, he would not have been able to stop us! Instead however, since the Church of the Nazarene stands in the Wesleyan tradition, and is now a member of the World Methodist Council, we decided to call the series the "Didsbury Lectures" to commemorate the former Methodist Didsbury College, famous in its day for the Greek scholar, J. H. Moulton, and the theologian, William Burt Pope. Five of the first ten Didsbury lecturers were Methodists.

In keeping with that heritage, I have addressed in these lectures the concern of the Wesleys and their heirs with Christian holiness, and particularly that difficult doctrine of Christian "perfection" which Wesley inherited from the church Fathers. I was in fact asked to address this topic, partly to expand and update the Collins Lectures, which I first gave in 1988 at the then Canadian Nazarene College in Winnipeg (now part of the Ambrose University College in Calgary). I was urged to publish these at that time by the president, Dr Neil Hightower, and the request has come from time to time from various quarters. The same material later formed the substance of the Rothwell Lectures at Southern Nazarene University in Oklahoma in 1995. The late Dr William Greathouse, General Superintendent Emeritus of the Church of the Nazarene, was most enthusiastic and insistent that I should publish them, and even went so far as to reference them in their unpublished privately-circulated version in his recent commentary on Romans, completed not long before he died. I was very conscious, however, that considerable work needed to be done before publication was possible.

In the privately-circulated version, these lectures were used as class texts for students at master's level at the college and also where I now teach, at Nazarene Theological Seminary, Kansas City. They have also served as a reasonably comprehensive introduction to Christian Theology for those whose undergraduate studies were in other disciplines. I have therefore retained chapter 1 on theological method, but this covers matters that are only preliminary. Too much so-called theology gets bogged down in these epistemological issues (like Christian in the Slough of Despond!) and never gets to real theology. The original Collins Lectures form the substance of chapter 1 and chapters 6 to 8, although much has been re-written. Chapters 2 to 5—summarizing the biblical and historical background, Wesley's own doctrine, and a contemporary reformulation of that—have been added. Chapter 9 is new.

My debts are great. My grounding in the Wesleyan tradition came primarily through the preaching of Dr Sydney Martin over twenty-five years during my childhood and youth. Following studies specializing in History and Education at the University of Glasgow and some years of teaching, I undertook theological studies at New College, Edinburgh, specializing in Christian Dogmatics under Professor T. F. Torrance. I well remember his encouragement when as a new student I explained to him my interest in investigating the question of Christian "perfection." Whereas some in the Reformed tradition would have discouraged such an interest, Professor Torrance, with his deep knowledge of the Fathers, was very positive. I would love to be able to discuss this book with him now. He also strengthened the conviction, already formed from my contacts with the Reformed tradition, that theology should be about *God* and not primarily about us. He also instilled in me the vision that whatever we evangelicals say about justification and sanctification (our heritage from the Reformation and the Evangelical revival), must be grounded in the patristic "dogma" and therefore be christocentric, and thus trinitarian. It was under his influence that I pursued my own doctoral studies in the Fathers. He also illuminated the obvious truth (obvious once you have seen it!) that Christian theologians ought not to be engaged in the task of perpetuating division within the church of Christ. Certainly, no tradition should simply abandon its insights, but the task of theology, in order "that they all may be one," is (as he would say) to "cut behind" our disagreements to the central core of Christian belief that "Jesus Christ is Lord" to see whether we could not resolve our differences. That is the spirit in which I approached these lectures: not to perpetuate a Wesleyan "distinctive" or to glory in our being "different" from others, but to persuade all Christians that this is the heritage of the one, holy, catholic, and apostolic church.

My more immediate thanks are due to Nazarene Theological College, Manchester, for the invitation to give the lectures; to my students over more than three decades in both Manchester and Kansas City for their thought-provoking questions; to my colleague, Dr David Rainey, for reading these chapters and for constructive and always convivial conversation; and to Chris Foster for his work in putting the book into the publisher's required house-style. As always, my thanks are due to my wife, Elaine, without whose support and encouragement (not to mention her proofreading) this project would never have been completed.

Thomas A. Noble
Didsbury, Manchester
United Kingdom
September, 2012

Abbreviations

ANF	*Ante-Nicene Fathers: The Writings of the Fathers down to A.D. 325.* 1867–73. Reprint. Edited by Alexander Robertson and James Donaldson. Peabody, MA: Hendrickson, 2004.
C. Ar.	Athanasius, *Orationes contra Arianos* (*Orations against the Arians*)
CCL.	*Corpus Christianorum, Series Latina*
CD	*Church Dogmatics.* Karl Barth. Edited by G. W. Bromiley and T. F. Torrance. Edinburgh: T. & T. Clark, 1956–75.
Civ.	Augustine, *De civitate Dei* (*The City of God*)
Conf.	Augustine, *Confessionum libri XIII* (*Confessions*)
Enarrat. Ps.	Augustine, *Enarrationes in Psalmos* (*Enarrations on the Psalms*)
Ep.	Gregory of Nazianzus, *Epistulae* (*Epistles*)
Epid.	Irenaeus, *Epideixis tou apostolikou kērygmatos* (*Demonstration of the Apostolic Preaching*)
Haer.	Irenaeus, *Adversus haereses* (*Against Heresies*)
Herm *Mand.*	Shepherd of Hermas, *Mandate*
Herm *Vis.*	Shepherd of Hermas, *Vision*
Ign. *Eph.*	Ignatius, *To the Ephesians*
NPNF [1]	*Nicene and Post-Nicene Fathers*, First Series. Edited by Philip Schaff. 14 vols. Edinburgh: T. & T. Clark, 1886–1900.

NPNF[2]	*Nicene and Post-Nicene Fathers*, Second Series. 14 vols. Edited by Philip Schaff and Henry Wace. Edinburgh: T. & T. Clark, 1886–1900.
Or.	Gregory of Nazianzus, *Orationes* (*Orations*)
Paed.	Clement of Alexandria, *Paedagogus*
PG	*Patrologia Graeca*. Edited by J.-P. Migne. 162 vols. Paris: Imprimerie Catholique, 1857–66.
PL	*Patrologia Latina*. Edited by J.-P. Migne. 217 vols. Paris: Imprimerie Catholique, 1844–55.
Psal. Don.	Augustine, *Psalmus contra partem Donati*
NIDNTT	*New International Dictionary of New Testament Theology*. Edited by Colin Brown. 4 vols. Exeter, UK: Paternoster, 1975–78.
Strom.	Clement of Alexandria, *Stromata*
TDNT	*Theological Dictionary of the New Testament*. Edited by G. Kittel and G. Friedrich. Translated by G. W. Bromiley. 10 vols. Grand Rapids: Eerdmans, 1964–74.
Trin.	Augustine, *De Trinitate* (*On the Trinity*)
Vit. Ant.	Athanasius, *Vita Antonii* (*Life of Anthony*)
Vit. Moy.	Gregory of Nyssa, *De Vita Moysis* (*The Life of Moses*)
Works (BE)	*The Bicentennial Edition of the Works of John Wesley*. 35 vols (projected). Edited by Frank Baker and Richard Heitzenrater *et al*. Nashville, TN: Abingdon, 1984–.
Works (Jackson)	*The Works of John Wesley*. 14 vols. Edited by Thomas Jackson. 1872. Reprint. Grand Rapids: Baker, 1979.

1

Preliminaries

Holiness is one of the core concepts of the Christian faith. It runs like a thread through the whole of the canonical Scriptures where we are taught to think of the God of Israel, named in the New Testament "the Father, the Son, and the Holy Spirit," as essentially and inherently holy. But because that is so, the people of God are to be holy. Christian theology must therefore include the concept of sanctification, an understanding of the way in which God "makes holy" (*sanctum facere*) not only a people corporately, but each one personally.

But Christians disagree in their teaching on sanctification. Clearly those who follow Christ will and should be changed by becoming his disciples, but in what ways, and how far? How like their Master can Christians become in this life? How well can they reflect the love of their heavenly Father? How far can they be filled with his Spirit? And can we possibly dare to speak of Christian "perfection"?

Several introductory books in recent decades have tried to set out the differing opinions on this, particularly among the heirs of the Reformation, evangelical Protestants. In *Justification and Sanctification* (1983) Peter Toon dealt with Catholic, Lutheran, Reformed, Anglican, and Wesleyan views.[1] Gundry's *Five Views on Sanctification* (1987) presented what were called the Wesleyan, Reformed, Pentecostal, Keswick, and Augustinian-Dispensational views. Donald Alexander's *Christian Spirituality: Five Views of Sanctification* (1988) included the same views, except that it replaced the last of these with the "Contemplative" view. J. I. Packer in

1. Books referred to in this paragraph are all listed in the Bibliography.

his book *A Passion for Holiness* (1992)[2] carried on the Reformed (or, more specifically, Calvinist) tradition of Bishop J. C. Ryle's book, *Holiness,* written to oppose the teaching given at the Keswick convention. Archbishop Rowan Williams was one of the compilers of a book sub-titled *The Anglican Quest for Holiness* (2001)[3] and an ecumenical and scholarly approach was taken in another compilation edited by Stephen Barton, *Holiness, Past and Present* (2003). The list could be extended.[4]

a) Wesley's Catholic and Evangelical Doctrine

The purpose of this book is to look particularly at the historic Christian teaching on Christian holiness as it was formulated by John Wesley. Stanley Hauerwas commented that in spite of the difficulties in Wesley's doctrine, particularly the troublesome word "perfection," he continued to think "that Wesley was right to hold that the peculiar contribution of Methodists to the church universal lies in our struggle to recover the centrality of holiness as integral to the Christian life."[5] William J. Abraham has characterized Wesley's doctrine of perfection as "an exercise in ascetic theology, which was also a form of realized eschatology that posited a distinctive phenomenology of the Christian life." He argues that the recovery and reformulation of this doctrine requires "much more serious endeavors in historical and systematic theology," and particularly calls for attention to "Methodist dogmatics."[6] Wesleyan theologians such Hauerwas, Dunning, Long, and Lowery have addressed the doctrine of Christian perfection creatively in the context of Moral Theology (*alias* Christian Ethics).[7] The aim here is to develop our understanding of the doctrine in the context of doctrinal theology, otherwise known as Christian Dogmatics. Samuel M. Powell differentiates "academic theology," which is close to philosophy of religion (and, we might add, apologetics), from confessional "church theology."[8] The former seems to attract much attention today, but the latter, church dogmatics, requires much more work for the sake of the

2. American title: *Rediscovering Holiness.*

3. The other editors were Geoffrey Rowell and Kenneth Stevenson.

4. Most recently, see Tidball, *Message of Holiness.*

5. Hauerwas, *Sanctify Them*, 124.

6. Abraham, "Christian Perfection," 597f.

7. Dunning, *Divine Image*; Long, *Wesley's Moral Theology*; Lowery, *Salvaging Wesley's Agenda.*

8. Powell, *Theology of Christian Spirituality.*

church. Philosophical theology may help to keep the wolves at bay (except of course when it is the work of a wolf in sheep's clothing!), but it is church doctrinal theology or dogmatics, working closely with biblical theology, that provides food for the sheep.

In keeping with Wesley's "catholic spirit," we will not present his doctrine of Christian sanctification as merely a series of sectarian "distinctives" of interest only to Wesleyans, but as a view that stands within the mainstream tradition of the Christian church. Sadly, the Wesleyan view has too often been presented in a sectarian way. In the disputes among evangelical Christians in the nineteenth and twentieth centuries, it was often attacked as "sinless perfection," and some of Wesley's heirs deserved to be rebuked for that distortion of his teaching. But unlike his more unbalanced followers, John Wesley was widely read and deeply immersed in the church Fathers and was an Oxford scholar who read the Fathers and the Scriptures in the original languages. He insisted on using the easily misunderstood word "perfection" because of his commitment to Scripture as "a man of one book" (*homo unius libri*). The Bible was Wesley's source of authority for his doctrine, interpreted in the light of the early Fathers and of his own tradition in the Church of England. His doctrine of Christian "perfection" was not, therefore, a new doctrine; it was simply his formulation of the doctrine within the mainstream tradition of the church catholic. The aim here therefore is not just to carry on a conversation within the Wesleyan tradition, but across the church.[9]

One of the key tasks of this book will be to understand from Wesley's own writings what he actually taught. It is necessary to distinguish that from the simplified (and indeed simplistic) teaching of some later teachers who regarded themselves as "Wesleyan."[10] But we will approach Wesley through first undertaking a survey of the ancient Christian tradition that shaped his interpretation of Scripture, noting particularly how far he was echoing the teaching of the Fathers of the church. But of course Wesley was not only an enthusiast for the "primitive Christianity" of the early centuries: he was also an evangelical Protestant. While listening to a reading from Martin Luther, he underwent a conversion in which he trusted in "Christ alone" and received assurance of the forgiveness of his sins. He embraced a doctrine of justification by faith, which, he said, did not differ

---

9. For an introductory textbook for students written from within the Wesleyan tradition, see Leclerc, *Christian Holiness.*

10. We will use "Wesleyan" rather than "Methodist" since not all Wesleyans are Methodists and not all Methodists are Wesleyan.

by a "hair's breadth" from that of John Calvin. It is this embracing of both the Fathers and the Reformers which makes him a figure of great ecumenical significance. His most original contribution to Christian thought was in "practical divinity."[11] He tried to think through how to integrate the teaching of the Fathers and the Reformers in this area of practical Christian living which Protestants have long referred to as "sanctification" and which today is often included in studies of "spirituality."[12] George Croft Cell, one of the pioneers of the twentieth-century rediscovery of Wesley as a theologian, famously wrote: "The Wesleyan reconstruction of the Christian ethic of life is an original and unique synthesis of the Protestant ethic of grace with the Catholic ethic of holiness."[13] That may not be exactly the best wording, but it does indicate that Wesley was what Kenneth Collins calls a "conjunctive" theologian.[14]

Once we have looked at the biblical roots of Wesley's doctrine, surveyed the earlier heritage of spiritual writers through the patristic and medieval periods, and tried to straighten out the tangled web of misunderstandings and distortions that abound about Wesley's own teaching at the popular level, we will then consider the limitations and weaknesses in Wesley's thought. This is important, for the aim is not to champion Wesley against all comers, but to further a deeper understanding among Christians that will help us all in the practical matter of following Christ. Therefore, we must recognize that, while Wesley was a careful scholar and a clear thinker, he was a man of his time. And while he should be regarded (in David McEwan's phrase) as truly a "pastoral theologian"[15] who took consistent theological positions, yet he was not a dogmatician. He did not engage in the kind of Christian dogmatics that tries to think out afresh Christian theology as an organic whole encapsulated in the creeds. He was clearly trinitarian, he clearly embraced orthodox Chalcedonian Christology, and he clearly stood in the Reformation tradition when it came to the doctrines of the atonement and justification by faith. But as a practical theologian of his time, it never occurred to him (or any of his contemporaries) to think through deeply and rigorously how his particular doctrines of "faith, repentance, and holiness" formed an organic whole with

---

11. See Langford, *Practical Divinity*.

12. Among recent works on Christian spirituality by Wesleyan theologians, see Collins, *Exploring Christian Spirituality*, and Powell, *Theology of Christian Spirituality*.

13. Cell, *Rediscovery*, 347.

14. See Collins, *Theology of John Wesley*, 4f.

15. McEwan, *Pastoral Theologian*.

the theology of the creeds.[16] In fact much theology since the Reformation has tended to regard the central doctrines of the faith as "ivory tower" matters. We have so often taken the trinitarian heart of the Christian faith for granted in order to get on with what is thought to be more practical and relevant. Specifically in Wesley's case, he did not engage in thinking through in depth and explaining how his doctrine of Christian perfection flowed out of these central Christian beliefs in the atonement, the incarnation, and the Trinity. As a man of his time, he cannot be blamed for that.

But that is the aim of this book. We begin with the belief of the mainstream of the Christian church—from the Apostolic Fathers through Clement and Athanasius, the Cappadocians, and through the spiritual writers of the Middle Ages up to Wesley and beyond—that Christians may be truly sanctified not only in outward consistency of conduct, but inwardly in such a way as to be truly among the "pure in heart." That is not a universal view, of course. Three of the church's greatest theologians, Augustine, Luther, and Calvin, question whether this level of Christian holiness is possible in this life. Our intention here is not to engage directly in polemics with these major doctors of the church, but we will keep their more pessimistic doctrine in mind as a helpful and necessary corrective and balance as we concentrate on the positive theological development of the long tradition from the Greek Fathers through the medieval writers to Wesley.

But the aim is not just historical. We do not have a merely antiquarian interest in Wesley or any of his predecessors. The aim is to address for today the theological question: what basis is there for this positive view of Christian holiness in the central Christian doctrines—atonement, incarnation, and Trinity? If we truly grasp God's action in the world in the incarnation of the Son by the power of the Holy Spirit in order to fulfill the redemptive will of the Father, does that imply that *already*, even in advance of the death of our bodies and our future resurrection, Christians may be pure in heart? Does the doctrine of the Trinity, focused in salvation from the Father in the Incarnate Son by the Spirit, and taken to be the comprehensive doctrine uniting the whole field of Christian theology, give us a basis for such a hope? Or does the trinitarian structure of Christian theology rather support the belief that the Fall is *so* deep and sin *so* entrenched that we can never love God with all our heart, soul, mind, and strength while we exist in these mortal bodies? Needless to say,

16. See the first two chapters of Campbell's, *Wesleyan Beliefs*, on the "Common Christian Beliefs" and the "Distinctively Methodist Beliefs" in Wesley's theology.

to address such questions within the scope of one little book calls for a broad-brush approach, or, to vary the metaphor, a wide-angle lens. The kind of academic specialism encouraged by minutely careful scholarship will (no doubt) find numerous points for critique. But the church, and particularly the student and the "intelligent lay reader," need to see the big picture. So we will take the risk.

First however, to pursue this aim we need to be clear on how to proceed and it will clarify the procedure we are going to follow to articulate in this first chapter some axioms of theological method. Eastern Orthodox, Roman Catholic, and liberal Protestant theologians will not agree fully with these, but here we are taking the Reformation view that these are essential to doing theology in a Christian way. We are not breaking new ground here, but simply attempting to state in a contemporary way the standard Reformation, evangelical position that Wesley shares.

b) First Axiom: Holy Scripture

The first axiom is that the only source of Christian doctrine is the biblical revelation. That is the Reformation position that Wesley accepted as a loyal member of the Church of England and it is clearly expressed in Article IV of the Thirty-Nine Articles:

> *Of the Sufficiency of the Holy Scriptures for Salvation.* Holy Scripture containeth all things necessary to salvation; so that whatsoever is not read therein, nor may be proved thereby, is not to be required of any man, that it should be believed as an article of the Faith, or be thought requisite or necessary to salvation.

This article asserts that it is part of the faith that the articles or doctrines of the faith must either be explicit in the canonical Scriptures, or implied by them. That is the evangelical or Protestant position of the Reformation. Eastern Orthodoxy may regard the historic ecumenical councils of the church as having equal authority, and Roman Catholics may ascribe to the Pope a certain infallibility. But for Protestants, the evangelical doctrine of the Reformation is that no pope or bishop, superintendent, council, or assembly is superior to the authority of the Word of God as expressed in Holy Scripture. The implication is that no church tradition formulated in any creed or confession or article of faith or statement of doctrine, be it ever so venerable or issued by any ecclesiastical dignitary, be he ever so high, is in principle final and binding, definitive and unrevisable. Every statement of doctrine made by Christians after the passing of the apostles is subject to the authority of the Word of God in Holy Scripture and must be evaluated as an expression of its teaching. The Bible is the one and only source and the one and the only ultimate criterion of Christian doctrine. God has spoken through the prophets and apostles, through the Old Testament and the New, and in drawing up the canon, the church, far from conferring authority on the Scriptures, recognized their authority as the voice and the Word of God.[17] This Reformation position, *sola scriptura*, does not, however, imply the later rationalistic understanding of "inerrancy" developed specifically within American (as distinct from European) Calvinism. Nor does it mean to say that there is no role for church tradition, and we shall come to that positive understanding of its role shortly.

But before we look at the necessary role of the church, several implications follow from this axiom about Scripture. First, it follows that it is not the task of theology merely to expound and elaborate and refine the church's doctrine: that would be a traditional Roman Catholic view of its function. Rather, this gives dogmatic theology a critical function, namely, in every generation to judge the doctrinal statements of the church against the criterion of Holy Scripture. Biblical exegesis, that is to say, must not be held in captivity to dogmatics, as it was in the pre-Reformation Catholic church or (in effect) in the age of Protestant scholasticism. As far as within us lies, exegesis must not become *eisegesis*, reading *into* the text our own doctrinal formulations. Rather, with the reverent, godly use of the tools of biblical criticism, purged from unbelieving and secular presuppositions, the text must be allowed to speak its own message and we must strive to allow it to call in question our understanding of the truth, our doctrinal formulations, so that they may be deepened and expanded and, if need be, corrected. In this way an ongoing dialogue takes place in which the living church of God with its doctrinal formulations listens again and afresh in every generation to the Word of God, and, in the light of new questions and new insights, deepens and corrects its understanding of the truth. That is the ongoing task that has been described as the hermeneutical circle or spiral,[18] and it is this living conversation that gives evangelical Protestant theology its vitality.[19]

17. For Wesley's view of the authority of Scripture, see Jones, *Conception and Use*, also Jones, "The Rule of Scripture," 39–61, and Bullen, *Man of One Book*.

18. See Osborne, *Hermeneutical Spiral*.

19. See McGrath, *Dangerous Idea*, on the revolutionary Protestant belief that each person could interpret the Bible.

To apply this directly to the doctrine of Christian sanctification, this means, to begin with, that biblical phrases such as "wholly sanctify," "filled with the Holy Spirit," "perfect love," "pure in heart," "indwelling sin," or "the mind of the flesh,"[20] have a priority and authority that cannot be accorded to such phrases as "the second blessing,"[21] "the sinful nature,"[22] or "original sin."[23] These latter words and phrases are not found in Scripture. Whether they offer a legitimate interpretation of Scripture is up for discussion, but they do not carry the same authority as the biblical phrases. Christians are free to reject this later terminology, but they are bound to come to *some* understanding of the biblical phrases, such as what Paul meant when he prayed that the Thessalonians be "wholly sanctified" or (as Luther translated it) "sanctified through and through."[24]

Secondly, this axiom implies that not only can Christian doctrine not be based merely on church tradition, but it certainly cannot be based on secular thinking. The doctrines of the church cannot be based on any metaphysical system, whether Platonist, Hegelian, or any other, nor can Christian theology find its source in the natural sciences, whether psychology or sociology, biology or cosmology. That does not mean to say that philosophy and science are to be excluded from the *articulation* of Christian theology. The Fathers used Platonism in this way, "spoiling the Egyptians" as they put it, and we may *use* other philosophies and the sciences in our contextualization of the Christian faith in today's multicultural world. But we are not to draw the doctrines of the faith from any of these. These may *shape* our expression of doctrine, but they are not *sources* of Christian theology. Applying that specifically to the doctrine of the Christian life, we may for example make use of psychology in articulating our understanding of Christian sanctification, but we cannot *build* our understanding of Christian sanctification on this modern secular science. The doctrine of the Christian life, including the corporate life of the church as well as our regeneration, justification, sanctification, and the

20. 1 Thess 5:23; Acts 2:4; 4:8; etc.; 1 John 4:17f.; Matt 5:8; Rom 7:17, 20, and 8:7.

21. Wesley had an ambivalent attitude to this term. Letters: 24 March 1757, L., III, 212; 3 April 1772, L., V, 315; 8 Oct. 1774, L., VI, 116.

22. The NIV unfortunately interprets *sarx* in various NT passages as "the sinful nature." This is a misleading interpretation, not a strict translation.

23. According to Williams, *Ideas of the Fall*, 327, the phrase *originale peccatum* first occurs in a discussion of Rom 7:7–25 in Augustine's treatise *de diversis quaestionibus ad Simplicianum* written in AD 397.

24. *Holoteleis* is an adjective meaning "wholly perfect." "Entirely" avoids confusing "wholly" with "holy."

work of the Spirit, must be drawn (like every other doctrine of the faith) from the Word of God in Holy Scripture. It is a doctrine of the faith, not a scientific theory.

c) Second Axiom: Tradition

If the first axiom is the authority of the Bible as the Word of God and its priority over the doctrinal statements handed on to us in the tradition of the church, the second is the legitimacy and necessity of church tradition.[25] It is essential that the church should formulate its doctrines in doctrinal statements, creeds, and articles of faith, and hand these on in its tradition from one generation to another. And while in principle the great creeds of the church are revisable and open to correction from further study of Scripture, yet in fact it is almost unthinkable for Christian theology that these should be abrogated or denied.

The historic creeds do not share in the final authority of the Scriptures, but all evangelical traditions follow the Reformers in believing that the ancient creeds are *in fact* a faithful summary of the teaching of the Scriptures and faithfully draw out their implications. They are indeed the church's hermeneutic for the interpretation of Holy Scripture. Even evangelical Protestants in the Anabaptist and Baptist traditions, who refuse to use the creeds in worship or to require subscription to them, generally accept them in fact in that role. But the creeds are always open to criticism. The Chalcedonian Symbol for example, not itself a creed, but a further clarifying of the second article of the Nicene Creed, is often subjected to criticism for the terminology and conceptuality of "two natures" which it employs to speak of the Person of Christ. It is only this freedom to critique the creeds in the light of Holy Scripture that guarantees that theology is a living, open dialogue between the Word of God and the church, with continuing development and increased understanding, and not a dead system of thought to be preserved like some precious antique and passed on undamaged to the next generation.

This idea of doctrinal development was advocated by John Henry Newman in his *Essay on the Development of Christian Doctrine* (1845), and he carried it from his Anglican heritage into the Roman Church, thus sowing the seeds that later bore fruit in the Second Vatican Council. But it was endorsed early in the twentieth century by the evangelical theologian, James Orr of Glasgow, in lectures later published as *The Progress of*

25. See Ted Campbell, "The Interpretive Role of Tradition," 63–75.

Dogma. It has indeed become a commonplace that Christian doctrines have developed over the centuries. The doctrine of the Trinity, that God is three Persons but one God, is not stated in so many words in Scripture, but had to be inferred as the *implication* of Scripture in a process of development that reached its climax in the late fourth century. The full doctrine of the Person of Christ as one Person in two natures is similarly not stated in so many words, but had to be drawn out as the implication of Scripture in a process reaching its climax in the middle of the fifth century. The doctrine of the atonement arguably did not begin to be fully developed as a distinct area of study until rigorous thinking was initiated by Anselm's work, *Cur Deus Homo*, in the eleventh century. It is no argument therefore against Wesley's understanding of Christian holiness that he reformulated this ancient Christian doctrine of Christian perfection in the language and concepts of the eighteenth century. Wesley was simply further drawing out and formulating the *implications* of Scripture with reference to Christian sanctification, as the Fathers did with respect to the Trinity, Anselm with respect to the atonement, and Luther with respect to justification by faith.

There is therefore a positive place to be assigned to the role of Christian dogmatics.[26] Over the centuries of the Christian era, it has formulated the major doctrines of the Christian faith in the light of Scripture. In this development over the centuries, it has been self-critical, repeatedly criticizing and developing its formulations. Sometimes, development has gone off in the wrong direction, as in the medieval Roman doctrine of Mary.[27] At times, particularly at the Reformation, whole lines of development have been written off as illegitimate in the light of Scripture. But valid development must continue to take place. In the parting words of John Robinson to the Pilgrim Fathers leaving Leiden on the *Mayflower*, "The Lord has yet more light and truth to shed forth from his Word."[28]

From one point of view, this is the ongoing work analyzed by hermeneutics, the study of methods of interpretation. And interpretation must go on in every age. It is now frequently described as the relating of the two

26. "Dogmatic theology" is a better term than "systematic theology." It implies that theological thinking is not a philosophical or metaphysical system but is centered on the *dogma* ("decree") of the church councils, particularly the Nicene Creed, that declaration of faith which articulates the centre and core of Christian convictions.

27. See Bauckham, *Chosen by God*, on "Mariological Excesses" in the medieval period, and the comment of Karl Barth, *CD*, I, 2, 139: "Mariology is an excrescence, i.e., a diseased construct of theological thought."

28. See the hymn based on these words by George Rawson (Hymn 230 in *Congregational Praise*, 259).

horizons,[29] the first-century world of the New Testament and the present day. Or it may be thought of as the "hermeneutical circle," or better still, as Grant Osborne suggested, a *spiral* moving round and upwards from interpretation to text to interpretation and so on.[30] But it is more than the interpretation of a text to make it speak to the present day or the relation of two widely separated horizons. If it is to be truly a spiral, penetrating ever more deeply into the truth, the history of interpretation must be taken into account. And it must lead to the distillation of the results of interpretation, the progressively more sophisticated and nuanced formulation of the truth about God in the creeds and later doctrines, while still inevitably limited to the fallible words and limited concepts of human language and culture. And just as the hermeneutical task is never finished, so the task of theology is never finished. In the light of new questions thrown up by changes in human culture, new aspects of Christian truth come to light. Neither Athanasius nor Augustine, neither Luther nor Calvin, neither Wesley nor any theologian since, has penned the last word.

As long as "this present evil age" lasts, the final definitive theology will never be written. The church must constantly live in the expectation of penetrating more deeply into the truth of God revealed once for all in Jesus Christ and expressed once for all in the Holy Scriptures. An important distinction is made here in the words of Jaroslav Pelikan, "Tradition is the living faith of the dead, traditionalism is the dead faith of the living." It is not a dead traditionalism we must cultivate, but a deeper study of Christian tradition. Any exposition of Christian theology which only takes note of recent writing and ignores the Fathers and the Reformers is bound to be superficial.

With particular reference to the doctrine of sanctification, this second axiom implies that our tradition should be a living one and not a dead one. A dead orthodoxy is a rigid corpse. Or it may be compared to a family heirloom, an antique increasingly useless and irrelevant, destined eventually for the museum. A dead orthodoxy is expressed in language and categories that have petrified. It imagines that it has said the last and final word and therefore in effect claims final authority for itself. But a living orthodoxy tackles the questions of each new generation. A living tradition goes humbly to Scripture with each new set of questions. It goes

29. The simile of the fusion of horizons seems to have originated with Gadamer in *Truth and Method*: trans. of *Wahrheit und Methode*, and was taken up by Pannenberg and Moltmann. Cf. Thistleton, *Two Horizons*.

30. Osborne, *Hermeneutical Spiral*.

to learn, and it develops new models and is not afraid to correct and refine or even perhaps to reject old theological categories in the light of deeper study of Scripture. It is faithful to the essential truth of the tradition, but longs to express it more adequately, more scripturally, with greater insight and penetration, more persuasively and compellingly. The Wesleyan tradition then needs to be a living one in ongoing conversation with the church catholic, not a fossilized and isolated one. That is why it is important to seek to penetrate afresh into the heart of Christian faith in Christ and through Christ in the Father by the Spirit, and to see that the truth of Christian holiness is built upon this foundation and no other.

d) Third Axiom: Rational Spiritual Experience

The third axiom of theological method that we will assume here is the role of what we shall call "rational spiritual experience." This phrase is intended to bring together "reason" and "experience," which have been misleadingly separated, and to qualify the rational experience we are talking about as "spiritual" or "relational."[31]

Since the patristic and Wesleyan scholar, Albert Outler, coined the phrase, the "Wesleyan Quadrilateral," referring to Scripture, tradition, reason, and experience, this has been thought to encapsulate Wesley's theological method. Outler claimed that this was distinctively Wesleyan: "Thus, we can see in Wesley a distinctive theological method, with Scripture as its preeminent norm but interfaced with tradition, reason and Christian experience as dynamic and interactive aids in the interpretation of the Word of God in Scripture."[32] He saw three of these factors—Scripture, tradition, and reason—in the classic Anglican methodology of Hooker and commented: "It was Wesley's special genius that he conceived of adding 'experience' to the traditional Anglican triad." But Outler's view has now become controversial.[33] Wesley certainly used the four terms, although never all at once, and Anglican theology from the time of Hooker is thought to have operated with Scripture, tradition, and reason,[34] and the claim was that, as an eighteenth-century thinker, Wesley added the fourth,

31. See Miles, "Role of Reason," 77–106, and Maddox, "The Enriching Role of Experience," 107–27.

32. Outler, "Wesleyan Quadrilateral," 9.

33. See Abraham, "Quadrilateral," and for a recent summary of the discussion, Thompson, "Outler's Quadrilateral."

34. See Bauckham and Drewery, *Tradition and Reason*.

experience. But the appeal to experience in theology is not original to John Wesley. Perhaps it is better to begin with the proposition that the so-called Wesleyan "Quadrilateral," although easy to remember and a useful teaching tool, is not exclusively Wesleyan and is not a quadrilateral! Just as budding physicists have to learn Boyle's Law and then later learn that it is not in fact true, so perhaps the so-called "Wesleyan Quadrilateral" needs to be treated in the same way.

The so-called quadrilateral is not exclusively Wesleyan because in fact in the modern era, evangelical preachers and theologians, at least since Calvin, have employed all four terms.[35] John Calvin frequently asserted, "Experience teaches . . . (*experientia docet*)."[36] And if by "experience" we are referring particularly to the "religious affections," then as Richard Steele documents, Wesley was to some extent following in the footsteps of the Calvinist theologian, Jonathan Edwards.[37] But more significantly, the so-called quadrilateral is not a quadrilateral, if that is taken to imply, as it appears to, four more or less equal factors, or four factors on the same level. Where it is really misleading is when the four factors are regarded as four distinct *sources* of doctrine. Timothy L. Smith suggested the figure of a three-legged stool, and that is certainly an improvement: Scripture is the floor on which the stool stands, the foundation of doctrine.[38] Doctrine itself is the seat of the stool, standing on this scriptural foundation on three legs, tradition, experience, and reason. The three "legs" then are figurative for the way we interpret Scripture. Randy Maddox expresses it as "a unilateral *rule* of Scripture within a trilateral *hermeneutic* of reason, tradition, and experience."[39] But while that is an improvement, even the figure of the three-legged stool is somewhat misleading. It seems to suggest a movement in only one direction, from Scripture to doctrine, instead of the hermeneutical spiral that is now recognized as more realistic. Further, the separation of reason and experience begs too many epistemological questions.[40]

35. See Noble, "Knowledge of God," and "Scripture and Experience"; also see Rossall, "God's Activity."

36. Torrance, *Hermeneutics*; cf. 24f. and 80.

37. Steele, *"Gracious Affection."*

38. Smith, "John Wesley," 12–15.

39. Maddox, *Responsible Grace*, 46.

40. See Abraham, "Quadrilateral," together with his other acute writings on theological epistemology.

"Reason" comprises not just our ability to reason abstractly following some kind of logical process like Descartes retiring into his stove.[41] Rather our rationality also includes the ability to *interact* with the world around us. It is when people lose that ability that we take them into care! Reason (or better "rationality") is not merely abstract, intellectual thought carried out by a mind in a vacuum. It also includes the intuitive activity of the mind in contact with the world around it in both its physical and personal (or spiritual) dimensions, interacting rationally with persons and things.

True experience is thus rational from the beginning and true reason is experiential. To speak of "Reason" and "Experience" (capitalized!) as distinct factors is a misleading abstraction, for there are no such entities. There are simply people, persons who *know* God corporately within the body of the church, but also personally, each one for himself or herself. That is experiential *knowledge*, as all first-hand knowledge is. As such, it is fully rational, for we are most fully rational when we interact with each other in personal, rational relationships. And we are most rational when God makes himself known to us through his Word and by his Spirit so that we know him and rationally respond in faith (trust) and repentance.[42]

The point of adding the word "spiritual" to the phrase "rational experience" is that, for Christian theologians, our thinking takes place as "faith seeking understanding" (*fides quaerens intellectum*). That is to say: theology takes place within the realm of the "spiritual," understood as the *relational*. Theological thinking *begins* within the *personal relationship* that God has established with his people through his Son by his Spirit.[43] While theology, therefore, engages the intellect, and while God's revelation is always in his Word and therefore conceptual from the beginning, theology is not *merely* an intellectual or academic exercise. It is not merely (as it appears to be in some forms of rationalistic, scholastic fundamentalism) the deducing of abstract doctrines from an inerrant text. It is not merely a rationalistic, scholastic knowledge of abstract "truths" or eternal

41. Descartes, *Discourse on Method*, 2. This presumably means that he sat in the seat which is part of the huge porcelain stoves one sees in the Low Countries. For the following alternative view of "reason" and "experience," see Macmurray, *Self* and *Persons*. See also Polanyi, *Personal Knowledge*, and Torrance, *Theological Science* and *God and Rationality*.

42. See Abraham, *Aldersgate*, for a study of Wesley's "evidences" for the knowledge of God.

43. See Gunter, "Personal and Spiritual Knowledge," on the similarity between Wesley's understanding of the knowledge of God and the understanding of "personal knowledge" in the thought of Michael Polanyi.

"principles." That is Platonism. It is rather analogous to the intellectual, conceptual dimension that is always inherent in relationships between sentient, rational persons. Theology is never merely knowledge of the Bible or knowledge of doctrines, an intellectual system to elaborate and to fight for as a kind of ideology. Theology is the articulation of intelligent, personal knowledge *of the living God,* the God revealed in his Word by his Spirit.

Christian doctrine then is the expression of that knowledge of God we all share in the body, the church. "Experience" is not therefore a distinct *source* of doctrine any more than "Reason" is. The One we experience is the God who makes himself known to his people by his Spirit, but never apart from his Word. Therefore, it is best to say that there is only one source of Christian doctrine, the Word of God.[44] God's revelation in the Word made flesh—known to us through the authoritative witness of the apostles and prophets in Holy Scripture, and experienced by us within the space-time creation by the Spirit—is the only reliable source of truth about God. Any other knowledge we think we have is shadowy and liable to be distorted and misleading. But *our expression* of the Word of truth, that is, church doctrine, is shaped by our rational, spiritual experience of God in and through his Word, and by our rational reflection upon that.

It is important then to emphasize the objective pole expressed in the phrase, "experience *of God.*" One of the dangers of the Pietist and Wesleyan traditions, followed by nineteenth-century revivalism and the twentieth-century Pentecostal and charismatic movements, is the danger of subjectiv*ism,* the seeking of subjective *experiences.* When the word "experience" is used as a noun in the plural in that way, it is used to speak of inner, subjective events happening within the mind and heart of the believer.[45] But Wesley never used the later phrase "crisis experiences": that language was coined in nineteenth-century revivalism and it subtly twists his meaning. The English word "experience" comes from the same root as "experiment" and Wesley used them as virtual synonyms. The famous preface to the *Hymns* explains that the hymns are arranged "according to the experience of real Christians, so that this book is in effect a little body of experimental and practical divinity."[46] "Experimental" religion (like ex-

44. Calvin, *Institutes,* I, xiii, 7: "Therefore, as all revelations from heaven are duly designated by the title the Word of God, so the highest place must be assigned to that substantial Word, the source of all inspiration, which, as being liable to no variation, remains for ever one and the same with God, and is God."

45. See Truesdale, "Reification," 95–119, on the reification of experiences.

46. *Works* (BE) 7:74. I have had the temerity to correct Wesley's punctuation to fit

perimental science) certainly requires a *subject* to do the experimenting or experiencing (so there must be a *subjective* pole), but it focused on the *object*, the *objective* reality that is experienced.[47]

Outler commented that in place of innate ideas or proofs for the existence of God, Wesley put an another notion of the self-evidence of God's reality as strictly implied in the faithful person's awareness of God's gracious presence towards him or her. This awareness of God's gracious "presence" is what Wesley meant by "experience," and it was for him as real and unmistakable a perception as any sensory awareness might be.[48]

Spiritual experience comes when, to complement our five physical senses, the Holy Spirit gives us the spiritual sense to be aware of the presence of the reality of God.[49] The inner subjective response is a response by the Spirit to the objective reality of the true and living God who encounters us. That is to say: while Wesley spoke of his heart being "strangely warmed" at his evangelical conversion, his faith in Christ was not based on his warmed heart: rather, his warmed heart was the consequence of his faith in Christ.

All of this is important since teaching about our own sanctification and talk of "religious experience" can too easily drop into a self-centered kind of subjectivism. But when a young man truly falls in love, it is not simply because he has been seeking for such a subjective event or "experience." Nor is it merely that he is undergoing certain emotional and volitional changes that are changing him subjectively. It is because he has met a person. *There* is the objective reality of his experience. He is not just experiencing some entity, or merely some subjective feeling or inner change called "love," but he is experiencing *her*. And he is never more rational, never more of a man, never more unselfish, never more devoted, never more lifted out of himself, never more full of life and energy, never more intelligent and sparkling and witty, never more at his best, than when he is with *her*! The real change in him is the result of the encounter with a person. *She* is the personal objective reality he experiences and the subjective change in him is the consequence.

---

his grammar!

47. Cf. Polanyi, *Personal Knowledge*, and T. F. Torrance, *Theological Science*, for a clarification of "subjectivity" and "objectivity" within the bi-polar relationship of subject to object.

48. Outler, *John Wesley*, 29.

49. For a recent study of this, see Joseph Cunningham, "Perceptible Inspiration."

Christian experience then is not merely the experiencing of theological abstractions called "salvation," or "sanctification," or "holiness." Nor is it merely the experiencing of inner subjective events or "crises," and certainly not of induced or self-induced crises. It only has objective validity, it is only real, when we experience or encounter the living God.

> My goal is God himself, not joy, nor peace,
> Nor even blessing, but himself, my God.[50]

The Lord God gives *himself* in grace to be known, to be experienced by us in his Word by his Spirit, to become, if you like, the Divine Object of our experience. God is the One we experience in "an experience," and it is only when we objectively experience *God*, that there is a genuine event, a genuine "crisis" with objective validity. Real inner and outer change, real sanctification, certainly requires self-knowledge and self-examination, but it occurs not when our eyes are inward in introspection but when we look *outward* and *upward* and our eyes are fixed on *him*. Real Christian experience is quite simply falling in love with God. And when we do that, we are never more rational, never more truly human, never more spiritually and intellectually awakened, never more at our best. It is objective experience of the real and living God that results in the subjective inner and outward change we call "sanctification."

Such experiential knowledge of God must not only be understood in a merely individualistic way. It is true, of course, that the tri-personal God enters into relationship with *each* of us as persons. We come to know with Paul, Augustine, Luther, and the Wesleys that Christ died "for me" (Gal 2:20):

> Died he *for me*, who caused his pain?
> *For me*? Who him to death pursued?
> Amazing love! How can it be
> That Thou, my God, shouldst die *for me*?[51]

And yet that *personal* encounter with God must not be understood *individualistically*, but within the fellowship of the people of God. Historically, the apostles experienced "God with us" in Jesus, the Incarnate Son, and ever and again as the story of the gospel is proclaimed and the Scriptures are opened and bread and wine are distributed, the people of God experience God's presence in the *corporate* worship of the church.

50. F. Brook, "My Goal is God Himself, not joy, nor peace," (Hymn 70 in *Redemption Hymnal*).

51. *Works* (BE) 7:322 (italics added).

"Reason" and "Experience" are thus not distinct factors in the shaping of Christian doctrine. The picture is much more unitary. When we experience the God who reveals himself to us in his Word by his Spirit, *that* is a fully rational event. We come to *know h*im. When we think about the God we know in Jesus and express our knowledge of him in words (also a rational act), *that* is theology. We do that together in the church and the result is church doctrine. When we formulate that doctrine in creeds and confessions and articles of faith and hand these on for the guidance of our children, *that* is church tradition.

There is thus one objective source of doctrine, God's own self-revelation, his Word. "Reason," "experience," and "tradition" are ways of speaking about the way we subjectively appropriate that revelation, personally and corporately, and express it. Christian doctrine is formed as the corporate church's rational reflection upon her experience of the living God who speaks to her in and through his Word. She expresses in her doctrine what she knows of God and his ways. That is why it is so important that our understanding of Christian sanctification should never be a separate doctrine, focused on ourselves. A doctrine of Christian sanctification can only be understood in the context of trinitarian doctrine. True Christian sanctification can only take place as the Holy Spirit indwells us, so focusing our attention not on ourselves, but on Christ, through whom alone we come to the Father and reflect his overwhelming, loving compassion.

e) Fourth Axiom: Trinitarian, Christocentric Shape of Christian Theology

The fourth and final theological axiom proceeds from this point. Since God's self-revelation takes place in his Word—by which we mean not only the written word of Scripture, but more fundamentally, the Word made flesh, our Lord Jesus Christ—then Christian theology is centered in him and built upon him. In short, this axiom is that Christian theology is christocentric. It is an organic whole in which the doctrines of Christ (Christology) and his atonement (soteriology) are central and the doctrine of God the Holy Trinity revealed in Christ provides the overall shape and contours.

This final axiom of method rejects two other ways of doing theology. The first is what is sometimes meant by "Systematic Theology," a kind of complete theological system of thought after the style of Origen or Augustine or Aquinas. Here a metaphysic or philosophy plays a determining role, and a system of thought (Platonist in the case of Origen and Augustine, Aristotelian in the case of Aquinas) is developed to account in a comprehensive, all-embracing way for all reality.

With Origen, the Platonist worldview distorted the doctrine of God in strange ways later judged heretical. With Augustine and Aquinas, the central doctrines remained orthodox but were married to a philosophically-based Christian worldview. This resulted in a systematic theology that can be so all-embracing that it smothers the natural and human sciences in its embrace and is indistinguishable from a philosophy or metaphysic. What this fourth axiom requires instead is a *dogmatic theology*, articulating the core convictions of the Christian faith, centered as they are in Christ, after the style of theologians such as Irenaeus, or Athanasius, or Luther, or Calvin, or Barth. With each of them (although we may disagree with them at many points) the centrality of the classic dogmas of Trinity, incarnation, and atonement makes Christian theology an organic whole with a profound unity and coherence to which Christ himself is the key.

This implies the rejection also of a second style of theology also exemplified by Aquinas, the scholastic model first formulated in the classrooms of the Middle Ages. In this style, doctrines were strung out in distinct, separate articles or *foci*, like washing on a line, as R. P. C. Hanson expressed it.[52] Instead, we need to aim at a holistic theology where, rather than a series of distinct doctrines conceived of almost as separate compartments of truth, the emphasis is on *connections* rather than *distinctions*. Doctrines are seen to inter-connect, to flow into each other, not in an amorphous way, but in a holistic theology that is shaped rather like the ancient creeds, trinitarian in its general shape and christocentric in its focus.

Scholasticism was a great intellectual achievement of the Middle Ages, reaching its highest point in Aquinas, but it can deteriorate into a dead text-book theology, a rigid system, fossilized by a static Aristotelian logic which cannot cope with life and movement. Perhaps some Pietists and revivalists like to have such a safely dead and rigid theology so that they can take it for granted and dismiss it as irrelevantly academic and unimportant for the life of the church! Or perhaps they assume that that is the only shape theology can take. But a theology that is concerned with expressing our experiential, rational knowledge of the living God is living theology.

What then is the implication of this fourth axiom for Christian holiness? It is this: that the doctrine of the Christian life, including

---

52. Hanson, *Attractiveness*, 47.

sanctification, cannot be articulated in isolation as a separate doctrine. If it is, the danger is that it will become an individualistic, introverted, subjectivist, and spiritually self-centered quest. The sanctification of the Christian can only be understood in the context of the sanctifying of human relationships within the church, the people of God. And the sanctifying of human relationships among those who are drawn into the church can only be understood in turn by seeing that the fellowship enjoyed within the church is the mutual fellowship of the Father with the Son, which is the fellowship of the Holy Spirit. Our understanding of Christian holiness finds its immediate context then in the third article of the creed, the doctrine of the Spirit, comprehending the doctrines of the church, the Christian believer, and the Last Things. But the Spirit leads us to Christ and speaks of him, and so the third article depends on the central article, that on Christ and his atonement. Consequently our doctrine of Christian holiness must begin there and find its foundation in him. But it is when we are "in Christ" that we can say, "Abba, Father," and so the doctrine of Christian holiness can only be understood within the context of the Holy Trinity.

It is to trace these inter-connections that we shall be concerned in this book. We shall look for the foundation of Christian sanctification in the atonement, and more profoundly in Christ himself, and then consider how what is his becomes ours through the work of the Spirit and in the context of the Holy Trinity. But before we attempt to do that, in the next four chapters we must consider first how the doctrine of Christian sanctification, or Christian "perfecting," is based in Holy Scripture; secondly how it has developed over the centuries from the earliest days of the church; thirdly how that tradition was expressed as part of the evangelical faith by John Wesley; and fourthly, how Wesley's doctrine may be re-expressed today.

2

Christian Perfecting in Holy Scripture

There are approximately seven thousand million reasons on this planet today why we should never use the word "perfect" in reference to human beings. And world population is rapidly increasing! We all know that we are not "perfect." And particularly since the Enlightenment, Christians have been criticizing the absurd notion of human perfectibility. Some of the great thinkers of the "age of reason" dismissed the Christian doctrine of sin and seemed to assume that human reason could produce the perfect society. "Man is born free," proclaimed Rousseau, "but is everywhere in chains." Reform, education, and democracy could abolish evil and could perfect human existence. Even the great human tragedies that began with the First World War and continued in wars, terrorism, and genocide throughout the twentieth century have not totally dislodged this Enlightenment myth of progress and human perfectibility from some minds.[1] But by the early twenty-first century it is surely clear that the Christian doctrine of sin gives us the most realistic perspective on the human condition and that the Enlightenment notion of human perfectibility is totally discredited. Only a blinkered rationalist could cling to the absurd fantasy that the human race could shrug off the inheritance of its past—violence, exploitation, and oppression—and attain "perfection." We all have a more sober estimate of humanity after the demonic atrocities of Hitler and Stalin and a dozen more monsters who have succeeded them around the world.

---

1. Niebuhr, *Nature and Destiny*, a classic work, presented a powerful analysis of human sinfulness.

Yet strangely, there are various biblical passages which speak not only of all of God's people as "saints"—"sanctified ones"—but which even speak of the sanctification or holiness of God's people as their "perfection." And there is a strong tradition running from the New Testament through all the centuries of the church which holds out the possibility of *Christian* "perfection." What are we to make of that?

a) The Meaning of "Perfection"

To begin with, it is necessary to remember that there have been fanatics throughout the history of the church who have claimed absolute "perfection." We do not have to search too far to find examples of unbalanced extremists who claimed to be "sinless," and clearly that claim has to be rejected. Wesley had to dismiss two of his preachers, Maxfield and Bell, who made such exaggerated claims.[2] And yet that does not account for some of the greatest teachers of mainstream Christianity—Clement of Alexandria, Athanasius writing about Antony, Basil the Great, Gregory of Nazianzus, Gregory of Nyssa, Cassian and Benedict, Bernard of Clairvaux, Thomas Aquinas, the Pietists Arndt and Spener, and the great evangelist John Wesley—who all gave measured teaching on Christian "perfection."

But also, and most importantly, it is essential to note that the biblical writers and these great teachers of the church through the centuries were working with a somewhat different understanding of the word "perfection." None of them ever taught "sinless perfection"—the idea that within this life, Christians could reach that final, absolute state of perfection where they were sinless and perfectly holy. Unfortunately, that is the idea our English word "perfect" conveys, a perfection of "zero defects." But these great teachers of Christianity were working with the *biblical* concept of perfection, which is rather different. It works essentially not just with a *negative* understanding of "perfection" as merely the absence of *sin*, but primarily with a *positive* understanding of "perfection" as a fullness of *love*. It has several shades of meaning.

First of all, to take the Greek words used in the New Testament, *teleios* (historically translated "perfect") and *teleiōsis* (translated "perfection"), the root idea is found in the word *telos*, meaning an "end" or "goal." Today *teleios* is often translated as "mature" and *teleiōsis* as "maturity," and that is helpful, since it gets us away from the misleading modern idea of an absolute perfection of zero defects. The idea of maturity does not imply

2. Rack, *Reasonable Enthusiast*, 337–42.

any arrival at a final goal, and no one is going to object to the idea that Christians may reach maturity through experience and growth and development in the Christian pilgrimage. So that is the first shade of meaning.

And yet the English words "mature" and "maturity" do not capture the full meaning of the Greek words. What they are missing is the second shade of meaning, the connection with the underlying idea of "end" or "goal." The Greek word has more of a dynamic sense of movement towards the goal or end or purpose. True, there is the idea of final *teleiōsis* when the person or thing has finally arrived and completed its reason for existence. But a person or thing may also be described as *teleios* if he, she, or it is on course for the goal, moving with undeviating impetus on the trajectory that will arrive at the final end and fulfill the final purpose. In this sense, the golfer has not only hit the perfect shot once the ball lands in the hole, but even while the ball is sailing so beautifully through the air, it is a "perfect" shot. In fact, only because it was a "perfect" shot from the moment he hit the ball, did he land that hole-in-one!

That means that for the biblical writers and the great tradition of Christian spirituality, there is not only the final perfection to be attained finally in the final resurrection when "we shall be like him [Christ] for we shall see him as he is" (1 John 3:2). But there is also a *relative* perfection or maturity which is only possible for the Christian who can say, like Paul, "This one thing I do," and who is heading unswervingly for the goal "that I may know him and the power of his resurrection" (Phil 3:10–15). None of us has reached that resurrection goal, but Paul numbered himself with those who were on the perfecting trajectory, aiming for it without deviation.

This leads us to the third shade of meaning in historic writing about Christian "perfection," the idea of wholeness. To be unswervingly committed to be Christ's men and women from head to toe is to have the whole of life and thought *integrated* around this one great goal. The Christian who is no longer divided in heart and mind is an integrated person, a whole person. There is no longer the divided mind which makes him unsteady or which makes her unreliable. In the title of a sermon on James 4:8, Kierkegaard put it this way: "Purity of heart is to will one thing." This wholeness or purity of heart is not to be understood in some kind of quantitative way: it is *qualitative*. This kind of Christian *teleiōsis* is holistic. It is an understanding of Christian holiness as personal "wholeness" or health.

But the fact that this is a dynamic kind of perfection, an unswerving trajectory towards the *telos*—a concept of "perfection" as movement rather than as rest—means that we may speak intelligently of stages or "degrees" of perfection, indications of how far we have advanced in our pilgrimage. Clement of Alexandria can write both about the "perfection" of the newly baptized Christian, but also the more advanced "perfection" of the mature. Medieval spiritual writers such as Walter Hilton refer commonly to the "ladder" of perfection with definable rungs indicating just *how* "perfect" or mature a Christian is.[3] There is the perfection of the newborn infant: but if there has been no growth a year later, then that once perfect child is now retarded. To continue on the pilgrimage, the Christian must advance "from glory to glory" (in the Pauline phrase highlighted by Gregory of Nyssa).[4] Practical advice which gives some specific measures and indications of growth can warn the careless by introducing an element of accountability and can encourage the faint-hearted to "press on toward the goal." Given that dynamic concept of the perfection of movement rather than final arrival, it may be preferable to express this meaning of the Greek word not by using the word "perfection," but by translating it as "perfecting."

Of course, all these shades of meaning in the biblical concept of "perfection" have to be taken together. The measuring of our spiritual progress or maturity can become a very self-centered business if it is not centered on the One who is the goal: "that I may know him and the power of His resurrection" (Phil 3:10). Christian "perfection" down through the centuries of the church has therefore been understood *not* as a self-centered, inwardly turned search for spiritual achievement or satisfaction, but as outwardly turned *love*. The great teachers of Christian spirituality define it in terms of the great commandments, loving God with all the heart, soul, mind, and strength, and loving our neighbors as ourselves. That means, of course, that it is cruciform-shaped. It is a dying and rising with Christ. It is learning in ever-deeper ways what it means to die to our own deep-seated sinfulness—to our own pride, idolatry, and self-centeredness—and to rise daily in Christ to his life of true, dynamic righteousness.

One major tradition in the church has generally rejected "perfection." It is that strain of Augustinian thought which issued in two of the great traditions of the Reformation, the Lutheran and the Calvinist or Reformed. But over against that, the Orthodox and Catholic traditions, along with many in the Anabaptist, Pietist, Anglican, and Methodist traditions, have carefully affirmed that we must take seriously the *biblical* idea

3. See Hilton, *Ladder of Perfection*.

4. See Daniélou, *Glory to Glory*.

of perfection. Those Augustinian traditions that have generally rejected the idea of perfection have not only often assumed that it must mean absolute, sinless perfection, but have also been deeply colored by Augustine's doctrine of original sin. The Lutheran tradition (even more than the Reformed) has been motivated by a deep fear that any such positive account of advance in Christian sanctification will compromise the great Reformation assertion of justification by faith alone.

In looking at the issue therefore, it is useful for us to concentrate on one major historic Protestant leader who held to *both* the Reformation doctrines of justification and original sin on the one hand and, on the other, to the majority view of the universal church that something positive must be said about Christian "perfection." That leader was John Wesley, and his synthesis of these different Christian doctrines at this point makes him a theologian and spiritual guide of ecumenical significance. But before we come to look at Wesley's own teaching in chapter 4, the aim in this chapter is to review the biblical roots of his doctrine. Our concern here is not with Wesley's own hermeneutic (which is a study of its own),[5] but with the resources within Holy Scripture which scholars today can see as providing a strong biblical basis. In the next chapter we shall similarly review the historical roots for Wesley's doctrine in the Christian tradition. But in both these chapters, we can only summarize this with extreme brevity. Each of these topics has been given scholarly treatment, and so we shall only attempt here to summarize the argument of relevant works of biblical and historical scholarship as a necessary prelude to addressing the theological task.

b) Biblical Roots

As a preacher, Wesley had a collection of favorite texts that he regarded as the basis of his doctrine of Christian perfection. W. E. Sangster listed fourteen of these passages, and judged seventy years ago that even after two centuries of advances in biblical studies, while there may be shadows of dubiety here and there on a translation or interpretation, by and large, "the stones stand."[6] Exegesis of specific biblical passages remains vitally

---

5. See Jones, *Conception Use*, and Bullen, *Man of One Book*.

6. Sangster, *Path to Perfection*, 51. The texts he lists are Ezek 36; 25; 26; 29; Matt 5:8, 48, and 6:10; Rom 2:29 and 12:1; 2 Cor 3:17f. and 7:1; Gal 2:20; Eph 3:14–19 and 5:27; Phil 3:15; 1 Thess 5:23; Titus 2:11–14; Heb 6:1; 7:25 and 10:14; John 8:34f. and 17:20–23; Jas 1:4; 1 John 1:5, 7–9; 2:6 and 3:8–10. See Cheatle, *Sangster*.

important. But the rise of Biblical Theology, often dated from the inaugural address of Johann Philip Gabler in 1787, just four years before Wesley's death, means that theologians have to be very wary of appearing to rely in the manner of scholastic "orthodoxy" on isolated "proof texts" taken out of "context" and used as a "pretext" to support their own categories and structure of thought. Further, developments such as James Barr's notable attack on "word studies,"[7] the emphasis that the Hebrew Bible does not work (like Western theologians) with abstract concepts but with concrete narrative, plus the deeper philosophical analysis of hermeneutics; all must make us rightly wary of how we base doctrine on Scripture. Nevertheless, despite Barr, we cannot totally abandon the view that words do retain a certain consistency of meaning even if we have to be highly sensitive to the variation indicated by specific context. If that were not so, we would have to throw away our dictionaries. Working with great care on this slippery territory, and taking into account not merely isolated "proof texts," but a scholarly grasp of the Hebrew Bible *as a whole* and the New Testament *as a whole*, there are some experienced scholars who provide guidance for the theologian in working with the concepts of "holiness" and "perfection."[8]

c) Old Testament

John T. Gammie summarized his study of holiness in the Old Testament with the conclusion: "Holiness in Israel was not first and foremost something for human beings to achieve, but rather the characteristic of ineffability possessed only by God, the Lord of Hosts, the Holy One of Israel."[9] And yet Gammie holds that holiness constituted "a commanding, inviting, summoning presence," a formulation not altogether different from Rudolf Otto's classic definition of "the holy" as a *mysterium tremendum et fascinans*.[10] So holiness was a "vocation" for Israel, and Gammie sees three strands in this: the "twin notions of separation and purity" in the priestly theology,[11] the "cleanness of social justice" in the prophetic tradition,[12] and the "profound summons to individual cleanness, inner integrity, and

7. Barr, *Semantics*.

8. They are not responsible of course for the line of argument which we develop here from their work.

9. Gammie, *Holiness*, 195.

10. Otto, *Idea*.

11. Gammie, *Holiness*, 43.

12. Ibid., 100.

purity of heart" in the Wisdom literature.[13] The "twin notions" to which Gammie refers in the priestly theology are linked but have to be distinguished, for to sanctify what is profane is not the same as to purify the polluted. Richard Bauckham gives a succinct summary of the difference when he explains that to purify is to make the polluted clean, but that it will still be profane until the further step in which it is made holy.[14]

John Oswalt develops his Old Testament theology of holiness by starting with the covenant.[15] This was God's way of teaching Israel that, unlike the surrounding religions of the ancient Near East, Israel was to draw strong boundaries between Creator and creation, the holy and the profane. A corporate holiness was required of Israel, "a kingdom of priests and a holy nation" (Exod 19:6), and within the covenant, this was strongly relational: "You shall be holy for I am holy" (Lev 19:2). The four major blocks of material from Exodus 10 continuously through to Leviticus 26 are connected with this holiness: the Decalogue, the tabernacle, the sacrificial system and priesthood, and the holiness code.

But perhaps it is particularly Deuteronomy which brings out the vital point that we cannot talk about this relational holiness, corporately required of Israel in order to reflect the character of their God, without talking about *love*. The *Shema* puts this right at the heart of Old Testament theology and ethics: "Hear, O Israel: the LORD [YHWH] God, the LORD [is] one. And you shall love the LORD your God with all your heart, and with all your soul, and with all your might" (Deut 6:4f.). Israel had not won or merited God's love: they had been redeemed by sheer grace. But within the covenant that followed their redemption from Egypt, the holiness that they were to demonstrate as a reflection of their redeeming God was faithful, consistent loyalty and love. That is what would constitute their righteousness, namely, their faithfulness to the relationship, their covenant with God, in other words, their *love*. And that love and faithfulness, reflecting the character of God, had to be exemplified in their love and faithfulness to each other (Lev 19:18). Justice lay in loving the neighbor.

According to Oswalt, the whole history of Israel can be captured in two motifs: "the constant and continuing failure of the mass of Israel to keep the covenant, and the constant and continuing faithfulness of God to Israel through the covenant."[16] And even when the covenant appears

---

13. Ibid., 149.

14. Bauckham, "Holiness of Jesus," clarifies this succinctly as the background to word usage in John's Gospel.

15. Oswalt, *Called*.

16. Ibid., 42.

to be abrogated at the exile, the promise is there of the new covenant in which by action of the Spirit of the Lord, they will be given new hearts (Jer 31:31–34; Ezek 36:25–29).

While the concept of holiness is a dominant one in the Old Testament, running in all its richness and variety through the whole narrative as well as the proclamations of the prophets and the reflections of the sages, the language of "perfection" is not so central. Nevertheless Oswalt identifies two relevant Hebrew words. The adjective *tamim* meaning "whole," "complete," or "without defect" along with the noun, *tam*, is most commonly applied to sacrificial animals, but also to humans such as Noah (Gen 6:9) and Abraham (17:1), when the idea is blamelessness or integrity.[17] The second is the adjective *shalem*, particularly when it is used to qualify the heart. The heart (*leb*) is an "all-inclusive term" indicating, according to Oswalt, "the centre of the personality," referring to "the powers of discernment, the will, and the motivations, as well as the affections."[18] It is not primarily associated with the emotions, which, in the very concrete Hebrew psychology, are resident in the bowels and the liver. The *leb shalem* therefore refers to someone who is undivided in thinking and willing, having an undivided heart of single-minded devotion to God.[19]

d) The Synoptic Gospels and Acts

When we turn to the New Testament with questions about holiness, the first thing to observe is that it is not any abstract concept or doctrine that is central, but the personal figure of Jesus. The Synoptic Gospels tell the story of one whose view of holiness was rooted in Israel's faith, but yet was different.[20] The surrounding Gentile religions had a notion of the holiness of the gods as mere power: Jesus shared Israel's ethical view of holiness as purity, faithfulness, and love. But in second temple Judaism, the priestly focus on safeguarding purity by separation had hardened from the time of Ezra onwards into an exclusivism particularly marked by observing the distinguishing markers of circumcision, the Sabbath, and the dietary laws. The Pharisees ("separatists") even regarded many of the Jewish population as unclean sinners. But whereas the Pharisees intensified the Torah, for Jesus the essence of holiness was "not separation but compassion." Kent

17. See ibid., 46–52.

18. Ibid., 52.

19. See ibid., 52–63.

20. See Brower, *Gospels*, for this section on the Synoptics.

Brower concludes, "In Jesus' view, holiness did not require protection and insulation from sources of defilement. Holiness was contagious and a transforming power."[21]

In Luke's Gospel, Jesus' compassion overrides concern for exclusive purity again and again, while his parables of the lost sheep, the lost coin, and (particularly) the lost son, vividly portray compassionate love as the heart of the holiness of God. In Mark's Gospel, while the language of holiness is absent, the theme of discipleship emphasizes that life as a Christian is not ticking off points on a moral code but "life lived in response to a relationship."[22] It is "following Jesus." This is undertaken not as an individual pursuit, but *together*: it is sharing together in the mission of Jesus. Discipleship has a starting point and requires full commitment from the start, but it also means progression, and the implications of the commitment only become evident after some time on the way. The journey that Mark narrates (which is not only geographical but theological) comes to a turning point when the disciples openly recognize Jesus as Messiah, but actually they still do not really understand what is going on and particularly the demand to take up the cross. Mark's narrative depiction of discipleship comes to its pinnacle in the temple where Jesus identifies love of God (the *Shema* of Deut 6:4) and love of neighbor as the greatest of the commandments and confirms the view of his questioner that that is the deeper meaning of the whole vast sacrificial system.

If faithful love of God with our whole being and compassionate love of neighbor are together the essence of holiness in Luke and Mark, it is in Matthew's Gospel that we find them explicitly expressed in the Sermon on the Mount, employing the Old Testament language of "perfection" and "purity of heart." The sermon is the first major block of Jesus' teaching that Matthew gives us, and in the key verse bracketing this section of the gospel (4:23 and 9:35), his teaching has to be taken along with his preaching or proclaiming of the imminent kingdom, and his healing. The greater righteousness he demands (5:20) is not a more detailed list of external commandments to tick off. As Brower puts it, "Jesus doesn't simply intensify the Torah: he radicalizes it by returning again and again to first principles and, hence, to a renewed emphasis on its inner purpose."[23] It is within that context that we need to interpret Jesus' adoption from the Wisdom writings of the phrase, "purity of heart" (5:8), and his requirement that his

21. Ibid., 41, with reference to Marcus J. Borg, *Conflict, Holiness*. See the whole section "Redefining Holiness" in Brower, *Gospels*, 54–59.

22. Brower, *Gospels*, 84.

23. Ibid., 122.

disciples are to be "perfect, as your heavenly Father is perfect" (5:48). This is not a legal requirement for entry to the kingdom, and it does not mean "flawless." It comes as the conclusion of the teaching that the disciples are to love not just their neighbor but also their enemy. "Perfection" once again, is not the outward legalistic observation of rules and regulations: it is the internal motivation of a heart filled with love. Kent Brower summarizes the point: "To be perfect like your Father is to have that perfect love, that single-minded devotion to God and love of neighbour that is the summation and fulfilment of God's great commands to us. Is it realizable now? Yes, it is, according to the Matthean Jesus. This is a present reality for the new people of God because disciples are called to a totally God-centered and neighbour-centered mindset."[24] It is in Matthew's Gospel too that it is most evident that this is a present reality for a new community, the community of the kingdom, a new eschatological people, called to faithfulness to the Torah as interpreted by the Messiah's teaching.[25]

This picture of the church as God's holy people is developed by Luke in Acts. Howard Marshall sums up this depiction: the holy people are committed to their Lord and their unity is demonstrated in their communal life as they give attention to teaching, to fellowship, the breaking of bread, prayer, and praise. The activities of this holy people are attributed to the Holy Spirit whose presence is evidenced by their readiness to forgive, their joyful good works, their honesty, and their total commitment to evangelism.[26]

e) Holiness in the Writings of Paul

The Gospels have too often been ignored in Western theology (particularly Protestant), which has been very Pauline. But the standard interpretation of Paul was deeply shaped by Augustine's fight with Pelagianism and by Luther's reaction against what he saw as the Pelagian "salvation by works" of late medieval Catholicism. The primary focus of this Protestant Paul has also been on salvation as the justification of the individual, where justification is understood in the forensic Western categories of the criminal court—guilt, punishment, and pardon. This understanding of salvation as essentially justification has been connected to a doctrine of the atonement understood as essentially penal substitution. Given those connections,

24. Brower, *Gospels*, 125.

25. See Hagner, "Holiness and Ecclesiology," 42–44.

26. Marshall, "Holiness," 114–28, esp. 125f.

"sanctification" seemed to have no real basis in the atonement and was easily reduced, in effect, to the individual's moral effort. A correction or modification of this whole understanding of Paul's gospel as centered on the forensic justification of the individual has been mounted by E. P. Sanders, James D. G. Dunn, N. T. Wright, and other scholars broadly grouped under the heading of the "New Perspective on Paul."

Despite the heat and dust of battle, the "New Perspective" should be seen as a modification but certainly not a rejection of everything the Reformers said. While opinions vary, generally the forensic element in the atonement and justification is not totally rejected, but seen within a wider view of Paul's theology. Indeed, this may be seen as a return to the Reformers, for certainly in Calvin and arguably in Luther, justification was seen as an aspect and implication of *union with Christ*. Calvin writes: "We expect salvation from him, not because he stands aloof from us, but because ingrafting us into his body, he not only makes us partakers of all his benefits, but also of himself."[27]

The New Perspective began with E. P. Sanders' argument that Second Temple Judaism was not a legalistic, Pelagian religion preaching "salvation by works," but should be described as *covenantal nomism*. The Law (*nomos*) or Torah was not the means of salvation, but the way in which Israel put into practice their loyalty to the God who had redeemed them from Egypt (by grace!) and entered into covenant with them at Sinai. The key then to Paul's particular slant on the gospel is that his vocation was to be the apostle to the Gentiles. He had not converted to a new faith ("Christianity") but rather had come to recognize the crucified and risen Lord Jesus as the fulfillment of Israel's faith so that the Gentiles might enter into the promises given to Israel and Jews and Gentiles together might become one in the church, the "body of Christ." Gentiles therefore did not need to become Jews, observing the Mosaic laws (circumcision, Sabbath, dietary regulations) but were "set right" with God (i.e., justified) through faith in Jesus alone. Salvation therefore is not only a matter of individual justification, understood as forensic pardon, but has to be understood in the wider historic perspective of corporate Israel.

Kent Brower, in his 2008 Didsbury Lectures, elucidates the place that Christian sanctification has as an integral part within this wider picture of Paul's theology. Holiness was a central concern of Paul throughout his

---

27. Calvin, *Institutes*, III, ii, 24. See Niesel, *Theology of Calvin*, 120–39, and Wallace, *Calvin's Doctrine*, 17–27 on "The Participation of the Church in the Sanctification of Christ."

entire life.[28] As a Pharisee, he was part of a movement that tried to extend the purity that the Torah required of priests in the temple to the entire land of Israel, and as an apostle of Christ he saw himself as "set apart for the gospel of God . . . to bring about the obedience of faith . . . among all the nations" (Rom 1:1–6). This gospel of God was "the gospel of his Son" (1:3), in which "the righteousness of God was revealed" (1:17). For Paul, the "righteousness of God" (as Martin Luther saw) was not primarily his retributive justice, but his restorative justice; that is, his redeeming and saving activity as part of his faithfulness, not only to his covenant with Abraham, but to the whole created order.[29] Retributive justice is not central, and yet it is the obverse of restorative justice. The judge will punish those who persist in opposing his good purposes (2 Thess 1:6–10), and therefore the judicial verdict of pardon is a necessary part of the picture. But it is not the goal: "The goal is reconciling and corrective rather than punitive judgement."[30]

f) Christian Holiness in Romans

Given that the human condition is not only being guilty, but also being enslaved to sin as a power, salvation cannot be only forgiveness (amazing though that is!) but deliverance or liberty. To show how this is integral to Paul's thought, William M. Greathouse draws on Leander Keck's analysis of the structure of Paul's exposition of the gospel in Romans as "spiral," "each time going deeper into the human condition, and each time finding in the Bible the appropriate antidote."[31] The first exposition in Romans 1:18 to 4:25 tells of the indictment of all, Gentiles and Jews, as guilty, and of justification by faith in the faithfulness of Christ as God's atoning sacrifice. At this point Paul is thinking corporately. The second exposition begins in 5:12–21 with the two realms of Adam and Christ and develops the theme of liberation through our incorporation into Christ from the sin that rules corporate Adamic humanity. This is achieved for all corporately by the obedience of the "one man," but as a consequence of that, the Spirit is now active, pouring God's love into our hearts (5:5). As N. T. Wright comments, "The *Shema* is at last fulfilled."[32] Peter Stuhlmacher comments

28. Brower, *God's Holy People*, 1.

29. On Luther, see Rupp, *Righteousness*, 121–37.

30. Brower, *God's Holy People*, 9.

31. Keck, "Romans Tick?" 25, and Greathouse, *Wholeness*, 87.

32. Wright, "Romans," 45.

that this is the fulfillment of Ezekiel 36:26ff.: those who are filled with the Spirit become capable of loving God.[33]

In the third exposition (7:17—8:17), as Keck defines it, Paul moves somewhat from the corporate to the personal, using the first person singular. He writes about "an illegal resident who usurped control of the house, thereby compelling the enslaved self to do opposite of what it intends." This is "sin that dwells within me" (7:17, 20). Because of the weakness of the flesh, Torah could not deal with this: but "what the law could not do," God has done by "sending his own Son in the likeness of sinful flesh" (8:3). This was in order that "the just requirement of the law" (summed up in the *Shema*) "might be fulfilled in us" (8:4) by the Spirit. Consequently, instead of walking "according to the flesh" we may walk "according to the Spirit," and instead of a "mind set on the flesh," we may have a "mind set on the Spirit."

God's salvation then, according to Paul, is not only justification in the sense of "pardon," being declared righteous, but a "rightwising" or being "set right" in relation to God in such a way that we are freed from the tyranny of sin, both outwardly in the Adamic sphere, but also inwardly in the heart and mind and disposition. Sanctification is inseparable from justification and all God's people are therefore "holy ones" or "saints" (*hagioi*).[34] True, we are not justified because we are sanctified, but we are justified and sanctified inseparably because of the coming of Christ and our incorporation into him by the Spirit. As Calvin saw, it is a matter of *union with Christ*. That is the key to both justification and sanctification. Accordingly, this salvation, which is already ours "in Christ," has still to be worked out in us as we walk "according to the Spirit."

Kent Brower notes that there is still a minority of commentators (mostly or all in the Reformed or Lutheran traditions) who take the view that the "wretched man" of Romans 7 is the "normal" Christian experience. Undoubtedly the life of the Christian is placed within the eschatological paradox of the "already" and the "not yet," but most commentators now take the view that this chapter is analyzing the situation of the unbeliever. Brower notes that even in this life "between the times," "Paul is quite clear that the Christian life is not to be characterized by a divided mind" (see 8:6–9). The believer continuously offers his or her life to God (12:1f.) so that character is transformed by a renewal of the mind. Further, it is very difficult to see how Romans 7:14 ("I am of the flesh sold under sin") can

33. Stuhlmacher, *Paul's Letter*, 80.

34. 1:7; 8:27; 12:13; 15:25, 26, 31; 16:2, 15. See Oakes, "Made Holy."

be a description of believers in the light of chapter 6 (particularly 6:17). He concludes that the tension of the "already" and "not yet" must be taken seriously. There is as yet no final perfection. "But to describe Paul's view of the Christian life in terms of Romans 7 rather than Romans 8 is to tip the balance too far towards a pessimism which does not take full account of Paul's optimism of grace." What this points to then is an understanding of the genuinely paradoxical nature of the Christian life, which does not topple over into the constant internal warfare of a divided mind and heart.

All of this is affected of course by how we understand the Pauline anthropology,[35] and part of the difficulty we have is the persistence of Platonist and rationalist ways of thinking which make us think individualistically rather than corporately about what it means to be human. Platonist thought divides the human being into two virtually independent substances, the body and the inherently immortal (indeed, divine) soul. Platonism shades away into outright Gnosticism when physical life is denigrated to the point where it is regarded as inherently evil. It is certainly true that Paul has a profound grasp of the reality of universal corporate human sinfulness, but we must not interpret that in a Gnostic way. It is perhaps too easy for the Augustinian tradition to understand "total depravity" in a way that actually makes "flesh" inherently evil.

The Old Testament word "flesh" (*basar*) refers essentially to "the human." Whereas the Platonist tradition equated the spiritual with the intellectual, and saw the spiritual realm as the unchanging, static, immutable eternal realm of the Forms, and the flesh as the realm of flawed matter, waxing and waning, being born and dying, and inherently unstable and sordid, the Old Testament usage of the words "flesh" and "spirit," is different. "Spirit" is life and dynamism, movement and power, and that comes from the dynamism of Israel's God: whereas "the flesh" is weak and inert without the power of the breath or spirit of God: "All flesh is grass, and all its beauty is like the flower of the field" (Isa 40:6). "The flesh" is "the human." It is human nature, corporate humanity viewed as physical. It is weak and fallen, but it is not evil, for though fallen, it is the good creation of God.

This Old Testament usage continues in the New Testament, and it is in this sense that we are to understand that "The Word became flesh" (John 1:14). But Paul adds a new twist to this by writing about "walking according to the flesh" and "the mind of the flesh." Being physically human (that is, "flesh") is not inherently sinful. What is sinful is to "walk according to

---

35. See Brower, *God's Holy People*, 30–33.

the flesh" (Rom 8:4f.), which we can interpret as "living for merely human goals and values." It is "the mind set on the flesh" (Rom 8:5f. NRSV) that is the problem, but that is what in fact characterizes the human race as a whole. Because we are born into the corporately fallen human race, all of us from our earliest days set our minds and our affections on the merely human—on the creature rather than the Creator. For Paul, all humanity is characterized by that mindset, and only through the sanctifying incarnation of the Son (8:2f.) and the coming of the Spirit into our hearts can we be delivered from that sinful orientation. But it is that real deliverance from sin, that genuine sanctification within this life, which leads into his vision of the final redemption of the cosmos (8:18–25), including these fallen, mortal bodies, and his paeon of praise that even in our present weakness and fallenness (v. 26), "we are more than conquerors" (v. 37).

g) Paul's Other Letters

Paul's view of Christian holiness, developed most fully in Romans, is coherent throughout his letters. In the early letters to the Thessalonians, the eschatological perspective is strong. The return of the Lord Jesus is expected imminently and Paul therefore prays that the believers in Thessalonica may be "sanctified entirely" (1 Thess 5:23). In the Greek sentence, the word translated "entirely" or "wholly" (*holoteleis*) is not actually an adverb modifying the verb "sanctify," but an adjective qualifying the pronoun "you" (*hymas*, plural). In other words, Paul is not praying that the sanctification of each individual be completed in the sense of being terminated, but that they may be sanctified "as a whole." It is a prayer for the *holistic* sanctification of this group of believers. And Paul is praying that that may occur now so that they will be ready for the coming of the Lord. (There would be no point in praying for what will be the case then!)

The prayer echoes an earlier prayer (3:12f.) which makes clear how we are to understand this: "And may the Lord make you increase and abound in love to one another and to all, even as we do to you so as to establish your hearts blameless (*amemptos*) in holiness (*hagiosunē*) before our God and Father at the coming of our Lord Jesus with all his saints." This *holistic* sanctification is the filling of their hearts with the love of God in such a way as to make them "blameless"[36] and ready for his coming.

In the comparatively lengthy Corinthian correspondence, Paul has to deal with a church that had enormous problems including party division,

---

36. See ibid., 100–105 on these two passages.

high-flown claims to "wisdom," questions of sexual ethics, class differences, and the whole question of how to live in an idolatrous and immoral world. In response, Paul emphasizes the centrality of Christ and the need for the Corinthian Christians to recognize that they are now the temple of God. They must therefore be corporately holy (1 Cor 3:16f.), keep their bodies holy (6:9), and recognize that they have been baptized into Christ (10:2–4) and are "the body of Christ," particularly as they participate in the Lord's Supper (11:17–31). These Corinthians are by definition "saints," God's "sanctified ones" (1:2), but Paul cannot speak to them as the "spiritual people" (*pneumatikois*) they are supposed to be. He can only speak to them as if they were still "fleshly people" (*sarkinois*). He does not deny that they are in Christ, but they can only be regarded as infants (*nepiois*) in Christ, to be fed with milk instead of meat (3:1f.). He can write to them, "You have been washed, sanctified, and set right in the name of the Lord Jesus Christ, and in the Spirit of our God." As Brower puts it, "These people do not need to become Spirit people. They need to become who they already are in Christ through the Spirit."[37]

They are interested in "spiritual things" (*pneumatikon*)—the word "gifts" is not in the text (1 Cor 12:1)—but Paul wants to direct their attention instead to "a still more excellent way" (12:31), the way of love. That is the key to the Christian life.

John Robert Walters comments: "Perfection is at the very centre of the Corinthian aberration from the faith. For all his struggles with them, Paul never disputes the truth of their claim. Instead he challenges their understanding of its implications. They have interpreted perfection absolutely. He understands it only in relative terms. To them it meant autonomy, to Paul it means dependency (2 Cor 12:5b–10)."[38]

In his letter to his beloved church at Philippi, Paul lays before them the Christian life as the way of the cross and the way of humility (1:19–24; 2:5–11; 3:8–11). That brings him to his exposition of the paradox of Christian perfection where he declares, on the one hand, that he is not yet "perfected" (*teteleiomai*), and yet numbers himself "among the perfect" (*teleioi*) three verses later! The paradox is unfortunately obscured by modern translations, which translate the verb in verse 12 as "not yet perfect," but translate the adjectival form of the same word in verse 15 as "mature." But in using the same word group, Paul is making a deliberate paradox. He is quite clear that he is not "perfected" in the sense that he has reached the

---

37. Ibid., 81.
38. Walters, "Perfection," 313f.

final perfection of the resurrection body, but he characterizes as "perfect" those who, like him, are "straining forward to what lies ahead."[39] They are those believers who "press on toward the goal for the prize of the upward call of God in Christ Jesus." Like Paul, they "count everything as rubbish" for the sake of Christ. Everything else is expendable for the overriding worth of knowing Christ. They are "this-one-thing-I-do" people, totally focused on him.

In Colossians, Paul again has this focus on Christ. His prayer is that the believers in Colossae may be "filled" with knowledge of God's will (1:9) and lead a life "worthy of the Lord" (1:10), their hearts "knit together in love" (2:2). As they have been reconciled to God through the dying and rising of Christ (1:22) so they are to replicate in their own lives that dying and rising which began with their baptism (2:8–15). They are not to be hung up on futile religious issues (2:16–23), but having died with Christ (2:20) and having been raised with Christ (3:1) they are to "set their minds on things above." Since they have put off "the old humanity" (*ton palaion anthrōpon*) with its practices and have put on the new and renewed one, Christ is to be "all in all" (3:9f.).

In Ephesians comes the great Triadic prayer. Since God's purpose is to "unite" or "sum up" or "recapitulate" (*anakephalaiōsthai*) all things (*ta panta*, the universe) in Christ (1:9), and since we have been saved by grace through faith "for good works" (2:8–10), Paul can bow his knees "before the Father," praying that his readers may be inwardly strengthened "through his Spirit" so that Christ may dwell in their hearts so that they may be "rooted and grounded in love," may know the love of Christ which is beyond knowledge, and be "filled with all the fullness of God."

Michael J. Gorman comments that it is ironic that the theme of holiness in Paul's writings is neglected today since he himself is "preoccupied with holiness." Not only is *hagioi* (saints, or holy ones) one of Paul's two favorite terms for believers, but the centrality of the theme appears in programmatic statements. Holiness is first of all difference from those who do not share in God's call or character, but it is also trinitarian in structure: "Holiness is the call and will of God the Father; it occurs in Christ, who defines holiness for the church; and it is effected by the Spirit, who is the *Holy* Spirit."[40]

---

39. See Walters, "Perfection," 327f. on the tension also between *kateilēphenai* (not yet arrived) and *ephthasamen* (already attained) and between *katantēsō* (yet to reach) and *katelēphthēn* (already taken hold of).

40. Gorman, "Be Cruciform." See also the other essays on Paul by Adewuya, Johnson, Lyons, Martin, Oakes, Wagner, Wall, and Winter in the same volume, Brower and

h) John: The Gospel and the First Epistle

Paul's teaching on the sanctification of the Christian is echoed in other terms in the writings of John. The Fourth Gospel has a narrative framework like the other Gospels, but there is more extensive teaching in which it is often difficult to distinguish the words attributed to Jesus from the words of the evangelist. The first letter of John shares many of the themes of the Gospel—incarnation, sin and atonement, light, and love.

If we come to these writings with questions about Christian holiness, we note first a number of themes directly related to Christ. He "tabernacles" in our "flesh" (John 1:14) and so is surely the One who is uniquely born "from above" (*anōthen*) (John 1:13 and 3:3–8.). He is the living water (4; 7:37f.), the bread of life (6), the true vine (15:1–6), all internal metaphors speaking of indwelling and more fully expounded in the farewell discourses as *mutual* indwelling (17:21–23). He is "the Lamb of God who bears away the sin of the world" (1:29) and so dies at Passover (19:14) and is the "propitiation" or "expiation" for our sins (1 John 4:10). *We cannot speak of Christian holiness therefore without speaking about Christ.* And it is not just a matter of what he has *done* for us (the bearing of our sins): it is a matter of who he *is* and what he has *become* for us. His incarnation is as integral to the holiness that we have *in* him as his death is. So also is his life and his consecration of himself. As we have already noted, Richard Bauckham carefully explains the difference between purification and sanctification in order to clarify how Jesus, who needed no purification from sin, nevertheless had to consecrate or sanctify himself in order that his disciples might be consecrated or sanctified to God.[41]

Secondly, the theme of love is prominent. The "new" commandment is similar to the second great commandment, but subtly deepened. That we are to love others "as we love ourselves" is usually taken to imply that there is a true and appropriate form of self-love. But in John, Jesus says that we are to love each other "as I have loved you" (13:34; 15:12; 1 John 2:7ff.), surely a much deeper love. John reaches the highest height when he goes on to assert that "God is love" (1 John 4:17–21) and that God's love is "perfected" (*teteleiōtai*) with us as we abide in God and he in us. John Robert Walters comments: "To be perfected in love is to be even in this world both the recipient of God's love and the conduit of God's love to others. To be 'perfected' in love is to be brought into the ongoing mission

Johnson, *Holiness and Ecclesiology.*

41. Bauckham, "Holiness of Jesus."

of Love's incarnation. . . . The 'perfection' of love is the ongoing incarnation of the divine love in this world."[42]

Thirdly, this has implications for our understanding of sin. Sin is slavery (John 8:33), and it is blindness that can only be relieved by light (John 9:41 and 1 John 1:5–7). We deceive ourselves if we say we have no sin (1 John 1:8–10), and yet John is writing to his readers so that they do not sin. If they do, they have an advocate with the Father, but John seems to assume that that would be exceptional, and that is made crystal clear a little later: "No one who abides in him sins. . . . No one born of God commits sin, for God's nature abides in him and he cannot sin because he is born of God" (3:6–9). That seems to run counter to the later emphasis in the Reformation traditions that Christians must confess daily that they are sinners and indeed it seems to sound uncomfortably like "sinless perfection." The church of the first two centuries generally took the line that sinning after baptism brings condemnation with no possibility of further forgiveness. Various ways of softening the text have been proposed, but however that is done, we have to begin by reconciling this repeated statement with 1:8: "If we say we have no sin, we deceive ourselves and the truth is not in us."

Walters suggests a distinction between the ontological claims to sinlessness and the functional assertion that the children of God do not in fact give expression to sin.

> Why is it that the ontological claims do not pass the test though the functional ones do? The answer is in the truth of Jesus' cleansing blood (1:7; cf. 3:5). Claims of ontological sinlessness nullify the very problem for which God sent his Son to be the remedy (2:2). . . . But to live sinless lives because of Christ's atoning mission is only proper and accords with the truth. [John] assumes that humanity is inherently sinful and in need of Christ's cleansing blood, but he also assumes that by virtue of Christ's blood those who belong to him do not sin.[43]

All of this has to be seen in the context of the eschatological tension. We are "not yet" delivered from the ontological weakness: that deliverance will come through our death and resurrection. But "already" the Spirit has been given: "The grace of God in giving the Spirit overcomes the weakness inherent in humanity and proves both the love of God and the reality of life in communion with him" (2:20, 27; 3:24). Consequently, "perfection

---

42. Walters, "Perfection," 254f.

43. Ibid., 244f.

in John is not absolute but a relative endowment, if one is even allowed to speak of Christian perfection at all. . . . The epistle speaks of being 'perfect in love,' not of being 'perfect.'" [44]

Fourthly, all of that means that Christians make progress "founded upon the 'already' of Christ's love, actualized in the past event of the cross and appropriated in present experience, and still 'not yet' fully disclosed in the life of this world (2:27)."[45] John therefore gives us the earliest passage in Christian literature referring to distinct stages in growth in the Christian life, those of infancy, youth, and parenthood (2:12–14).

i) Sanctification in Hebrews, 1 Peter, and Revelation

The epistle to the Hebrews provides the fullest exploration in the New Testament of the Person and work of Christ understood from the "types and shadows" (Heb 8:5) of the Old Testament sacrificial system. The cultic model and specifically the priesthood of Christ are the focus of the entire epistle, which is the most sustained piece of theological reflection in the New Testament apart from Paul's epistle to the Romans. Despite this focus on the centrality of the death of Christ as a sacrifice, the words "justify" (*dikaioō*) and justification (*dikaiosunē*) do not appear, but (as one would expect from the Old Testament) the sacrificial model is instead associated with sanctification. It was "in order to sanctify the people through his own blood" that Jesus suffered (13:12). David Peterson comments that this book has more to say about the sanctification of believers, using transformed cultic terms, than any other book in the New Testament, and this takes place through the self-sanctification of the Son. "By the will of the Father, revealed in Scripture and carried out by the Son, Hebrews proclaims that 'we have been sanctified through the offering of the body of Jesus Christ once for all' (10:10). Believers are sanctified because of his definitive sanctification, 'once for all' (Gk. *ephapax*) in death. Jesus is 'the sanctifier' of the people of the new covenant (2:11, Gk, *ho hagiazōn*), because he was perfected 'through sufferings' (2:10)."[46] This definitive "once-for-all-time" sanctification is "the once-for-all cleansing from sin that the law of Moses could not provide," and Jesus' perfect sin-offering inaugurates the new covenant promised in Jeremiah 31:31–34 (10:11–18). This single offering has also "perfected for all time those who are sancti-

44. Ibid., 261f.

45. Ibid., 257.

46. Peterson, *Possessed*, 34.

fied" (10:14). Gordon J. Thomas commented that, more than any other book in the New Testament, "the main thrust of Hebrews is to attribute the sanctification of all believers to the all-sufficient sacrifice of Christ. For this writer, sanctification is Christocentric."[47]

But what was objectively achieved in the death of Christ must become subjectively effective in the heart and conscience of the believer. There must be "repentance from dead works" (6:1) and yet it is not our repentance that is said to purify or sanctify us, but the sacrificial death of Christ. "If animal blood purified and sanctified at a ceremonial level under the Old Covenant, the writer goes on to insist, 'how much more will the blood of Christ, who through the eternal Spirit offered himself without blemish to God, purify our conscience from dead works to worship the living God' (9:14)."[48] Perfection is not synonymous with cleansing, and yet, according to Peterson, it involves the latter. Nor is it synonymous with sanctification, although the two concepts are closely related. It looks towards the final fulfillment for which the other two are necessary. We are therefore to "go on to perfection" (6:1).[49]

As it is clear from the opening greetings of most of Paul's letters that the "saints" or "sanctified ones" include the whole church, so also in 1 Peter, those who are "sanctified by the Spirit" are the whole people of God, the believing exiles of the Diaspora (1 Pet 1:2).[50] But perhaps the most neglected book when it comes to Christian holiness is John's Revelation. That may be because, instead of dealing with the personal dimension of holiness, the book is strongest on the communal and cosmic dimensions. The question confronting John's readers, according to Dean Flemming, is whether they will let their hearts and minds be captivated by the deceptive worldview of imperial Rome or by the vision of Christ's victorious kingdom. The only appropriate response to the holy God and the slaughtered Lamb in John's vision is *worship*.[51] "A holy God requires a holy people" and so: "In Revelation the holiness of Christians is portrayed largely in corporate terms." Resisting the earthly powers calls for a "heavy accent on ethical holiness,"[52] and an emphasis on "the public and political dimensions of

47. Thomas, "Perfection of Christ," 293–310.
48. Peterson, *Possessed*, 37f.
49. Ibid., 36.
50. Green, "Living as Exiles," 311–25.
51. Flemming "On Earth," 344–46.
52. Ibid., 347–49.

holiness."[53] The vision of a holy church reaches its climax in the "stunning image of the New Jerusalem."[54]

j) Conclusion

In this chapter we have attempted to summarize a biblical theology of the holiness of God's people. We have not simply produced a list of isolated "proof texts" for the idea of "perfection," but rather have used contemporary biblical scholarship to sketch a comprehensive overview of the understanding of the holiness of God's people in each of the major blocks of writing in the Old and New Testaments. We have then tried to see the concept of "perfection" within this overall horizon. This brief summary suggests several conclusions.

First, holiness, sanctification, perfection, and purity are not exact synonyms, but the concepts are closely connected. In the Old Testament, "holiness" uniquely refers to the God of Israel, but his people have a vocation to reflect God's holiness. This implies priestly separation from sin, prophetic social justice, and the sage's inner integrity or purity of heart. But at the heart of the holiness of the people of God is loving God with all the heart, soul, mind, and strength, and love of neighbor.

Secondly, in the Synoptic Gospels, Christian holiness is understood as discipleship, following Jesus on the way, taking up the cross: it is a pure heart, being filled with outgoing, inclusive compassion, rather than protecting oneself with exclusive separation.

Thirdly, in Paul, it is the transformation of those who are "in Christ"; it is dying and rising with Christ; it is walking according to the Spirit rather than according to the flesh; it is holistic inner and outer sanctification, that wholehearted single-minded perfecting to be finally perfected on the last day.

Fourthly, in John, it is no longer living in sin but a perfecting in love, and in Hebrews it is that entering into the once-for-all sanctifying of humanity in the blood, that is, the sacrificial death, of Christ.

Finally in Revelation, holiness is corporate and cosmic.

Those, in very brief summary, are the biblical themes that must be part of any understanding of Christian sanctification and Christian perfecting. But of course, we cannot stop there. Christian theology does not just summarize what is *explicit* in Scripture, but interprets it by drawing

53. Ibid., 351.
54. Ibid., 355.

out what is *implicit*. The outstanding example of that is the doctrine of the Holy Trinity. That God is three Persons in one Being is not explicit in the New Testament, far less the Old. But the doctrine was developed by the church Fathers over four centuries from what was *implied* by Scripture, and without it, the faith of the New Testament in the Father, the Son, and the Holy Spirit collapses into incoherence. Systematic (or better, dogmatic) theology has to work at this task in every area of doctrine, while also ensuring that it is not just a ragbag of themes, motifs, or disparate doctrines, but a coherent whole. We now turn therefore in the next chapter to the way in which this particular area or theme of Christian theology, our understanding of Christian sanctification, and particularly Christian "perfecting," developed historically. Later in the book we shall be concerned with how this doctrine fits into trinitarian Christian theology as a whole.

3

Christian Perfecting in Church Tradition

Having looked at the roots of the doctrine of Christian sanctification in Scripture, we come in this chapter to the historical development of the doctrine through the patristic and medieval eras. Once again, this is an enormous task. The amount of primary material to be taken into account is even greater, and once again we shall have to be highly selective. We cannot engage here in any frontline research but will simply summarize very briefly the research and writings of scholars and students of church history who have studied the writings of the most prominent Christian figures in depth. Once again we are interested in an overview, tracing the concept of the holy and of what it means to sanctify or "make holy" (*sanctum facere*). But within that we are also concerned to trace the more specific language of "perfection."

It is worth repeating that both of these terms are problematic in the contemporary world. "Holiness" tends to be interpreted as "other-worldliness." "Perfection" was a problematic word for Wesley and he only insisted on using it because it was biblical. But he also repudiated those who interpreted it in a legalistic way to mean absolute sinless perfection. That was a particular aversion in Protestant culture, and remains a bugbear. As we have suggested, it might not be such a stumbling block if in our contemporary culture we spoke of "Christian perfec*ting*," for in none of the great teachers of the church did it imply *arrival* at final sinless perfection in this life.

For Wesley, Christians could be perfect in one way only, perfect in *love*. But even that meant only whole-hearted, undivided love and was not a static final perfection so that they floated two feet off the ground with some esoteric spirituality which made them inhuman by losing contact with practical daily life. Quite the contrary, it meant that they were immersed in the practicalities of living and were so filled with an all-consuming love for God, and therefore a practical love for their neighbor, that they developed an integrity and maturity of character.[1] In short, it made them more truly and compassionately human. But it did not at all guarantee perfect performance. It was *not* sinless perfection. It did *not* mean that anyone was flawless. Christians always remain fallen creatures. Despite his attempt to give this carefully balanced view of "perfection," Wesley nevertheless found himself at odds with his Calvinist friends and allies in the evangelical revival. He was using a scriptural term, "perfection," and was drawing on long centuries of Christian spirituality, but sadly the word seemed to trigger (as it still does) an instinctive reaction.

The pioneers (at least among Protestants) in tracing this tradition of Christian spirituality through the centuries appear to have been two Methodists, Harold William Perkins, and the Cambridge scholar, R. Newton Flew, whose book, *The Idea of Perfection in Christian Theology*, was first published in 1934.[2] We shall draw on that and on more recent works of scholarship in summarizing very briefly and selectively the tradition Wesley inherited. We are not primarily interested at this point in defending Wesley, but in tracing this ancient, central, mainstream teaching of the Christian church in which he stood.

a) The Greek Fathers

The Second Century

The early Greek bishops and teachers of the church had the advantage that they still operated in the same Hellenistic culture in which the apostles had evangelized. Moreover, the Christian Scriptures (the New Testament writings), while they were the product of minds steeped in the Hebrew Scriptures, were in their own language, the common Greek of the day. That gives those Hellenes an authority in the interpretation of Scripture that we barbarians need to respect.

---

1. See the significant development of Christian holiness in terms of character development in Hauerwas' *Character* and *Sanctify Them*.

2. See Perkins, *Doctrine*, and Flew, *Idea of Perfection*.

The writings of the "Apostolic" Fathers (the name given only to the generation immediately after the apostles) include those from the pen of three bishops, Clement of Rome, Ignatius of Antioch, and Polycarp of Smyrna, as well as a letter attributed to Barnabas, and *The Shepherd*, which was a collection of visions from a Roman called Hermas. Since the Roman church still used Greek we may include it here. In Ignatius we find a passing reference to "perfect faith and love toward Jesus Christ," and an assertion that appears to echo 1 John 3:6: "No one professing faith sins, nor does anyone possessing love hate."[3] He also develops the Pauline metaphor of the church as a holy temple of living stones, writing to the Ephesians that they were "stones of a temple, prepared beforehand for the building of God the Father, hoisted up to the heights by the crane of Jesus Christ, which is the cross, using as a rope the Holy Spirit."[4] Paul Bassett sums up Ignatius's teaching: "While he clearly advocates perfection, perfection in love, as the Christian norm for this life, he says nothing of how one enters upon this perfection, nothing of its relation (whether theological or experiential) to justification, and nothing of its connection with the notion of sanctification, although he does relate it to the work of the Holy Spirit."[5]

In *The Shepherd*, Hermas takes up the problem of post-baptismal sin. It is striking that, in contrast to later tradition, the earliest churches appeared to share the belief that sin after baptism could not be forgiven. That seems to have been a deduction from the teaching of 1 John 3:6–9 as well as Paul in passages such as Romans 6:1 and (especially) Hebrews 6:4–8, but from our perspective today, it appears to destroy the Christian's sense of security. Presumably open and obvious acts of sin were in mind—theft, adultery, murder, and so on—but Hermas raises the question of inner sins of thought. After imagining a beautiful woman he would like to have as his wife, the dreamer falls into condemnation in case that constituted lusting after her in his heart.[6] In *The Shepherd*, he argues for the more moderate view that repentance *is* possible after baptism, but he still holds to the norm that Christians do not repeatedly sin. Among the commandments that Hermas attributes to the angel-shepherd is this: "For the one who has received forgiveness of sins ought never to sin again, but to live in purity."

---

3. Ign. *Eph.* 14:2 (Holmes, *Apostolic Fathers*, 195).

4. Ign. *Eph.* 9:1 (Holmes, *Apostolic Fathers*, 191).

5. Bassett and Greathouse, *Historical Development*, 30.

6. Herm *Vis.* 1 (Holmes, *Apostolic Fathers*, 455).

He adds, "If, after this great and holy call, anyone is tempted by the devil and sins, that person has one opportunity for repentance."[7]

What is clear from all this is the serious importance of baptism. While the Fathers did not teach the later, medieval, *ex opere operato* view, that the very going through the waters of baptism automatically effects regeneration, they did encourage catechumens to look on the moment of baptism as the moment of regeneration. Having totally renounced the devil and all his works, they would be born of the Spirit while looking to Christ in faith at that moment.[8] They were then "washed" clean and utterly committed to the new life. Baptism was the beginning of radical sanctification.

Clement and Origen

In fact, it became common to refer to baptism as the "perfecting" of the Christian. Clement of Alexandria, a leading Christian teacher and thinker at the end of the second century, particularly developed this terminology for baptism in his work, *The Instructor (Paedagogus)*: "Straightway, on our regeneration, we attained that perfection after which we aspired." Clement's contemporary Irenaeus, a native of Asia Minor who became missionary bishop in Lugdunum in Gaul (now Lyons in France), developed the teaching that Jesus "recapitulated" our human life, growing and perfecting each stage of life. Clement similarly, while he rejects the idea that Jesus was ever imperfect, writes of his baptism as his "perfection." Consequently we too are "perfected" in baptism: "But he is perfected by the washing of baptism alone, and is sanctified by the descent of the Spirit? Such is the case. The same also takes place in our case, whose exemplar Christ became. Being baptized, we are illuminated; illuminated we become children [lit. 'sons']; being made children, we are made perfect; being made perfect, we are immortal."[9] According to Piotr Ashwin-Siejkowski, "The Irenaean 'childhood analogy' was thus adopted by Clement and incorporated into his own programme of education."[10]

We too can understand today that regeneration is in some sense a completed work. Since the human person is an indivisible whole, we cannot be partially born again. We are either "in Christ" by faith or we are not;

---

7. Herm. *Mand.* 4.3, 31 (Holmes, *Apostolic Fathers*, 513f.).

8. See Cyril of Jerusalem, *The Catechetical Lectures* 3.4 (*NPNF*[2] 7.15).

9. Clement, *Paed.* I, vi (*PG* Vol. VIII, 280C–281A) (*ANF* 2:215).

10. Ashwin-Siejkowski, *Clement of Alexandria*, 148. See the whole of chapter 5, "The Path to Perfection," 147–87.

we have either confessed and believed, repented and turned to Christ, or we have not. In that sense, our regeneration is "perfect." But in another of his major works, *The Miscellanies* (*Stromata*), Clement develops his teaching about a more mature perfection.

Clement was educated in Athens itself and was teaching in Alexandria, the greatest Greek city of the ancient world. Debate was hot and furious in this university city where Jews and Hellenists, philosophers and differing faiths and religions shared in robust and ongoing discussion. Philo of Alexandria, a contemporary of Jesus almost two centuries earlier, had formulated a Hellenistic kind of Judaism there, and Clement himself had studied Judaism and the Hebrew Scriptures, but was also contextualizing his Christian teaching using Platonist and Stoic notions. The philosophy of the day was not merely rationalistic abstract thinking, but had a religious dimension in which the life of the body was disciplined in order to contemplate the mysteries of the spiritual or intellectual realm. It was in that context that some teachers who regarded themselves as Christians developed the highly imaginative and vivid teaching about the ascent of the soul through the heavens that we call "Gnosticism."

Clement believed that, while these heretical Gnostics had some strange ideas, Christians had the true knowledge (*gnōsis*) and that mature Christians were therefore the "true Gnostics." Being intensively loving souls, they have a vision of God attainable by "the pure in heart." "This is the function of the Gnostic, who has been perfected, to have converse with God through the great High Priest, being made like the Lord up to the measure of his capacity."[11]

Clement enumerates the virtues that will be part of the character of these holy persons. One of the first is impassibility (*apatheia*), meaning control of the passions rather than not having any. To "bring themselves into captivity" and die to the old humanity, by "becoming free from sin, both the Gospel and the apostle enjoin." They will therefore be characterized by prudence, righteousness, wisdom, fortitude, moderation, and liberality.

Clement employs his Greek heritage here in enumerating these Aristotelian virtues that characterize a person of character. But for the Christian, the beginning of this character development is faith in Christ. "Christ is both the foundations and the superstructure," by whom are both the beginning, which is faith, and the end or goal (*telos*), which is love. By this we gain true knowledge through grace. "And this takes place, whenever one

11. Clement, *Strom.* VII, iii (*PG*, Vol. IX, 416C–417A) (*ANF* 2:526).

hangs on the Lord by faith, by knowledge, by love, and ascends along with him to where the God and guard of our love and faith is."[12] This knowledge of God purifies "and by its own light conveys humanity through the mystic stages of advancement till it restores the pure in heart to the crowning place of rest, teaching to gaze on God, face to face with knowledge and understanding." "And in my view, the first saving change is that from heathenism to faith, as I said before; and the second, that from faith to knowledge. And the latter, terminating in love thereafter gives the loving to the loved, that which knows to that which is known."[13] Ashwin-Siejkowski comments: "The crucial distinction between *pistis* [faith] and *gnōsis* [knowledge] in Clement's theory reflects two stages of Christian life. The first stage *pistis* is directly related to conversion and baptism/illumination and introduces the newly baptized into the spiritual realm (or into salvation). The second stage associated with *gnōsis* [knowledge] is a further growth in holiness and experience of God."[14]

These advances are part of the Christian's education. The first stage is preceded by catechesis, instruction in the doctrines of the faith and teaching in ethical discipline, "while the second calls for more advanced hermeneutics and intellectual abilities."[15] For Clement, as for all the Fathers, the spiritual and the intellectual are not contrary to each other (as in some superficial forms of modern pietism), but require each other.

According to Mayeul de Dreuille, these two changes distinguish three stages in the progress of the "true Gnostic." The transition from unbelief to belief is brought about through faith, by which "Clement understands the starting point of conversion and a comprehensive knowledge of the essentials, which have to be perfected by knowledge or *gnosis*." The knowledge of God is purifying and produces a continuing repentance or turning away from sin producing control of the passions (*apatheia*), a state of tranquility, and a consequence of perfect self-mastery. "Beyond faith and knowledge there is a third stage, leading to contemplation that is *agapē* or love."[16] Here we must understand that knowledge of God can never be exhaustive or controlling, for God is infinite and while we apprehend him with the intellect, we can never comprehend him.[17]

12. Clement, *Strom.* X (*PG*, Vol. IX, 480A) (*ANF* 2:538f).

13. Clement, *Strom.* VII, x (*PG* Vol. IX, 481A) (*ANF* 2:539).

14. Ashwin-Siejkowski, *Clement of Alexandria*, 164.

15. Ibid., 165.

16. Dreuille, *Absolute Love*, 5.

17. See Hägg, *Clement of Alexandria*, on Clement's apophaticism.

Origen succeeded Clement as head of the catechetical school in Alexandria and developed his scheme of spiritual ascent. He outlined several stages.[18] In the first, where faith is primary, conversion comes in realizing that, although we are created in the image of God, this has been defaced by sin. The second stage is that of union with God. Origen interprets the story of the exodus and the wilderness wanderings of the children of Israel as an allegory by which we may understand this spiritual journey. There is first the struggle against sin and the passions in order to cultivate *apatheia*, understood as self-control. But there is progress in spiritual understanding coming to a climax in *ecstasis*, which is awe before God. The third stage, developed in his commentary on the Song of Solomon, is that of perfect union in love. The soul is captivated by the beauty of God, wounded by the arrow of love (a common ancient metaphor),[19] and receives the five spiritual senses to "taste and see that the Lord is good." Divine light is a gift of the Spirit putting the soul in direct contact with God.

The Later Greek Fathers

The spiritual theology of Clement and Origen had a lasting influence on later writers. Among these, none was greater that Athanasius, Archbishop of Alexandria, the major defender of the full deity of Christ expressed in the creed of Nicaea, who had the key role in formulating the church's trinitarian faith. But in addition to his monumental theological contribution, Athanasius also wrote the life of his friend Antony, the pioneer of the monastic movement.[20] Antony was challenged by hearing the text, "If you would be perfect, go and sell what you have and give to the poor, and come and follow me" (Matt 19:21), and retired into seclusion for fifteen years in a tomb or mausoleum which symbolized dying with Christ. There he practiced prayer and hard manual work, triumphing over severe demonic temptation by his devotion to Christ. After a further twenty years secluded in an abandoned fort in the desert, he emerged to become an example of the "pure in heart," inspiring many to aspire to holiness through lifelong discipline.[21]

---

18. For this paragraph, see Dreuille, *Absolute Love*, 9–14.

19. Think of Cupid!

20. Athanasius, *Vit. Ant.* (*NPNF*[2] 4:195–221); *PG* 26, 835–976; cf. Dreuille, *Absolute Love*, 17–25.

21. See also Burton-Christie, "Place of the Heart."

The three great Cappadocian bishops, Basil of Caesarea, Gregory of Nazianzus, and Gregory of Nyssa, completed the formulation of appropriate language to express and safeguard the deity of Christ and the doctrine of the Trinity. Their work lay behind the final form of the Nicene Creed, the church's most definitive expression of the faith. But our interest at this point lies in Basil's work as the one who also developed the more moderate "coenobitic" monasticism, correcting the extreme asceticism of the Egyptian desert hermits. Derived from *koinos* (common) and *bios* (life), the word denotes living as a community devoted to work and prayer rather than as isolated hermits. Protestants were much later to react against a corrupt monasticism and to emphasize that the holy life must be lived in the world rather than by withdrawal from it. Nonetheless, it must be recognized that Basil and his elder sister Macrina, by turning the life of their rich, landowning family with their servants into a Christian community where all shared equally in prayer and manual work, were setting a powerful example of community Christian life.[22] Basil drew up rules for communal life in the *Asceticon*, later called by Benedict, *The Rule of Saint Basil*. De Dreuille puts his finger on what is crucial: "But at the base of the whole structure he puts the twofold aspect of charity—the love of God which leads to total renunciation of the world, easier of attainment in a solitary life, and the love of one's neighbour which excludes eremitical life."[23] Harriet Luckman sees Basil as in harmony with the Syrian tradition of prayer "that a pure heart is a heart that has but one purpose and aim."[24]

Basil's friend, Gregory of Nazianzus, great orator and poet and Archbishop of Constantinople, prays to the "Light that knew no dawn" for purity of heart:

> From sin Thy child in mercy free
> And let me dwell in light with Thee:
> That, cleansed from stain of sin,
> I may meet homage give,
> And, pure in heart, behold
> Thy beauty while I live;
> Clean hands in holy worship raise,
> And Thee, O Christ my Saviour, praise.[25]

22. See Sunberg, "Cappadocian Mothers."

23. Dreuille, *Absolute Love*, 54. See also Rousseau, *Basil of Caesarea*, 190–232.

24. Luckman, "Basil of Caesarea," 101.

25. Brownlie, *Hymns of the Early Church*, 20.

Nazianzen also employs the concept of "deification" (*theōsis*) probably more than any of the Fathers.[26] Inheriting this language from Irenaeus and Athanasius, Nazianzen is clear that a Christian understanding of deification is not like the ascent of contemporary Neo-Platonism, but for Christians, being united to Christ, comes only through *kenōsis*, self-emptying. It is possible because of the incarnation, but initiated in the Christian by the Spirit at baptism.[27] Gregory is quite clear, however, that deification is a metaphor, model, or figure. It is not to be taken literally or strictly (*kyriōs*).[28] We do not share in God's essence or being, but rather reflect his character. Deification has attracted much recent interest as a synonym for sanctification, but Nazianzen's clarification needs to be clearly understood.[29]

Gregory of Nyssa, Basil's younger brother, developed the concept of "perfection," following Nazianzen, it has been suggested,[30] by adopting the doctrine of Clement of Alexandria on the infinity of God. For material things, "perfection" always implies definite limits, but since God is infinite perfection, and since Christian perfection comes through participation in God, it is "utterly impossible to attain perfection." Since we must obey the divine command, "Be perfect as your Father in heaven is perfect," Gregory Nyssen suggests that "it may be that human perfection lies precisely in this—constant growth in the good."[31]

In the *Life of Moses*, Moses climbing Mount Sinai becomes the symbol for the Christian's ascent to God. In *The Christian Institute*, Nyssen writes about the importance of directing one's love towards the right "goal." For Plato, "love" is that which draws us to our goal, and for Christians, this focus for our love must be God. But we can love him only as the Spirit draws us and as we are guided by the Scriptures. There has to be a synergy between the gracious work of the Holy Spirit and the effort of the Christian in self-discipline.[32] "He who applies himself to prayer, taking the Spirit as his guide and support, burns with the love of his Saviour and

26. Winslow, *Dynamics*, 34.

27. See McGuckin, "Strategic Adaptation."

28. See Gregory Nazianzen *Or.* 42.17 (*NPNF*² 2:391; *PG* 36, 477C).

29. See Christensen, "Christian Perfection": the concept is more fully explored in the volume as a whole, Christensen and Wittung, *Partakers*; cf. also Kärkäinen, *One with God*, and Finlan and Kharlamov, *Theōsis*.

30. Otis, "The Throne," 162.

31. Gregory Nyssen, *Vit. Moy.* (*PG* 44, 300–301), translated by Bassett in Bassett and Greathouse, *Historical Development*, 81.

32. See Dreuille, *Absolute Love*, 61–68, on Gregory of Nyssa.

throbs with desire, never finding satiety in his prayer but always inflamed with the good." De Dreuille comments: "In this continual transport the soul is purified, abandoning itself to the attraction of divine beauty, and perceives the love of God (*agapē*) descending to fill its yearnings (*erōs*) to the full."[33] John Chrysostom similarly urges his congregation to aspire to "perfection," which he understands in terms of love. Not only monks, but all Christians are to aspire to this.[34]

A Syrian Writer: Macarius/Symeon

A version of part of Nyssen's *The Christian Institute* appears also in the work of an anonymous writer, thought at one time to be Macarius the Egyptian, and so known today as "Pseudo-Macarius." It appears, however, that this anonymous writer was a Syrian Christian, possibly Symeon, but scholars are divided on the question of who influenced whom. George Maloney argues that while the Hellenistic influence in Clement, Origen, and their Alexandrian successors led them to think in terms of abstract and logical ideas, the tradition of Antioch in Syria reflected the more Semitic focus on the dynamic, voluntaristic, and existential, and this certainly characterizes the Macarian homilies.[35]

Newton Flew noted the strong individualism in the homilies and a piety seemingly independent of the liturgical worship of the church. This "true life of the soul" is God-given however, and "Macarius" grounds his confidence in the incarnation: "His mysticism is a Christ-mysticism."[36] Yet, like all the Fathers, he has a strong belief in the freedom of the human will and his doctrine of progress in the Christian life has a strong insistence on moral purification. "Experience of struggle against sin makes the warriors firmer and wiser."[37] Consequently, as an infant only gradually grows to maturity, and crops only gradually ripen, "so likewise also in spiritual things, where there is a question of so much wisdom and subtlety, man makes progress gradually 'and reaches to a perfect man, to the full measure' (Eph 4:13), and not as some say: 'To put off one garment and put

---

33. Ibid., 66, taking the quotation from *Gregori Nysseni Opera* (W. Jaeger, ed.), 8:78.

34. See Dreuille, *Absolute Love*, 72f., also McCormick, "Wesley's Use of John Chrysostom."

35. Maloney, "Introduction," 2; see also Golitzin, "Temple and Throne."

36. Flew, *Perfection*, 181.

37. Ibid., 183.

on another."[38] Moral transformation comes at the beginning of the new life, but the ethical virtues develop gradually. There is no quick and easy path to sanctity:

> Real perfection does not consist in refraining from evil, but only if, entering into your darkened mind, you put to death the serpent that lies inside your mind, deep down in your thoughts. That serpent kills you by digging itself deeply into the secret chambers of your soul, and there sets up its nest (for the soul is an abyss). Unless, I say, you put it to death and get rid of all the uncleanness that dirties you.

How then can we obtain purity of heart?

> There is no other way than through him who was crucified for us. For he himself is the way, the life, the truth, the door, the pearl, the living and heavenly bread.[39]

The key to purity of heart, cleansing from this inner sin, is therefore a heart filled by the Holy Spirit with love for Christ.[40] "Macarius" writes of such believers: "Being completely attached to the cross of Christ, they daily perceive in themselves that they are spiritually progressing toward their spiritual Bridegroom." But this is the great paradox of Christian holiness: "The richer they become spiritually, the poorer they consider themselves, as they burn interiorly with an insatiable spiritual yearning (*pothō*) for the heavenly Bridegroom."[41]

Given then that those who desire to know Christ in this way are the pure in heart, "Macarius" quite clearly teaches that this inner sin is "rooted out" or "eradicated." The verb he uses, *ekrizoō*, comes from the noun *riza*, a root, but of course this is clearly a metaphor. He is not thinking of this inner sin as some kind of thing or entity, but he is clear that the pure in heart are cleansed (to substitute another metaphor) from this "indwelling sin" (to use the Pauline phrase). But how is this related to natural desire? Macarius addresses this very question, but his answer is not entirely clear:

38. Pseudo-Macarius, *Homily* 15:41 (*PG* 34, 604C), Maloney, tr., *Spiritual Homilies*, 124.

39. Pseudo-Macarius, *Homily* 17:15 (*PG* 34, 633B), Maloney, tr., *Spiritual Homilies*, 140f.

40. See Flew, *Perfection*, 184f. for Macarius's focus on love. On the emphasis on the Holy Spirit in Macarius-Symeon, see Hoo-Jung Lee, "Experiencing the Spirit in Wesley and Macarius."

41. Pseudo-Macarius, *Homily* 10:1 (*PG* 34, 541B), Maloney, tr., *Spiritual Homilies*, 88.

"Is natural desire (*hē physikē epithumia*) rooted out (*synekrizoutai*) with the sin (*meta tēs hamartias*)? Answer: Sin is rooted out, and humanity (*ho anthrōpos*) receives the original formation of pure Adam. . . . Humanity is deified (*apotheoutai*)."[42] And yet, Macarius has a warning:

> Simple-minded and foolish persons, when grace begins to some degree to work in them, believe that they are simply freed from sin. . . . Very often we have found certain ones among the brethren who have received so much joy and grace that, for five or six years, they asserted, desire (*epithumia*) had been burned up and from that time on they thought themselves free from it. Yet the hidden potential for evil rose up in them and they so burned with the fire of desire (*epithumia*) that they were amazed and crushed. . . . Therefore, no one in his sane mind should dare to say: "Because I am in grace, I am thoroughly freed from sin."[43]

(b) The Latin Tradition

Greek Christianity was the direct result of apostolic evangelism (as was Syrian), and the New Testament Scriptures emerged from these early Jewish and Gentile churches, written (significantly) in Greek. Latin Christianity resulted from further cross-cultural mission into a culture that was politically and militarily dominant, but intellectually less sophisticated. Latin culture was under Greek tutelage. This difference is reflected in the Latin Fathers, whose theology tends to be more characterized by legal and judicial categories of rules and regulations, guilt and pardon. That also influenced their concepts of holiness and perfection.

Hippolytus and Tertullian

Hippolytus, an elder in Rome and contemporary of Origen in the early third century, was the last leading figure of the Roman church to write in Greek. He led a schism when he was elected bishop in opposition to Callistus, whom he regarded as too lenient in his treatment of penitents guilty of mortal sin. His strict views on the purity of the church are illustrated in *The Apostolic Tradition*, a book of church order, which among other things

---

42. Pseudo-Macarius, *Homily* 26:2 (PG 34, 676B), author's own translation.

43. Pseudo-Macarius, *Homily* 17:5-6 (PG 34, 628AB), Maloney, tr., *Spiritual Homilies*, 137 (slightly altered).

lays down rules for admitting non-believers to hear the gospel preached.[44] By custom, they were then dismissed from the Christian assembly before the celebration of the Holy Communion. But even to be admitted to the "Liturgy of the Word" required passing a rigorous test. Not only were astrologers, magicians, prostitutes, and heathen priests debarred, but also actors, charioteers, soldiers, and magistrates, and even teachers of young children came under scrutiny. That sinners should be debarred from hearing the gospel until they reform is hardly believable in the context of today's evangelical Christianity, but the context must be remembered. Rome in the third century was a dangerous, deeply corrupt, and mercilessly cruel society where promiscuity, child abuse, and perversion of all kinds were rife, often as expressions of idolatrous and indeed demonic "religion." This was not just a matter of outward practices: the corporate sin of a whole culture shaped deeply disturbed and warped people. That they were clamoring to come into the fellowship of the church is witness not only to the fears of those who were vulnerable, exploited, and so themselves warped, but to the moral example of Christians and their loving compassion for those around them. In that context, the concern of Hippolytus for the holiness of the church and the deep and true sanctification of those coming to faith was not only understandable but imperative.

The same concerns motivated his more creative contemporary, Tertullian, from the Roman province of Africa. Gerald Bray sees sanctification as the main theme of his writings.[45] Human beings were guilty before God and the problem was rooted in the will. Sin had penetrated to the will through the flesh, and therefore, even before the flesh was cleansed in baptism, there had to be deep and true repentance before baptism so that the Spirit could enter the soul. But it was only then that the real battle began—the struggle between the Spirit and the lusts of the flesh. And to lose that battle because of the fragility of the flesh was to risk an eternal hell. The key word in Tertullian's doctrine of sanctification is therefore *discipline*.

Tertullian was disgusted at the way in which the Eastern fertility religions had infiltrated Rome and corrupted the old Roman morality. For the old Roman republic—where the temple to Vesta, the goddess of the hearth, was inhabited not by priestess-prostitutes, but by the Vestal Virgins—sanctity was closely linked to chastity. Whereas the Old Testament celebrates marriage, Tertullian's reaction against promiscuity turned into

44. See Dix and Chadwick, *Treatise*, for a translation.

45. Bray, *Holiness*, 66.

misogyny and a strongly negative attitude to human sexuality. He saw the Bible as a *regula*, a rule for life, and therefore the answer to the problem of decaying morality. But Christians were to practice an even more rigorous ethic. The discipline of the Old Testament had been incomplete, even allowing polygamy. The coming of Christ brought an end to this period of *indulgentia*, but even then the apostles had been lenient in enforcing the new standard. But now, through the Montanist prophets (Tertullian was attracted to this charismatic and millenarian movement), the Holy Spirit was giving more detailed instructions. Since Christ was soon to return to Phrygia (where Montanus prophesied!), Christians were now to abstain from all sexual relations, even within marriage. The entire sanctification of the human race was now possible at last in the dawning age of entire chastity!

It has to be said that Tertullian's legalism and his negative attitude towards human sexuality and the biblical ideal of joyful marriage has had a deep and lasting effect on many Western Christians right down to the present. While sexual temptation is real and sexual promiscuity and perversion represent possibly the most deeply damaging dimensions of human sinfulness, Christian holiness has too often been understood in this merely negative and legalistic way.

Augustine

Something of these attitudes also characterized the greatest of the Latin fathers, Augustine, whose powerful rhetoric has made the whole Western tradition of Christianity thoroughly Augustinian. Augustine's theology is more deeply shaped by Platonism than the Nicene Greek fathers, who were perhaps more aware of the dangers of their own Hellenistic heritage. His focus is less on the centrality of Christ and more on the church and the experience of the individual believer. Even his doctrine of the Trinity owes more to his anthropology and his understanding of human psychology than to its true root in the biblical narrative of salvation. The newly converted Augustine understood religion as a matter of "God and the soul, the soul and God," so that there is a highly individualistic and introspective strain to his thought. It can be argued that all the distortions of Western subjectivism, and of a theology which is little more than anthropology in disguise (Feuerbach's stinging critique of liberalism), can be traced back to this.

Nevertheless, there is much that is positive and indeed profound about Augustine's theology, not least that he was the great champion of grace. It was this that made him the great opponent of Pelagius, the Celtic monk who seemed to be proclaiming salvation by works. It also made him the great opponent of Donatism. That African movement of extreme loyalty to the faith rejected the *traditores*, presbyters who had handed over the sacred Scriptures to the persecuting authorities, as unworthy to dispense the sacraments. Augustine insisted that no one was "worthy" to dispense or receive the sacraments and that the church was holy, not because of the holiness of its members, but because of the holiness of Christ, its Head. We come to the table not to proclaim our worthiness, but with empty hands, invited in grace because of our need. That the church was to be viewed as a school for sinners rather than a society of saints was something of a departure from previous ecclesiology, not least that of Hippolytus. But it was a powerful repudiation of the idea that Christian holiness is to be equated with any kind of legalistic perfection.

Of greatest interest here, however, is the way in which Augustine's doctrine of grace and his concept of love shaped his understanding of both human sin and Christian holiness. And at this point it is important for Protestants to understand not only how Augustine was a forerunner of the Protestant Reformation, but also the ways in which his theology was quite different from Luther. Both Augustine and Luther (and indeed Calvin) were theologians of grace, but they had different ways of thinking about grace and they differed in their views of justification.

As a Platonist, Augustine tended to speak of grace as a kind of substance coming from God; a medicine or influence that operated in an interior way to heal the human will (*voluntas*). What began as a metaphor became a definitive model until eventually in later Augustinianism it seems to have been taken literally. When the will was healed by grace, the believer would ("freely" but certainly!) believe and obey. This medicinal grace was infused into the Christian through the sacraments, regenerating grace by baptism, persevering grace by the Holy Communion, so that the Christian was made (*facere*) increasingly righteous (*iustus*) or holy (*sanctus*). Justification (*iustum facere*) and sanctification (*sanctum facere*) therefore referred to the same process. Clearly, while Luther was also a theologian of grace, it was at this point that in effect he repudiated Augustine and the Augustinian tradition. He concluded through his study of Paul that "justification" was to be *declared* righteous or holy and that this came through faith. Historically, therefore, Protestant theology works with a clear distinction between justification (being *declared* righteous or holy) and sanctification (being *made* righteous or holy).

What is important for us at this point, however, is to see how Augustine's doctrine of grace connected with his doctrine of sin. Scholars debate whether his view of grace shaped his doctrine of sin or *vice versa*, but all we need to note here is their close interconnection. If Augustine was to insist, in opposition to Pelagius, that salvation was totally by grace and that good works made no contribution at all, then he needed a concept of "total sin" to match his belief in "total grace." Somehow, despite any apparent moral goodness, humanity as a whole must be corporately sinful. That was what required a doctrine of *original sin*.

It is important to see that Augustine did not invent the doctrine of original sin: most of the elements of the doctrine are there in the Greek Fathers. They invented the term "the Fall" to refer to the disobedience of Adam and Eve. They took seriously Paul's assertion in Romans 5 that this brought death to the human race, and it was this ontological dimension, death, on which they focused. But they also taught that sin was universal and that it was not merely outward action but inward condition. Yet although all that is common to all the Fathers, Augustine did shape the doctrine in his own way. What he added was a clearer assertion that all shared in Adam's guilt for the Fall, although he also said that this share in original guilt was washed away in baptism. But most significantly for our concerns here, he also developed a more profound analysis of the psychological dynamic of "indwelling sin" (to use Paul's phrase again), but unfortunately added to it a bizarre theory that this "disease" of original sin was passed on through sexual transmission. We can forget the last point as totally unbiblical and incoherent, but his analysis of the psychological dynamic of inner sin is indeed perceptive, and it is best approached as an aspect of his concept of love.

If Augustine was the greatest theologian of grace since Paul, he was also the greatest theologian of love. We have seen the importance of love in the homilies of "Macarius" and the theology of Gregory of Nyssa, but Augustine develops this much more comprehensively. His concept of love runs through his works. His great work on the Trinity includes the idea that the Trinity should be thought of as the Lover (the Father), the Beloved (the Son), and the Love between them (the Spirit).[46] He eventually arrives at what he considers the best model for understanding the Trinity, found in the true "image of God," which as a Platonist he identifies as the human

46. Augustine, *Trin.* 13:10 (*NPNF*[1] 3:124).

mind. This is the trinity of memory, understanding, and will, and "will" is interpreted as love. Also in his great theology of history, *The City of God*, in which he traces the two cities—the earthly and the heavenly—through time, he similarly finds the concept of love to be pivotal: "Two loves built two cities. Love of self to the contempt of God built the earthly city: love of God to the contempt of self, the heavenly."[47]

What is most significant for us here is that he also employs this idea of the two kinds of love to analyze the psychology of the motivation of the individual. The basic idea is the Platonist one that we are drawn to what we love. We cannot be human without being drawn to what we love, and every human being is therefore motivated by love. The key question is *what* we love:

> Love (*amor*) itself cannot be empty. For what person is there who does anything at all, except by love? Show me the love that is empty and does not do anything! Shameful deeds, adulteries, acts of violence, murders, all excesses—is it not love which produces these? Therefore purify your love! Turn into the garden the waters flowing into the drain! Whatever desires it had for the world, let it have for the Creator of the world! Love! But be careful what you love! The love of God, the love of our neighbour is called *caritas*: the love of the world, the love of this life, is called *concupiscentia*. Let *concupiscentia* be tethered, *caritas* stirred up![48]

For Augustine then, *amor* may be given two different names, depending on the object to which it is directed. If it is drawn towards the things of the world, it is *concupiscentia*, a selfish love that is out to own, to possess, to consume for self-gratification. That is the motivation behind all sin, whether violence, theft, murder, or boasting, lying, and deceit. Elsewhere Augustine uses the word *cupiditas*, greed. At the root of both words is the Latin verb *cupido*, I desire, from which also comes the name of the god Cupid, son of Venus, whom the Greeks called *Erōs*. But it is important to see that while this includes that most powerful desire, sexual desire, it is not limited to that. *Concupiscentia* covers *all* forms of self-centered desire—greed for riches, hunger for position and power, the longing to be praised and feted and famous.

For Augustine, the only possible antidote to this deep-seated "disease" of inner sin at the heart of all human motivation was *caritas*, love

---

47. Augustine, *Civ.* 14:28 (*NPNF*¹ 2:282f.).

48. In Augustine, *Enarrat. Ps.* XXXI, ii.5 (*CCL.* 38.228).

for God. But this was not something we could cultivate on our own. Here Augustine departed from pagan Platonist morality. Only the gift of the Holy Spirit could counteract powerful sinful desire and hence his favorite text from the New Testament, quoted more than any other, was Romans 5:5: "God's love has been poured into our hearts by the Holy Spirit who has been given to us." Augustine took that to refer not to God's love for us, but to our consequent love for God. Our hearts can only be filled with *caritas*, love for God, by being filled with the Holy Spirit.

Gertrude Gillette notes that Augustine expresses the concept of the resulting purity of heart in a number of ways: "simplicity of heart," a "clean heart," and a "single" or "simple heart." It is an inner disposition of the heart focused on God alone and it results, in the light of the sixth beatitude, in seeing God. Augustine "wobbled on the question of whether it was possible to have a direct vision of God in this life," and although he gradually became more negative, he "never totally abandoned the possibility."[49] The "eye of the heart" by which we ultimately pierced the mystery of God was "the intention with which we perform our actions." Sin has obscured our vision and diverted our attention to other objects, but even when we "act for our own selfish motives, yet in our deepest self the heart is sadly divided for we still yearn for true and lasting happiness while trying to find it in transitory and false objects of happiness."[50] To be rid of this duplicity, there had to be a cleansing of the heart by faith, and, as Gillette notes, Augustine was continually quoting Acts 15:9, where Peter declares that God had cleansed the hearts of the Gentiles by faith. But what kind of faith makes the heart pure? Augustine quoted Paul: "faith working through love" (Gal 5:6). "Unless God is loved by faith, the heart cannot be cleansed so as to be fit and ready to see him."[51]

It is impossible to overestimate the importance of this analysis of human motivation for shaping the subsequent Western understanding of sin and sanctification, and particularly (through this long tradition) in shaping the thought of John Wesley. The key is this concept of love. But it is important to see too how the Augustinian concept of the two forms of *amor*, expressed in Latin as *caritas* and *concupiscentia,* related to the Greek vocabulary for love. Early in the twentieth century, the Lutheran theologian Anders Nygren published a biblical study of the motifs of *agapē* and *erōs*, maintaining that the former—*agapē*, the love that is not desire but

49. Gillette, "Purity of Heart," 175f.

50. Ibid., 178.

51. Ibid., 183, quoting Augustine, *Trin.* VIII, 4, 6 (*PL* 42, 951).

generous grace (*charis*), love of the *unlovely*—was the peculiarly Christian form of love over against pagan *erōs* or desire.[52] John Burnaby's important study, *Amor Dei*, pointed out that this was an over-simplification.[53] In the thought of Augustine, our love for God cannot be called *agapē*, if by that we mean love of the undeserving and *unlovely*, for quite clearly, God is supremely beautiful and deserves—indeed, demands—our love and loyalty. Christian love for God, therefore, what Augustine called *caritas* in Latin, is *not* the equivalent of the Greek *agapē*, but the equivalent of *erōs*. In other words, there is not only evil desire: there is also good desire—aspiration, desire to know God and be known by God. That is the kind of love that the Lord demanded of Israel in *Shema*. The Hebrew word *hesed* includes both meanings, loving grace towards the unlovely, and also loyal love toward God and desire to know him, love him, follow and obey him.

Sadly however, although Augustine gave us this psychologically acute and perceptive analysis of human motivation and particularly of the supreme love or desire for God that can purify the heart from the wrong kind of self-centered love or desire, he did not connect this with his concept of Christian "perfection." This was partly because he took a legalistic concept of perfection as perfect performance, and partly because, in his later years at least, he interpreted Romans 7 as referring to the Christian, and held that as long as we are in the "flesh"—that is, in the mortal body—the desires of the flesh mean that we cannot love God with all our hearts. This is a question to which we shall have to return.

Bernard

The pursuit of purity of heart was also a theme in Augustine's contemporary, Cassian.[54] A century later, Benedict's formulation of the rules for the monastic orders, drawing on *The Rule of St. Basil* and other eastern texts, enabled the church not only to survive the challenge of the collapse of Roman civilization with the invasion of the barbarian tribes, but also to re-evangelize Western Europe. The theology and the spiritual life of this Western church through the Dark Ages and into the high Middle Ages were deeply Augustinian, but did not necessarily endorse Augustine's view in every detail (predestination, for example). One of the corrections was in thinking about the spiritual life, the life of holiness. Augustine's concept

52. Nygren, *Agape and Eros.*
53. Burnaby, *Amor Dei.*
54. See Dreuille, *Absolute Love*, 103–10.

of love and his corresponding analysis of human motivation were brought into close connection with the concept of Christian "perfection."

The powerful personality of Bernard of Clairvaux dominated the Cistercian reform of monasticism in the twelfth century, and it was he who developed the more positive understanding of the power of love to perfect the Christian. He discovered the idea of the ladder (*scala*) of love in the seventh chapter of the Rule of St. Benedict and developed it in his treatise, *On the Love of God.*

Bernard bases his spirituality on experience, particularly the experience of the love of God. Jean Leclercq writes that according to Bernard, "Love is the sole object of the sacred texts that recount the history both of salvation and of personal experience. Everything comes from and must lead to love. Salvation history is a love story between God and his people, between God and his church, between God and each person."[55]

But Leclercq adds, "The point of departure for Bernard's entire doctrine is an intense personal experience of the interior struggle." Humanity had lost the spiritual freedom that allowed union with God, and experienced "anxiety, loneliness, failure, absurdity, reason's inability to explain everything, the tendency towards discouragement, and anguish in face of death."[56] To recognize that that is our condition is the starting point. Contemplation brings one to true humility, which Bernard defines as "the virtue by which a man recognizes his own unworthiness because he really knows himself."[57] But at the same time this contemplative knowledge includes faith in God's kindness. All of Bernard's writing about this presupposes both trinitarian theology and taking seriously the *human* experience of Christ. His learning obedience through suffering (as Hebrews emphasizes) is the key to the remedy for our plight. We must imitate his humility. Bernard's great work on the Song of Songs sees it as a song of praise to Christ and "also expresses the longings of the sanctified soul."[58] Because of Christ and the work of the Spirit, there is a way open to us from misery to ecstasy.

It is this way of progress that Bernard develops in his treatise *On the Love of God.* He writes about four degrees, four rungs on the ladder (*scala*), and starts on the lowest rung, the love of self *for self.* This is where we

55. Leclercq, "Introduction," 32.

56. Ibid., 36.

57. Bernard, *On the Steps of Humility and Pride (De Gradibus humilitatis et superbiae)* 1:2, Evans, tr., *Bernard*, 103.

58. Leclercq, "Introduction," 46.

all begin since it is innate and it includes love of the body, which is God's good creation. There is no Gnosticism here, but this love of self becomes selfish and so must be checked by the commandment to love our neighbor. The second degree of love is love *of God for what he gives*. We cannot love our neighbor as we ought till we love God, and yet this is still a mercenary kind of love, loving God for the benefits he gives us. The third degree is to love God *for his own sake*. When the kindnesses of God are experienced, "it will not be difficult for the man who has had that experience to keep the commandment to love his neighbour. . . . He truly loves God, and therefore he loves what is God's. He loves chastely, and to the chaste it is not a burden to keep the commandments; the heart grows purer in the obedience of love, as it is written (1 Pet 1:22)."[59]

This degree of perfection of love means loving God with one's whole body. The bodily desires are not evil in themselves but, in our fallen condition, they are a reality of "the flesh" in the peculiarly Pauline sense. Jean Leclercq comments: "This is what Bernard expresses when he says at times that concupiscence is found not in the body, but in the 'heart.' When the heart has been healed, purified, and redirected, it takes the body with it on its flight to God."[60]

But the dynamic that heals, purifies, and redirects the heart is the desire for God. Here is the thoroughly Augustinian model: the only power that can nullify *concupiscentia* (self-centered desire) is *caritas* (loving desire for God), poured into our hearts by the Holy Spirit.

The fourth degree of perfection in love is a rapture or ecstasy in which we *love ourselves only for God's sake*. This is for hereafter and only a few experience it in this life, and that rarely and momentarily. But the third degree of perfection in love *is* possible in this life.

Thomas Aquinas

With Thomas Aquinas we come to one of the greatest minds of the church, and to a concept of perfection that is not just to be seen within the context of the doctrine of the Christian life, but as a major concept in his whole systematic theology. Perfection is twofold (*duplex est perfectio*), a perfection of *form*, seen in creation from the beginning, and a perfection of *operation*. The latter has been lost in the Fall, the former has not. One must distinguish, therefore, between the first perfection (*perfectio prima*),

59. Bernard, *On the Love of God* (*De diligendo Deo*), 9:26, Evans, tr., *Bernard*, 194.
60. Leclercq, "Introduction," 41.

which creation still has, and the second perfection (*perfectio secunda*), which it will one day have. Perfection may only be attributed analogically to God since God is not composite as creatures are, but being free from all composition is altogether simple. Creatures participate in the perfection of God, since he created them, but not in a pantheistic way.

It is the perfecting of humanity specifically that can be seen as shaping the whole structure of the *Summa Theologica*. Christ *is* the image of God (the exemplar): humanity is *in* the image of God. Humanity retains the "first perfection" of form—that is to say, remains fully human—but must regain the "second perfection" of operation. Edgardo A. Colón-Emeric explains the structure of the *Summa* like this: "The object of the science of theology is God and also humans as they proceed from God and are directed by God. These two objects, the exemplar and the image, constitute the foundation of the *exitus-reditus* [exit-return] schema of the *Summa*. The *Prima Pars* presents the procession of the image from the exemplar; the *Secunda Pars* the movement of the image toward the exemplar; the *Tertia Pars* the union of the image with the exemplar in the person of Christ."[61]

The image of God in us is an image of the Trinity, and in Augustinian fashion, it is the human mind that reflects the Trinity in that there is a procession of knowledge in the word, and a procession of love in the will. The *perfectio prima* of humans is that they are intellectual creatures capable of knowing and loving God. The *perfectio secunda* will be achieved when humans actually do know and love God. This is to be achieved by "grace" through "faith," which are "habits" infused into us by the Holy Spirit. *Caritas* is also an infused habit that perfects the intellect and the will.

There are, therefore, distinguishable states on the way to Christian perfection. Humanity was originally in a state of innocence, but this no longer obtains. Yet we are still in the *status naturae*, the state of nature. Sin has not and could not destroy our natural perfection as human beings, but resulted in a state of fallen or corrupt nature. This did not erase the original image, but has made it impossible to attain final perfection. Christians however, having been infused with grace in baptism, are now in the *status gratiae*, the state of grace, and will move on by grace to the *status gloriae*, the state of glory.

In the light of that, how are we to understand perfection? Aquinas starts from the commandment of Jesus: "Be perfect as your heavenly father is perfect" and concludes from that, that it is possible for a human

61. Colón-Emeric, *Wesley, Aquinas.*

being to be *in some sense* "perfect" in this life. "Perfection" must be understood in terms of love, *caritas*, particularly love of God, and he envisages four possible levels of perfection. The highest conceivable level, the absolute, is where "God is loved as much as he can be loved." That is obviously impossible for any creature: only God can or ever will love like that. The second level is where love for God fills the lover to full capacity continuously and constantly. That may be possible for us hereafter, but not now in the circumstances of this present life. But for Aquinas, the lowest level of perfection *is* possible in this life:

> The lowest degree of perfection requires that everything inimical to God's friendship is excluded. Augustine remarks that cupidity is poison to charity, while the absence of cupidity is charity's perfection. Such perfection is possible here below, and in two ways. First, when human affection excludes everything contrary to charity, in other words, mortal sin. Charity cannot exist without this perfection, which is commanded as necessary for salvation. Next, when human affection excludes everything which hinders our being wholly in love with God. Charity can exist without such perfection, as it does in those who are beginners and in those who are making progress in the life of perfection.[62]

Aquinas's view of the possibility of perfect love in this life is therefore very similar to that of Bernard. All Christians have the grace of *caritas* infused into them at baptism and this love for God excludes all mortal sins. Such sins are not impossible, and, if committed, require the grace of penance, but Christians do not live committing flagrant acts of intentional sin contrary to their love for God. That is incompatible with the state of grace. But those who are no longer beginners, but making progress in the life of perfection, come to the point where everything contrary to being wholly in love with God is excluded: they love God with all their hearts.

Edgardo Colón-Emeric is surely correct in concluding that, despite the many theological differences between Aquinas and Wesley, when it comes to the doctrine of Christian "perfection" understood in terms of love, or specifically *caritas*, there is a remarkable similarity.[63]

---

62. Aquinas, *Summa Theologica*, 2a–2ae, Q. 184, Gilby, tr., *Thomas Aquinas*, 268.

63. See esp. Colón-Emeric, *Wesley, Aquinas*, 149–81. See also Long, *John Wesley's Moral Theology*, 199–201, for parallels.

(c) The Reformation Context

When we come to the theologians of the Reformation, we find a much more negative approach to the idea of Christian "perfection." Their theology is rightly described in Luther's word as "Evangelical," in preference to the political term, "Protestant," which has become more common in the English-speaking world. After all the religiosity and the hypocritical claims to "holiness" and "perfection" in a church that was largely corrupt, the Lutheran Reformation was a return to the scriptural *evangel* or gospel, particularly Paul's gospel, summed up in "justification by faith." The distinction between justification, being *declared* righteous or holy, and sanctification, being *made* righteous or holy, in contrast to the old Augustinian equation of the two, was basic. The justification of the *ungodly* by faith was the article by which the church stood or fell. Salvation was *sola gratia, sola fide*, and *a solo Christo* and this doctrine was to be held against all comers, even in the church, along with the concomitant "formal principle," the *sola scriptura*.

Martin Luther

However, what may seem a clean break was not such a completely new start as some might believe. The Reformation was not the founding of new churches, but the reforming of the "one, holy, catholic, and apostolic church." And while Luther's passionate focus on justification by faith *alone* might lead him at times to be very suspicious indeed of any claims to sanctity or monkish "perfection," or any formal doctrine of sanctification that might compromise justification, there are aspects of his thought that indicate continuity with the piety of the Middle Ages. First there is his re-publication of the *Theologia Germanica*, an anonymous tract emerging from the small groups of *Gottesfreunde* ("Friends of God") who met for prayer and mutual spiritual encouragement in the fourteenth century.[64] Luther's breakthrough was not simply the abstract intellectual discovery of a forensic doctrine, but, like the *Gottesfreunde*, the *sapientia experimentalis* (experimental wisdom), which was the "practice of the presence of God." Secondly, Luther views faith as not just mental assent to what God has done for us in Christ, but as "the wedding ring" that unites us to Christ, the heavenly Bridegroom. Faith is relational and therefore transformative: "Faith, however, is a divine work in us which changes us and makes us to

---

64. See Hoffman, *Theologica Germanica*, for an accessible translation.

be born anew of God. . . . O it is a living, busy, active, mighty thing, this faith. It is impossible for it not to be doing good works incessantly. It does not ask whether good works are to be done, but before the question is asked, it has already done them, and is constantly doing them. Whoever does not do such works is an unbeliever."[65]

The implication is that what is traditionally labeled "sanctification" (the "real change" as Wesley called it) is inseparable in Luther's understanding from the "relative change" of justification. As the Methodist Philip Watson put it sixty years ago, Luther brought about a "Copernican revolution" by moving Christian piety from an anthropocentric or egocentric type, revolving around the needs of the worshipper, to a theocentric type where God is sovereign.[66] The insight that *homo religiosus* is too easily *homo incurvatus in se*, a man turned in on himself, and needs to be delivered from the self-love which is at the heart of his sinful condition, is a truly Augustinian insight.[67] Further, recent interest in the thought of deification in Luther's theology would also strengthen the view that he thinks of real change (i.e., "sanctification") in the Christian, and never merely a forensic change of status.[68]

But like Augustine, Luther did not think that there was any deliverance from this condition of "original sin" in this life. Paul Bassett quotes his amusing and vivid comments in his "table talk":

> The original sin in a man is like his beard, which, though shaved off today so that a man is very smooth around his mouth, yet grows again by tomorrow morning. As long as a man lives, such growth of hair and beard does not stop. But when the shovel slaps the ground on his grave, it stops. In just this way original sin remains in us and exercises itself as long as we live, but we must resist it and always be cutting off its hair.[69]

65. Luther, "Preface to the Epistle of Paul to the Romans," *Luther's Works*, 35:370.

66. Watson, *Let God*.

67. See Jenson, *Gravity of Sin*.

68. See Mannermaa, "Why is Luther"; also Kärkäinen, *One with God*.

69. Bassett & Greathouse, *Historical Development*, 158, with reference to *Weimar Ausgabe, Tischreden*, I: No. 138.

John Calvin

John Calvin has perhaps a more explicit doctrine of Christian sanctification, although again the word may not often be found.[70] He has a different word usage, using "regeneration" for the life-long change, with "repentance" (*poenitentia*) as a synonym. He analyzes this "real change" into two parts, *mortificatio* and *vivificatio*, a participating in the dying of Christ and in his rising to new life. This requires an inner transformation, a "circumcision of the heart," that is, of our internal affections, in such a way that impiety is "eradicated," for God hates "a double heart."[71] Yet, this regeneration takes place gradually and is never completed in this life. He writes that the concupiscence in us, which may be regarded by some as a weakness until it leads to actual sin, "we regard as sin." Consequently "there is always sin in the saints, until they are free from their mortal frame, because depraved concupiscence resides in their flesh."[72] Yet sanctification proceeds in believers as they practice self-denial. Where Luther is influenced by the *Theologia Germanica*, Calvin is influenced here by the fifteenth-century writer Thomas à Kempis. We are to present our bodies as living sacrifices (Rom 12:1), for self-denial leaves no place for the vices "engendered by self-love."[73] When we deny ungodliness and worldly lusts and live soberly, righteously and with godliness (expounding Titus 2:11–14), then "these, connected together by an indissoluble chain, constitute complete perfection." But "nothing is more difficult" and only at the final advent of Christ will this salvation have full effect.[74]

For Calvin, according to R. S. Wallace, Christian perfection meant a wholehearted response to the grace of God. It was a "perfection of faith," and it "will express itself in wholehearted self-denial." Calvin notes that Job is called a "perfect man": "But he prefers to use the words '*rondeur*' or '*integrité*' to describe Job's 'perfection,' since what Scripture really means by perfection is the dedication of the whole heart and mind to God with one single aim, without any doubleness or hypocrisy or holding back in any part." Calvin holds, according to Wallace, that such perfection can never be attained in this life, and that yet "there is a state of achieved

70. Calvin's doctrine is to be found particularly in two chapters of the *Institutes*, III, iii, entitled "Regeneration by Faith. Of Repentance" and III, vii, "The Sum of the Christian Life. The Denial of Ourselves."

71. Calvin, *Institutes*, III, iii, 3.

72. Calvin, *Institutes*, III, iii, 7.

73. Calvin, *Institutes*, III, iii, 1–2.

74. Calvin, *Institutes*, III, iii, 3.

victory over sin and whole-hearted surrender which by the grace of God may be called 'perfection.'"[75] Here again is the idea we noted in Bernard and Aquinas that there is a level of perfection possible in this life and a level of perfection that is not.

Puritans, "Arminians," and Pietists

Two centuries separated the Wesleys from the Reformers and in that intervening time the different movements of evangelical Christianity in the Reformation tradition had different approaches to Christian sanctification and to the idea of Christian "perfection." The Puritan party within the Church of England wanted to reform it further according to "the best Genevan model," abolishing bishops and liturgy. Their Calvinism developed into a scholastic system shaped by (among others) William Perkins, the great John Owen, and the Westminster Confession of Faith (1647), drafted during the years of the Cromwellian revolution. Since justification by grace through faith was linked to an exclusively penal substitutionary view of the atonement, sanctification could very easily become a matter of law and discipline. It was seen as "growth in grace," a pilgrimage pictured for the faithful in that great work of English literature, Bunyan's allegory, *Pilgrim's Progress*. That narrative doctrine of Christian sanctification shaped the life of the people.

During the same decades of the seventeenth century, the opposing "high church" party in the Church of England strongly disavowed "papacy" yet wanted to conserve the ancient catholic forms of episcopacy and liturgy.[76] They were known as "Arminians" (although they owed little directly to Arminius) since they rejected much of the Calvinist tradition beloved by the Puritans, and eventually triumphed with the Restoration of both the monarchy and the Elizabethan settlement of the Church of England in 1660. This was the party of the Wesley family in Epworth in the early eighteenth century, and of particular significance for the Wesleys' doctrine of Christian sanctification, particularly "perfection," was the "holy living school" of George Herbert, Jeremy Taylor, the seventeenth-century Bishop of Armagh, and of Wesley's older contemporary, William Law. It was from

75. Wallace, *Calvin's Doctrine*, 321–26.

76. It is important not to confuse this older "high church" party of Archbishop Laud, which was clearly Protestant, with the later nineteenth-century "high church" party of Tractarians led by Pusey, Keble, and Newman, who regretted the Reformation and moved closer to Rome.

them that the Wesleys derived their love of the "primitive Christianity" of the pre-Nicene Fathers and their doctrine of Christian "perfection."

Less influential on the Wesley brothers were the Dutch Pietists, including the Catholic, Dirck Coornhert, and the Reformed Pietist, Willem Teelinck, both of whom emphasized that alongside justification one must talk of regeneration, the beginning of the genuine, actual sanctification of the Christian, including an understanding of "perfection." Jodocus Lodenstein, one of the leading Reformed pastors in the seventeenth-century *Nadere Reformatie*, wrote about *volkomen Heiligheid* ("entire sanctification").[77] A similar emphasis may also be traced in the German Pietism of Johann Arndt and Philipp Jakob Spener. The pietism of these representative figures spans the sixteenth and seventeenth centuries.[78]

Conclusion

This chapter has been an exercise in noting very selectively and in a very compressed form the tradition in which Wesley stood. That is not to say that he was consciously following all of these theologians. His particular veneration was for the Ante-Nicene fathers of the second and third centuries. He was especially influenced by Clement of Alexandria and the homilies attributed to Macarius, but references can be found to all of the Fathers mentioned here and more.[79] But although Wesley attributes no direct influence to Augustine, he was an heir of the whole Augustinian tradition which so profoundly shaped Western Christianity, particularly the way in which Augustine shaped the theology of love with his polarization of *caritas* and *concupiscentia*. That is the underlying model that shapes the Augustinian doctrine of original sin, so strongly defended by Wesley in the longest treatise he ever wrote, and which underlies the way in which *caritas*, love for God, is the dynamic of the perfection that frees Christians from sin, reflected in the thought of Bernard and Thomas Aquinas. Here, throughout this whole tradition is the idea of "love excluding sin." No matter how aware or unaware Wesley was of the source of this heritage, as part of the tradition of the Church of England, he was deeply influenced by the whole Augustinian tradition of Western Christianity as well as by his beloved Eastern Fathers. But Wesley also rediscovered his

77. Overduin, *Searching*, private circulation, 37.

78. For an introduction to these four Pietists see Bassett and Greathouse, *Historical Development*, 177–99.

79. See the useful Appendix 2 in Campbell, *John Wesley*, 125–34.

Reformation heritage, becoming a true evangelical centered on the gospel of justification by faith. That put the music of Christian "perfection" in a whole new key.

4

Wesley's Doctrine of Christian Perfecting

Wesley's doctrine of Christian perfection did not arise out of nowhere. It was a formulation of the tradition of the church catholic which we briefly reviewed in the last chapter. But there was also, as we saw, a transformation of the doctrine which resulted from the more immediate influence of the Reformation traditions. The whole of Christian sanctification had to be seen in the light of justification by grace through "faith working by love." In this chapter, we will try to summarize the outlines of Wesley's own version of the doctrine of Christian perfection, trying to be sensitive to the subtleties and the development in his thought. But some words of caution need to come first.

a) Understanding Wesley's Doctrine

John Wesley's doctrine of Christian perfection is easily misunderstood. That is often because the reader comes with some other doctrinal scheme in mind, along with its particular concepts and terminology, and so jumps to the conclusion that Wesley is confused. However, given that Wesley was an expert on Aristotelian logic that conclusion is *prima facie* unlikely. It is more likely that the reader has not given Wesley's writings sufficiently deep attention. But one further difficulty is that Wesley never really set out his doctrine in clear systematic form: his writings are all occasional. *A Plain Account of Christian Perfection* is undoubtedly a classic of Christian spirituality, but it is a compendium of his writings put together in 1766 to prove that he had taught the same doctrine for forty years, and so it tends to be repetitive. And while there is amazing consistency over that time span, it is only to be expected that there will be developments and modifications. Scholars refer now to the "early" Wesley (1725–38), the "middle" Wesley (1738–65), and the "late" Wesley (1765–1791); but while it is important to take note of the modifications in his thought, there is an underlying consistency. At the same time, we have to have an awareness of semantics, and we have to recognize that Wesley's doctrine is a subtle and sophisticated construct. It takes careful and patient reading to understand it.

Further, one must be careful not to read into Wesley some of the doctrines of those who claimed to be his heirs and successors. While Wesley did not openly disagree with the views of his saintly colleague, John Fletcher, the vicar of Madeley, we must not read Fletcher's dispensational pneumatology into Wesley.[1] Nor must we read into him the later developments in the holiness movement of the nineteenth century, either the "shorter way" or the "altar theology" of Phoebe Palmer with its new language of "consecration," and even less so, the proto-Pentecostal, "baptism of the Spirit," interpretation of the "second blessing" by Asa Mahan and Charles Finney of Oberlin College.[2] Mahan and Finney particularly employed an interpretation of Acts 2 that was foreign to Wesley and was an attempt to provide a biblical basis for the "secondness" of what was increasingly called "the second blessing." The lack of a deep immersion in classical literature and biblical languages of the kind that Wesley had, together with the attempt within the subculture of nineteenth-century American revivalism to simplify and to use the arts of persuasion, tended to produce a simplistic and even a well-intentioned but sometimes manipulative presentation of the doctrine. New vocabulary, such as "crisis" and "process," changed its balance and focus. Further, the "Higher Life" movement spread across the Protestant denominations and led to the teachings of the Keswick Convention, also presenting a different scheme of sanctification. As careful historians, therefore, we must strive not to read these developments back into Wesley and must try to understand his own eighteenth-century way of thinking.

But there is another caution we must bear in mind. We must not expect too much from Wesley. Christian theology is by its very nature

1. See Wood, *Meaning of Pentecost*, for the case that Wesley approved of Fletcher's views.

2. See, however, the insight into Phoebe Palmer's "Mystical Theology" in Heath, *Naked Faith*; on Mahan, see Dayton "Asa Mahan"; and Dayton, "Doctrine of the Baptism."

open-ended. We are talking about the infinite God, not one who is finite and so may be "defined." And in speaking of the Christian life, we are dealing with personal or spiritual realities, not mechanical, quantitative realities. There is always therefore an "apophatic" dimension, the dimension of mystery. No science can claim to have reached exhaustive understanding of what it studies, even if it is one of the physical or natural sciences, never mind the human sciences. And that is certainly even more true of theology. Any doctrinal or intellectual scheme is always an oversimplification compared to the reality it tries to describe and analyze. Specifically, any doctrine of the Christian life is merely a map for the journey, and the map is not the territory itself. The map does not answer all the questions for us: every map has to be *interpreted* by the traveler, and the territory never looks *exactly* as we expect from the map. Every traveler also has a peculiar and unique history and the map is concerned with what we share in common: it cannot take account of what is unique to each of us. We therefore cannot escape from the necessity of having to interpret thoughtfully how Wesley's map applies to each of us, to our peculiar history, experience, and personality.

And there is a further reason why we must not expect Wesley to answer all our questions for us. In any area of intellectual endeavor, the mark of a good scheme of thought, a "hypothesis," is not that it answers all our questions, but that it answers many of them but at the same time stimulates new questions for further exploration so that our understanding can advance. Wesley did not write the last word on Christian sanctification or how this area of doctrine is to be articulated in relation to all other areas of doctrine. The task of historical theology, undertaken in the last chapter and in this one, is only preliminary to the real task of theology: to deepen our understanding further. Therefore, we will have to take note of those areas where Wesley's doctrine raises pertinent questions for further development.

With these cautionary points then, we turn to the attempt to summarize Wesley's doctrine of Christian sanctification as succinctly as possible in this one chapter. Needless to say, we are depending on the vast and detailed endeavors of scholarship. Harald Lindström's classic work remains particularly valuable in this area along with the more recent standard studies of Wesley's theology as a whole by Randy Maddox and Kenneth Collins.[3] But every interpretation has to be brought to base in Wesley's own writings.

---

3. Lindström, *Wesley*; Maddox, *Responsible Grace*; Collins, *Theology*; see also

b) Wesley's Pilgrimage

Wesley's discovery of the key concept at the heart of his doctrine of sanctification came in 1725. He tells the story in a significant passage included at the beginning of *A Plain Account of Christian Perfection*:

> In the year 1725, being in the twenty-third year of my age, I met with Bishop Taylor's *Rules and Exercises of Holy Living and Dying*. In reading several parts of this book, I was exceedingly affected; that part in particular which relates to purity of intention. Instantly I resolved to dedicate all my life to God, all my thoughts and words, and actions; being thoroughly convinced, there was no medium; but that every part of my life (not some only) must either be a sacrifice to God, or myself, that is, in effect, to the devil.

> In the year 1726, I met with Kempis's *Christian Pattern*. The nature and extent of inward religion, the religion of the heart, now appeared to me in a stronger light than ever it had done before. I saw, that giving even all my life to God (supposing it possible to do this, and go no farther) would profit me nothing, unless I gave my heart, yea, all my heart to him. I saw that "simplicity of intention, and purity of affection," one design in all we speak or do, and one desire ruling all our tempers, are indeed "the wings of the soul," without which she can never ascend to the mount of God.

> A year or two after, Mr Law's *Christian Perfection* and *Serious Call* were put into my hands. These convinced me more than ever, of the absolute impossibility of being half a Christian; and I determined through his grace . . . to be all devoted to God, to give him all my soul, my body, and my substance.[4]

The key concept in this passage is that of a *total, undivided devotion to God* and the key phrases are "purity of intention," "inward religion," "the religion of the heart," "simplicity of intention," "purity of affection," "one desire ruling all our tempers," and "all devoted to God." This was the vision that became the lodestar for Wesley's pilgrimage, and he caught the vision from Thomas à Kempis (who also influenced Calvin), and from two

---

Wood, *Excluding Sin*; Gunter, *Limits*; and McGonigle, *Scriptural Holiness*.

4. Wesley, *Works* (Jackson) 11:366–67. The *Christian Pattern* was the name then given to the *Imitation of Christ*.

writers of the "holy living" school in the Church of England, Jeremy Taylor and William Law.

In 1729, he returned to Oxford as a Fellow of Lincoln College and became the leading figure in the student group nicknamed the "Holy Club," "Bible Moths," or "Methodists," started by his younger brother, Charles. They visited the sick and imprisoned, attended all the "means of grace," and read the early Fathers, particularly Clement of Alexandria, "Macarius," and Ephraim Syrus. In 1733, in his first university sermon, the young don expounded this very patristic, "high church" view of "Christian perfection":

> "It is that habitual disposition of the soul which, in the sacred writings, is termed holiness; and which directly implies the being cleansed from sin, 'from all filthiness both of flesh and spirit'; [2 Cor 7:1] and, by consequence, the being endued with those virtues which were in Christ Jesus; the being so 'renewed in the image of our mind,' [conflation of Eph 4:23 and Col 3:10] as to be 'perfect as our Father in heaven is perfect' [Matt 5:48]."[5]

But these years were a time of increasing frustration, as Wesley attempted to reach this level of Christian devotion by discipline and methodical living which became somewhat neurotic and ended up in the great fiasco of his ministry in Georgia.

It was at this point that Wesley encountered the Moravians and, through them, Luther's doctrine of justification by faith. Peter Böhler convinced him that this implied that one must have an instantaneous conversion, and the subsequent searching and spiritual travail led him to the event of 24th May 1738, which Wesley recounted in his *Journal* in words that have become famous:

> In the evening I went very unwillingly to a society in Aldersgate Street, where one was reading Luther's preface to the Epistle to the Romans. About a quarter before nine, while he was describing the change which God works in the heart through faith in Christ, I felt my heart strangely warmed. I felt I did trust in Christ, Christ alone for salvation; and an assurance was given me that he had taken away *my* sins, even *mine*, and saved *me* from the law of sin and death.[6]

---

5. *Works* (BE) 1:402, Sermon 17, "The Circumcision of the Heart," also quoted in *Plain Account*, 6, from *Works* (Jackson), Vol. XI, 367.

6. *Works* (BE) 18:249f.

The revolution in Wesley's thinking in 1738 was profound. He had discovered for himself the reality of the doctrine of justification, which he had to recognize was already stated in the Thirty-Nine Articles of the Church of England. Why then was it so new to him? One has to conclude that in the "high church" tradition in the Church of England, this was no longer part of the living, existential faith. Through the Moravians and the writings of Luther himself, he had rediscovered the evangel, the gospel of justification by faith. He had become a true evangelical, and the consequence was that he became an evangelist. He wrote to his mentor, William Law, to rebuke him for neglecting to point him to the heart of the gospel. And yet he did not abandon his roots in the "holy living" school. From this point on, we have what George Croft Cell described as "an original and unique synthesis of the Protestant ethic of grace with the Catholic ethic of holiness."[7] Wesley recounted the development like this (referring to himself and Charles):

> In 1729, two young men, reading the Bible, saw they could not be saved without holiness, followed after it, and incited others so to do. In 1737 they saw holiness comes by faith. They saw likewise, that men are justified before they are sanctified; but still holiness was their point. God then thrust them out, utterly against their will, to raise a holy people.[8]

It took Wesley some years to work this out. At first he seems to have believed that this instantaneous conversion would bring him to the perfection or purity of heart that he had been seeking, and the consequence was a time of some spiritual struggling when this did not prove to be so. But over the succeeding decades, it was not so much introspection, but his pastoral counseling and questioning of thousands of his Methodists that led him to the overall shape of a doctrine hammered out through biblical study, wide reading in the Christian literature of the ages, and the "experimental" religion of those who consulted him, wrote to him, questioned and discussed with him. His doctrine was biblically based, but Scripture was interpreted through the traditional teaching of the ages and the experience of "real Christians." We shall attempt to lay out the doctrine of the Christian life at which he eventually arrived, Wesley's own version of the pilgrim's progress, the *via salutis* (way of salvation), informed both by the

---

7. Cell, *Rediscovery*, 347.

8. Minutes of Several Conversations [= The Large Minutes], *Works* (Jackson) 8:300; *Works* (BE) 10:875.

patristic and medieval model of "degrees" or levels of perfection and by the Reformation insistence on the priority of justification by faith.

c) Justification and the New Birth

Wesley's deeper understanding of justification by faith came from Luther through the Moravians, but in debate with his Calvinist allies in the revival he could also identify with Calvin and declare, "I think on justification . . . just as Mr Calvin does. In this respect I do not differ from him an hair's breadth."[9] But along with the other leaders of the eighteenth-century evangelical revival, Wesley had inherited from Puritans and Pietists a stronger emphasis on regeneration or "the new birth" as the initiation of the Christian life. He understood justification and regeneration as occurring simultaneously:

> Though it be allowed that justification and the new birth are, in point of time, inseparable from each other, yet are they easily distinguished, as being not the same, but things of a wholly different nature. Justification implies only a relative, the new birth a real change. God in justifying us does something *for* us; in begetting us again he does the work *in* us. The one restores us to the favour, the other to the image, of God. The one is the taking away of guilt, the other the taking away the power, of sin.[10]

It is important to understand here that for Wesley, regeneration was the beginning of sanctification. Those influenced by the teaching of the later nineteenth-century holiness movement tend to jump to the conclusion that every time they see the word "sanctification," they must take it as referring to a later moment in the Christian life, a "second blessing." But while (as we shall see) Wesley did speak of a second moment, which he called *entire* sanctification, it is very important to understand that that was not the *beginning* of sanctification. For Wesley, *the sanctification of the Christian begins at regeneration*, that is, at the "new birth," which is simultaneous with justification.

Wesley himself recognized that confusion can arise at this point: "We grant . . . That the term *sanctified*, is continually applied by St Paul to all that were justified. That by this term alone he rarely, if ever, means 'saved

9. Letter to John Newton of 14th May 1765, in Telford, *Letters*, 298. For Wesley's doctrine of justification see Sermons 5 and 6, *Works* (BE) 1:181–216.

10. Sermon 19, "The Great Privilege of those that are Born of God" (1748), *Works* (BE) 2:431f.

from all sin.' That consequently, it is not proper to use it in that sense, without adding the word *wholly, entirely* or the like."[11] Unfortunately he himself did not always obey this rule and so the confusion persists. At its worst, it leads to the popular idea that at conversion, *only* justification takes place. The new follower of Christ is therefore said to accept Christ as Savior, *but not as Lord*; there is forgiveness of sins, but consecration is something delayed to a "second blessing." This is a travesty of Wesley's understanding of the New Testament. For Wesley, the beginning of sanctification is at the new birth, the moment of regeneration, which is simultaneous with justification. One cannot be a Christian without being sanctified. Sanctification may not be complete or "entire" at this point, but it has begun. There may be a deeper act of consecration later when the full implication of consecration is understood from within in a new way, but we must surely concur with Wesley that the new Christian does not partially consecrate himself or herself to the Lord. It would be complete nonsense to pray, "Lord, please forgive my sins, but you know that I cannot consecrate my life to you till later!" As far as he or she is aware, there must be a total commitment to be a disciple. Without that, there is no genuine regeneration.

Wesley makes all this abundantly clear in his two sermons, "The Marks of the New Birth," and "The Great Privilege of those that are Born of God."[12] The marks of the new birth are faith, hope, and love. Faith is the foundation of the rest since we are born again through faith in Christ, but faith is not only assent to doctrines, but a "disposition" that God works in the heart, a renouncing of all confidence in one's own righteousness and a sure trust and confidence that our sins are forgiven "through the merits of Christ." This faith brings power over sin and peace with God. A sure hope is the second mark of the new birth, but the third and greatest mark is love, even "the love of God shed abroad in their hearts by the Holy Ghost which is given unto them."[13] Wesley develops his thought on this new relationship with God in the second of the two sermons by beautifully expanding the New Testament metaphor of birth. The unborn child hears little, sees nothing, and is not aware of the world that is sustaining it. However, once born, the child feels the air, sees the light, and hears the endless diversity of sounds. In the same way, before spiritual rebirth, we actually subsist by the power of God, but we are not aware of that. The new birth is the opening of the spiritual senses and entering into a new relationship with God.

11. Wesley, *Plain Account*, 17, quoting from the Minutes of Conference, 1747.

12. Sermons 18–19, *Works* (BE) 1:415–43.

13. *Works* (BE) 1:425, quoting Rom 5:5 (AV).

As the newborn child breathes in the air for the first time, so the Spirit or Breath of God is breathed into the newborn Christian. "As it is continually received by faith, so it is continually rendered back by love, by prayer, by praise and thanksgiving—love and praise being the breath of every soul which is truly born of God." This beautiful metaphor of a new "spiritual respiration" speaks then of the new loving, trusting relationship with God. The Spirit "bears witness" that we are the children of God so that we too may cry, "Abba! Father!"

To be so intimately related to God and to have such a love for God in the heart and mind and shaping the will *is* sanctification, for God is holy. But it is important to see that this new *inner* commitment to Christ has the immediate *outward* consequence of "power over sin." Wesley draws this conclusion from Romans 6 and from 1 John 3:9 in the first of these two sermons, and the latter passage, "Whosoever is born of God doth not commit sin" (AV), is the basis for the second sermon. In the first sermon, Wesley refuses to allow this text to be softened by adding the word, "habitually," but in the second sermon, he softens it himself by qualifying what is meant here by "sin." A common definition of his day was that given in the Catechism accompanying the Westminster Confession of Faith: "Sin is any want of conformity unto, or transgression of any law of God."[14] Clearly if one were to understand "committing sin" in this text according to that definition, then the only result would be utter despair. Who could claim to be born again? So Wesley softens the text by adopting a more limited definition of sin appropriate in this specific context: "By 'sin' I here understand outward sin, according to the plain, common acceptation of the word: an actual, voluntary 'transgression of the law' [cf. v.4], of the revealed, written law of God; of any commandment of God acknowledged to be such at the time that it is transgressed."[15]

Truly regenerate Christians, according to Wesley, do not deliberately flout the law of God—murdering, stealing, lying, cheating, committing adultery, or in any way intentionally disobeying God's clear written commandments. And in this, Wesley is not saying anything substantially different from Aquinas, who, as we saw, taught that "mortal" sins were incompatible with a "state of grace." Nor is Wesley saying anything different in effect from any of the Reformation traditions. The Reformed, Anglican, Lutheran, or Baptist minister may lead his people each week in confession

14. The Westminster Shorter Catechism (1647), Question 14, Schaff, *Creeds*, 678.

15. Sermon 19, "The Great Privilege of those that are Born of God" (1748), *Works* (BE) 1:436.

of their sins, but in each tradition that is clearly understood to apply in effect *primarily* to "venial" or involuntary sins or sins of thought rather than to flagrant outward acts of disobedience to the written moral law of God. Let any such minister be caught red-handed in theft or adultery, and he will not be in his pulpit the following Sunday leading the congregation in confession! In practice then, all Christian traditions make a distinction between "mortal sins," outward actions that are voluntary transgressions of known laws of God, and involuntary transgressions, particularly if these are inner actions of thought but not outward acts.

But the implication of Wesley's softening of the text that is sometimes missed (particularly in the "holiness" tradition) is that the born-again Christian may, indeed will, continue to be guilty of involuntary transgressions. Wesley rather pedantically refused to call those "sins," insisting on using the word "sins" to refer *only* to voluntary transgressions. However, if we adopt the common usage of extending the category of "sins" to all transgressions, then Wesley is quite clear that no Christian is "sinless" in the sense that he or she never transgresses the perfect law of God. On the contrary, we transgress the law of God in involuntary ways every day, constantly falling short of perfect performance. Every Christian and every congregation should therefore practice the discipline of regular confession, and that is in fact what Wesley himself did every time he participated in Holy Communion according to the *Book of Common Prayer*.

According to Wesley, the newly regenerate Christian should also quickly expect to conquer inner sinful acts of thought. Of course, there may be thinking *about* sin that is not itself sinful: one may think about hatred, lust, or jealousy without oneself hating, lusting, or being jealous. But actually hateful, lustful, or jealous thoughts—inner mental acts in which one hates, lusts, or is jealous—are incompatible with this new love which the new child of God has for the Lord Jesus Christ, the one through whom we call God, "Abba, Father."

And yet while voluntary, intentional sins of thought or deed do not characterize the Christian life, falling into such voluntary sin is by no means impossible. Although it need not and should not happen, it does happen. The statement in 1 John 3:9 that the one born of God "*cannot commit sin*" does not mean that voluntary sin is an *absolute* impossibility, but, according to Wesley, only a *conditional* impossibility. The regenerate Christian cannot commit sin *as long as* he or she is actively trusting in God through Christ and living in the divine presence. But Wesley gives a long analysis in nine steps of how what should be impossible can in fact happen.[16] And yet, *if* Christians do sin voluntarily and deliberately, "we have an advocate with the Father" (1 John 2:1).

Many later teachers in the Wesleyan "holiness" tradition were to leave the impression that the Christian may sin regularly and voluntarily until a later moment in their pilgrimage. They may live a defeated life until the "second blessing" brings them into a life of victory. And that remains a stubbornly persistent belief at the popular level. But that is *not* Wesley's teaching! For regenerate Christians to live with voluntary, deliberate, intentional sin in their lives is abnormal, and to come to a new consecration that deals with that problem (which seems to be the "Keswick" view) is not to experience what Wesley called "entire sanctification." For Wesley, such a new consecration would simply be the abnormal belated completion of their true *regeneration.*

But it is important to understand that, for Wesley, it was not the ability to live the life of victory over voluntary transgression that defined the Christian life. That would be to put the cart before the horse. The new moral life is the *consequence* of, not the qualification for, regeneration. Even at this initial level of the Christian life, this lowest level of Christian perfection, it is (in the words of the Scottish Presbyterian, Thomas Chalmers) "the expulsive power of a stronger affection" which is the key.[17] The secret is not victory over temptation: that is the consequence. The secret is a heart newly filled with love for God. It is the new Christian's faith in Christ which impels and empowers their new life. It is the power of the Holy Spirit that enables the Christian to confess, "Jesus is Lord," and to cry, "Abba! Father!"

d) The "Gradual Work" of Sanctification

In keeping with the great tradition of Christian spirituality down through the centuries, Wesley speaks of a "gradual work" of sanctification that follows regeneration. He states this explicitly for example in his 1765 sermon, "The Scripture Way of Salvation," which lays out the doctrine of the Christian life which he had more fully formulated by then:

16. Sermon 19, II, 9, *Works* (BE) 1:440, also repeated in Wesley, *Plain Account.*

17. The actual title of Chalmer's sermon is "The Expulsive Power of a New Affection," Discourse IX, on 1 John 2:15, *Works* (BE) 7.

> From the time of our being born again, the gradual work of sanctification takes place. We are enabled "by the Spirit" to "mortify the deeds of the body" . . . and as we are more and more dead to sin, we are more and more alive to God. We go on from grace to grace, while we are careful to "abstain from all appearance of evil," and are "zealous of good works," as we have opportunity, doing good to all men.[18]

But although he had been guided in his understanding of this by Clement and other writers of Christian history, as *homo unius libri* (a man of one book), Wesley grounds his understanding of different stages in this "gradual work" again in a favorite epistle, First John.

> There are several stages in the Christian life as well as in the natural: some of the children of God being but new born babes, others having attained to more maturity. And, accordingly St John, in his first Epistle, applies himself severally to those he terms little children, those he styles young men, and those whom he entitles fathers [1 John 2:12ff.]. . . . But even babes in Christ are in such a sense perfect, or "born of God" . . . as, first, not to commit sin. . . . In conformity therefore both to the doctrine of St John, and to the whole tenor of the New Testament, we fix this conclusion: "A Christian is so far perfect as not to commit sin. This is the glorious privilege of every Christian; yea, though he be but a 'babe in Christ.'"[19]

But this is the lowest level of Christian perfection. The "young men" to whom John refers are those who have moved on beyond that and who have experience of victory over temptation, particularly in the thought life: "But it is only of those who are 'strong in the Lord,' and 'have overcome the wicked one,' or rather of those who 'have known him that is from the beginning,' that it can be affirmed they are in such a sense perfect as, secondly, to be freed from evil thoughts and evil tempers." The "fathers," according to Wesley, are those who are mature in the faith and who have advanced further in Christian perfection so as to be filled with the love of God.

A significant dimension of this growth is a growth in self-understanding, a deeper and more realistic perception of the depth of inner sin. The greater our love for God and neighbor, the deeper our self-awareness

---

18. Sermon 43, "The Scripture Way of Salvation," *Works* (BE) 2:160.

19. Sermon 40, "Christian Perfection," *Works* (BE) 2:105f., 116f., quoted in *Plain Account*, 12.

and our perception of our own sinfulness. "The conviction we feel of inbred sin is deeper and deeper every day. The more we grow in grace, the more do we see the desperate wickedness of our heart. The more we advance in the knowledge and love of God, through our Lord Jesus Christ ... the more do we discern of our alienation from God, of the enmity that is our carnal mind, and the necessity of our being entirely renewed in righteousness and true holiness."[20]

The continuation of "inbred sin" in the Christian after regeneration was standard doctrine for both Protestant and Catholic traditions. Wesley specifies what he means by it and gives his biblical basis by quoting the Pauline phrase from Romans 8, translated in the Authorized Version as "the carnal mind." Elsewhere he goes so far as to quote the original Greek phrase when he writes of this conviction of inner sin: "It is properly a conviction, wrought by the Holy Ghost, of the *sin* which still *remains* in our heart, of the *phronema sarkos*, the carnal mind, which 'does still *remain*' ... although it does no longer *reign* ... the tendency of our heart to self-will, to Atheism, or idolatry; and, above all, to unbelief."[21]

Thus far, Wesley is at one with Augustine and the Reformers. But at this point he goes instead with the Greek Fathers and the medieval tradition of the ladder of perfection formulated by Bernard, Aquinas, and many other spiritual writers. This gradual deepening of understanding of one's own inner sinfulness is not a dead end. With the Greek Fathers and the medieval theologians, Wesley believed that there is deliverance at the point where the Christian (taking a phrase from 1 Thess 5:23) is "entirely sanctified." Wesley was the one who popularized this particular phrase, and we have already seen that in the Greek text, the word *holoteleis* is not an adverb qualifying the verb "sanctify," but an adjective modifying the pronoun "you" (plural). It is not that sanctification is completed or finished or comes to an end: it is rather that Paul was praying that these Thessalonians be *holistically* sanctified, or, as Luther translated it, sanctified *through and through*.

---

20. Sermon 21, "The Sermon on the Mount—Discourse 1," *Works* (BE) 1:482f.
21. Sermon 43, "The Scripture Way of Salvation," *Works* (BE) 2:165.

e) Perfection in Love through "Entire" Sanctification

But for Wesley, this "entire sanctification" was merely a means to an end, not something to be sought for its own sake. In itself, the phrase has something of a negative ring since, rightly or wrongly, "sanctify" tends to be equated with "purify,"[22] and seems to prompt the question: *from what* are we purified or sanctified? But in Wesley's thinking, the positive is primary. For him, as Mildred Bangs Wynkoop saw so clearly, holiness is not primarily a negative, freedom or purification from sin, but a positive. Like Paul and John, Nyssen and Augustine, Bernard and Aquinas, his understanding of Christian holiness was a "theology of love."[23] If "entire" sanctification is understood as purification from "inbred sin," then it is only a means to an end: the end is that we should be filled with the love of God. Wesley's hermeneutic is not so much a "hermeneutic of sin" or cleansing from sin: it is rather a "hermeneutic of love."[24] It is best understood in his key phrase that gives priority to the positive: "Love excluding sin."[25]

Wesley's focus was on "perfect love," rather than on the "entire sanctification" that brings us to that point. That is seen in his characteristic answers when asked to explain his doctrine. Near the conclusion of *A Plain Account*, he sums it up like this:

> In one view, it [Christian perfection] is purity of intention, dedicating all the life to God. It is giving God all our heart; it is one desire and design ruling all our tempers. It is the devoting, not a part, but all our soul, body, substance to God. In another view, it is all the mind which was in Christ, enabling us to walk as Christ walked. It is the circumcision of the heart from all filthiness, all inward as well as outward pollution. It is renewal of the heart in the whole image of God, the full likeness of him that created it. In yet another, it is loving God with all our heart, and our neighbour as ourselves. Now, take it in which of these views you please (for there is no material difference), and this is the whole and sole perfection, as a train of writings prove to a demonstration, which I have believed and taught for these forty years, from the year 1725 to the year 1765.[26]

22. In the biblical languages these are not in fact synonyms: see Bauckham, "Holiness of Jesus."

23. Wynkoop, *Theology of Love*.

24. See McGonigle, *Scriptural Holiness*, 20.

25. Sermon 43, "The Scripture Way of Salvation," *BE* 2:160.

26. Wesley, *Plain Account*, 17.

In this classic explanation, both positive and negative aspects mingle, but the former predominate. The first sentence gives what we may call the positive psychological model, purity of intention, which he first read in Jeremy Taylor but which goes all the way back to Augustine. This is explained in terms of devoting the whole of oneself to God. The second model he gives is the christological model and he appears to have Philippians 2:5–11 in mind. The third is the model of *Herzensreligion* so characteristic of German Pietism, and gives both negative and positive aspects, the renewal of the heart in the image of God and the circumcision or cleansing of the heart. This is explained in terms of the great commandments. The phrase, "entire sanctification" does not even appear in this classic definition, for it is merely that which brings us to the life that really matters, "perfect love," understood as living in a way which is centered on God and neighbor. That is what matters.

That sanctification must be understood in terms of positive love, and that it is love that matters, rather than seeking for particular spiritual "experiences" or "blessings," is seen too in this passage:

> It were well you should be thoroughly sensible of this, the heaven of heavens is love. There is nothing higher in religion; there is, in effect, nothing else; if you look for anything but more love, you are looking wide of the mark, you are getting out of the royal way. And when you are asking others, "Have you received this or that blessing?," if you mean anything but more love, you mean wrong; you are leading them out of the way, and putting them on a false scent. Settle it then in your heart, that from the moment God has saved you from all sin, you are to aim at nothing more, but more of that love described in the thirteenth chapter of Corinthians. You can go no higher than this, till you are carried into Abraham's bosom.[27]

Nor is this the beginning of the life motivated by love for God and neighbor. This love has been the believer's motivation since the new birth, but it now increases in degree so that it comes to a new fullness rather perhaps like a glass that is steadily filled until it becomes full. Everything opposed to this love is "excluded":

> From the moment we are justified, till we give up our spirits to God, love is the fulfilling of the law; of the whole evangelical law, which took the place of the Adamic law. . . . Love is the

27. Wesley, *Plain Account*, 25 ("Farther Thoughts on Christian Perfection," 1763), Ans. to Q. 33.

> sum of Christian sanctification; it is the one *kind* of holiness, which is found, only in various *degrees*, in the believers who are distinguished by St John into "little children, young men, and fathers." The difference between the one and the other properly lies in the degree of love.[28]

And yet the positive ("love") also implies the negative ("excluding sin"):

> In the same proportion as he grows in faith, he grows in holiness; he increases in love, lowliness, meekness, in every part of the image of God; till it pleases God, after he is thoroughly convinced of inbred sin, of the total corruption of his nature, to take it all away; to purify his heart and cleanse him from all unrighteousness; till he fulfil that promise which he made first to his ancient people, and in them to the Israel of God in all ages: "I will circumcise thy heart, and the heart of thy seed, to love the Lord thy God with all thy heart, and with all thy soul."

Quite clearly here Wesley is *not* referring to "sins" in the sense of sinful actions or even sinful thoughts, defined as "voluntary transgressions of known laws." According to Wesley's map of the pilgrim's progress, those ceased *at the new birth*. Now he is claiming that at this later point the heart is cleansed so that the believer loves God with all the heart, soul, mind, and strength, and loves the neighbor accordingly. That implies the cleansing from "inbred sin," from "the total corruption of his nature." We shall have to look closely at that claim, for it is this which has been interpreted as a claim to "sinless perfection," but here at this point, we simply need to be clear that he is not talking merely about the ceasing of acts of sin, but of God's dealing with our sinful condition, the inner sinfulness of the "heart."

How then does the Christian pilgrim come to this point in the journey? Wesley is not thinking here of "backsliders" or people who have not realized or made actual in daily life the consecration they made at conversion. Rather Wesley has in mind those who live in God's presence, motivated by his love, going out in loving action and reaction to those around them, putting their consecration into practice in daily life and in all their relationships. Those are the Christians who are close to this more mature level of Christian "perfection." How then do they come to this new stage in their spiritual journey? Wesley poses the question and puts the answer like this:

---

28. Sermon 83, "On Patience," *Works* (BE) 3:174f.

How are we to wait for this change? Not in careless indifference, or indolent inactivity; but in vigorous, universal obedience, in a zealous keeping of all the commandments, in watchfulness and painfulness, in denying ourselves, and taking up our cross daily; as well as in earnest prayer and fasting, and a close attendance on all the ordinances of God. And if any man dream of attaining it any other way (yea, or of keeping it when it is attained, when he has received it even in the largest measure,) he deceiveth his own soul. It is true we receive it by simple faith; but God does not, will not, give that faith, unless we seek it with all diligence, in the way which he hath ordained.[29]

It is clear then that the "gradual work" of sanctification and "entire sanctification" need each other: they are mutually dependent. If one is not progressing in the consecrated life, loving God and neighbor in the power of the Holy Spirit, then there is no prospect of coming through "entire sanctification" to the "perfection" or fullness of that love. But conversely, unless the pilgrim believes that God will fill him or her with his love, thus dealing with the problem of the sinful condition, he or she is less likely to press on. Only if this level of perfection can in fact be reached is the pilgrim going to go all out to reach it. And yet, in the end, it is not an achievement: it is the gift of God.

Wesley discusses the question whether this moment of "entire" sanctification must be instantaneous. For him, this is not such a big issue as it later became among some of his followers who were perhaps shaped more by the dynamics of later American revivalism. In that subculture with its "altar call," some kind of great public "crisis" came to be expected. Wesley *did* in fact believe that "entire" sanctification was "instantaneous," but for him that was a minor question. It was not something that could be determined by reference to Scripture, therefore it was not a necessary point of doctrine, and rather than becoming exercised about a rather abstruse point (perhaps rather like the notorious scholastic question about the number of angels who could stand on the point of a pin!), believers should be more concerned about whether right now they loved God with all their hearts:

But it may be inquired, in what manner does God work this entire, this universal change in the soul of the believer? This strange work, which so many will not believe, though we declare it unto them? Does he work it gradually, by slow degrees?

29. Wesley, *Plain Account*, 19, quoting "Thoughts on Christian Perfection" (1759).

> Or instantaneously, in a moment? . . . The Scriptures are silent upon the subject; because the point is not determined, at least in express terms, in any part of the oracles of God. Every man therefore may abound in his own sense, provided he will allow the same liberty to his neighbour. . . . Permit me likewise to add one thing more. Be the change instantaneous or gradual, see that you never rest till it is wrought in your soul.[30]

And yet Wesley himself *did* believe that entire sanctification was instantaneous. Scripture did not require anyone to believe that, but on the basis of his own pastoral experience of thousands of his Methodists and by simple logic, he himself came to the conclusion that it had to be.

> But is it in itself instantaneous or not? In examining this, let us go step by step. An instantaneous change has been wrought in some believers. None can deny this. Since that change, they enjoy perfect love; they feel this, and this alone; they "rejoice evermore, pray without ceasing, and in everything give thanks." Now this is all I mean by perfection; therefore these are witnesses of the perfection which I preach. "But in some, this change was not instantaneous." They did not perceive the instant it was wrought. It is often difficult to perceive the instant when a man dies; yet there is an instant in which life ceases. And if even sin ceases, there must be a last moment of its existence, and a first moment of our deliverance from it.[31]

The balanced and sophisticated position he adopts then is that while logically there must be an instant when for the first time the believer comes to love God with an undivided heart, the focus must *not* be on the "instant," the "blessing" (later called a "crisis"), viewed as a specific happening or event. Wholehearted love for God does not come about when we are peering into the depths of our own souls trying to find (or even worse, to induce or work up or reproduce) a particular spiritual or emotional "experience," but rather when, fully aware of the depth of our own sin, our eyes are quite simply fixed on God!

f) An Imperfect Perfection

For Wesley then the Christian could be perfect in one respect only, perfect in love. It was not an absolute or legal perfection, perfection in

---

30. Sermon 83, "On Patience," *Works* (BE) 3:176f.
31. *A Plain Account*, 26, *Works* (Jackson), 11: 442.

performance, a perfect observance of rules and regulations. Of course, since in common usage the very word "perfection" conveys the idea in English of absolute perfection, it is unfortunately misleading. But "perfection" in love simply means *undivided love*. Such Christians may love many people, family and friends, and many things—country, places, pursuits, causes, interests, hobbies, skills, games, or sport—but will love nothing that *conflicts* with their love for God. Even their love for themselves has been purified. And yet even those who love God with all their hearts in this way still fall short of "perfection" of performance. They still have faults and flaws.

Wesley constantly struggles, particularly in his later years, to clarify what he meant by this "imperfect perfection" and explains it in terms of two linked areas of imperfection. First there is our physical constitution as fallen creatures, and secondly there is our consequent liability to involuntary or unintentional transgressions and to faults of character as long as we live in the body. The consequence of this continuing fallen condition and the continuing involuntary transgressions is that we are always dependent on forgiveness through the atonement of Christ.

> To clear this point a little farther: I know many that love God with all their heart. . . . But even these souls dwell in a shattered body, and are so pressed down thereby, that they cannot always exert themselves as they would, by thinking, speaking, and acting, precisely right. For want of better bodily organs, they must at times think, speak, or act wrong; not indeed through a defect of love, but through a defect of knowledge. And while this is the case, notwithstanding that defect, and its consequences, they fulfil the law of love. Yet, as even in this case, there is not a full conformity to the perfect law, so the most perfect do, on this very account, need the blood of the atonement, and may properly for themselves, as well as for their brethren, say, "Forgive us our trespasses."[32]

Wesley sees this in eschatological perspective. Only when the Lord comes and the creation is redeemed will we be "perfected" as he is: "The Son of God does not destroy the whole work of the devil in man so long as he remains in this life. He does not yet destroy bodily weakness, sickness, pain, and a thousand infirmities incident to flesh and blood. He does not destroy all the weakness of understanding, which is the natural consequence of the

---

32. Wesley, *Plain Account*, 25 ("Farther Thought on Christian Perfection").

soul's dwelling in a corruptible body; so that still, *humanum est errare et nescire*; 'Both ignorance and error belong to humanity.'"[33]

As the heir to centuries of Platonist influence in theology, and particularly in the area of theological anthropology, Wesley does tend to write about the "eternal soul" in a way that contemporary biblical scholarship has made us tone down today. But remarkably, and presumably because his mind was so steeped in Scripture, he does have a remarkable grasp of the psychosomatic unity that is closer to biblical and particularly Hebrew ways of thinking. In one of his last sermons, only a year before he died, Wesley makes this clear: "From a disordered brain there will necessarily arise confoundedness of apprehension, showing itself in a thousand instances; false judgements . . . and wrong inferences . . . and from these innumerable mistakes . . . mistakes in judgement . . . mistakes in practice . . . wrong words or action . . . wrong tempers . . . error in ten thousand shapes."[34]

He is quite clear therefore that Christians who love God with an undivided heart must not be proud of their great spirituality. That would be the most ridiculous hypocrisy, a complete and self-refuting denial of what they claim. Rather they must live in an attitude of daily confession, daily recognizing how far they fall short and in daily dependence on the atonement of Christ.

> To explain myself a little farther on this head: (1) Not only sin, properly so called (that is, a voluntary transgression of a known law), but sin, improperly so called (that is, an involuntary transgression of a divine law, known or unknown), needs the atoning blood. (2) I believe there is no such perfection in this life as excludes these involuntary transgressions which I apprehend to be naturally consequent on the ignorance and mistakes inseparable from mortality. (3) Therefore *sinless perfection* is a phrase I never use, lest I should seem to contradict myself. (4) I believe a person filled with the love of God is still liable to these involuntary transgressions. (5) Such transgressions you may call sins, if you please: I do not, for the reasons above mentioned.[35]

Perhaps we should avail ourselves of the permission Wesley gives us here to call these "involuntary sins," but the point is merely a semantic

---

33. Sermon 62, "The End of Christ's Coming," *Works* (BE) 2:482. The phrase "corruptible body" does not imply that for Wesley the body as such is sinful. See Rainey, "Wesley's Doctrine," 248, quoting Wesley, *Works* (BE) 3:79f.

34. Sermon 129, "Heavenly Treasure in Earthen Vessels," (1790), *Works* (BE) 4:165.

35. Wesley, *Plain Account*, 19 ("Thoughts on Christian Perfection").

one. Whatever label we put on them, these require the regular discipline of confession. Any believer who does not confess his or her faults and failings, or any company of believers neglecting to engage in corporate confession, is in danger of the worst of all possible forms of pride, namely, religious pride, pride in one's own spiritual perfection.

Those who have been "perfected in love" (by which Wesley means simply that their hearts are undivided in their love for God) must be conscious of two vital truths: that they are still pilgrims on a journey, and that they are totally dependent on Christ. At the end of a passage in which he emphasized that the "perfection" he was writing about was neither freedom from ignorance nor from temptation, Wesley wrote about the continuing journey and the lack of absolute perfection: "Yet we may, lastly, observe that neither in this respect is there any absolute perfection on the earth. There is no 'perfection of degrees,' as it is termed; none which does not admit of a continual increase. So that how much soever any man hath attained, or in how high a degree soever he is perfect, he hath still need to 'grow in grace,' and daily to advance in the knowledge and love of God his Saviour."[36]

He was equally clear in various passages that such "perfection" was not a holiness that the Christian has inherently in himself or herself independently of Christ. He makes this clear writing to one correspondent, also showing his awareness of the semantic problem around the word "sin":

> These very persons feel more than ever their own ignorance, littleness of grace, coming short of the full mind that was in Christ, and walking less accurately than they might have done after their Divine Pattern; and are more convinced of the insufficiency of all they are, have, or do to bear the eye of God without a Mediator; and are more penetrated with the sense of the want of him than ever they were before. . . . "Are they not sinners?" Explain the term one way, and I say, "Yes"; another, and I say, "No."[37]

It is clear then that, fully aware of the paradox of this "imperfect perfection," Wesley would give guarded assent to Luther's dictum that the Christian is *simul iustus et peccator*, at once a sinner and justified. If by that is meant that the regenerate Christian deliberately and intentionally flouts God's known laws every day, then he would reject such an idea as

36. Sermon 40, "Christian Perfection," *Works* (BE) 2:104.
37. Wesley, *Letters* IV, 189–90.

antinomianism. But if it means that, no matter how far we advance in holiness, even if we love God with an undivided heart and our neighbors as ourselves, we still fall short, still have faults and failings of character, still do not merit our salvation, still err and do the wrong thing, still must pray, "Forgive us our trespasses," then Wesley agrees. "Explain the term [sinners] one way, and I say, 'Yes'; another, and I say, 'No.'"

The underlying theological reason for this is that we are never holy in ourselves. We can become genuinely holy people filled with God's love and compassion, but only because we are "in Christ" and indwelled by his Spirit. The christocentric nature of the believer's holiness and our dependence on Christ in all his "offices" is quite clear. Only in dependent relationship to him, only because by the Spirit we are "in him and he in us," is such a level of holiness possible for the Christian.

> The holiest of men still need Christ, as their Prophet, as "the light of the world." For he does not give them light, but from moment to moment; the instant he withdraws, all is darkness. They still need Christ as their King; for God does not give them a stock of holiness. But unless they receive a supply every moment, nothing but unholiness would remain. They still need Christ as their Priest, to make atonement for their holy things. Even perfect holiness is acceptable to God only through Jesus Christ.[38]

Since then no one has a "stock of holiness," the Christian filled with the love of God must continue to pray "from moment to moment" to be filled *anew* with the love of God. Anything else would be presumption and spiritual pride. Charles Wesley's great prayers for "full redemption" give us prayers in biblical language that need to be often on the lips and constantly in the heart:

> O for a heart to praise my God,
> A heart from sin set free!
> A heart that always feels thy blood,
> So freely spilt for me!

> A heart resigned, submissive, meek,
> My great Redeemer's throne,
> Where only Christ is heard to speak,
> Where Jesus reigns alone.

38. "Farther Thoughts on Christian Perfection," answer to question 9, published in Wesley, *Plain Account*, 25.

O for a lowly, contrite heart,
Believing, true and clean,
Which neither life nor death can part
From him that dwells within!

A heart in every thought renewed,
And full of love divine,
Perfect, and right, and pure, and good—
A copy, Lord, of thine.

Thy tender heart is still the same,
And melts at human woe;
Jesu, for thee distressed I am—
I want thy love to know.

The nature, gracious Lord, impart;
Come quickly from above;
Write thy new name upon my heart,
Thy new, best name of love![39]

g) Conclusion

Let us be clear: Wesley has not answered all the questions by any means. But once we have cleared our way through the thicket of occasional writings, which show some change and development, and once we clear our heads of other versions of the doctrine of sanctification, and once we stop jumping to premature judgments through inadequate and careless reading, we have here a coherent understanding of Christian sanctification and a very thoughtful version of the central Christian tradition on Christian "perfection." As in Clement, Origen, the later Greek Fathers, and in Bernard and Aquinas (to name only some of those we selected from the great tradition), there is no thought here of easy, instant holiness. Rather there is a concept of different levels or stages or "degrees" of "perfection"—rungs on the ladder. We have suggested that, given the great suspicion of the word "perfection," it may be better to refer to these as *degrees of "perfecting,"* indicating that our growth and development into Christian maturity continues as long as we live. Wesley's immense stature as one of the greatest evangelists and church-builders of the whole Christian era demands

---

39. Hymn 334 in *A Collection of Hymns for the Use of the People Called Methodists*, *Works* (BE) 7:490f.

that we pay close attention and do not jump to snap judgments. His careful scholarship and clear logical thinking also command respect. And above all, his life-long commitment to mapping out the path of pilgrims as a true pastor engaged in the "cure of souls," along with this immense experience of decades of spiritual counseling, call us to study his thinking in depth.

However, what he has given us is merely a model, a map, a paradigm. It has not reached final perfection either! It calls for development. R. W. Dale, the nineteenth-century Calvinist preacher, commented:

> There was one doctrine of John Wesley's—the doctrine of perfect sanctification—which ought to have led to a great and original ethical development; but the doctrine has not grown; it seems to remain just where John Wesley left it. There has been want of the genius or courage to attempt the solution of the immense practical questions which the doctrine suggests. The questions have not been raised—much less solved. To have raised them effectively, indeed, would have had a far deeper effect on the thought and life—first of England, and then of the rest of Christendom—than was produced by the Reformation of the sixteenth century.[40]

There is the challenge that Wesleyans today are called to meet.

---

40. The quotation from Dale appears in Sangster, *Path to Perfection*, 168, referencing R. W. Dale, *The Evangelical Revival and Other Sermons*, 39.

5

Reformulating Wesley's Doctrine Today

> Enormous changes have taken place in the world, in culture, in philosophy and society and thought, since Wesley's death in 1791. Schleiermacher, Hegel, and Kierkegaard; Marx, Darwin, and Freud; Einstein, Wittgenstein, and Barth, to name only a few, have revolutionized our ideas of the cosmos, of what it means to be human, and of the role and nature of Christian Theology. We cannot think as Wesley thought in the eighteenth century. Insofar as our theology cannot but be contextual, there are many assumptions that Wesley made about humanity and the world which we can no longer share.[1]

While we paid close attention to Wesley's doctrine in the last chapter, therefore, and while we are indebted to historical theologians who can help us to dispense with many of the simplistic and inaccurate versions of what Wesley himself taught, and while Wesley himself is a towering figure whose Christian commitment and achievements few if any of us can ever hope to match, our greater concern is to understand what Christian holiness means for us in the language and concepts of the twenty-first century. We cannot stop therefore at a merely antiquarian interest in this eighteenth-century Oxford don. Our focus must rather be on how he (and indeed the saints of the ages) can guide us as we think today about the holiness that is possible by grace for the Christian in this life. On the other hand, of course, while our doctrine must be *articulated* in the context of

---

1. Noble, "To Serve the Present Age," 74.

twenty-first century cultures, it can only be *drawn* from Holy Scripture as interpreted through the Christian tradition.

That is why our aim in this book is to set our understanding of sanctification or Christian holiness particularly in the context of the great central doctrines of the Christian faith. These are summarized in the creeds and shaped within that most comprehensive of Christian doctrines, the doctrine of the Holy Trinity. The christocentric-trinitarian shape of Christian theology is the way it has been shaped and developed by the Christian tradition from its roots in Holy Scripture. But before we come to that in the final four chapters, we shall attempt in this chapter to critique, assess, and to some extent re-express the doctrine of Christian "perfection." As we have seen, that doctrine is not an invention of John Wesley. He stood in the great tradition that we have traced briefly and selectively from the New Testament and the earliest Fathers of the church right up to his day. But we will focus our attention on his particular formulation since it recasts the doctrine of perfection in the light of the Reformation focus on justification by faith. Wesley is the one major figure of Christian history who uniquely gives us a synthesis of evangelical and ancient catholic strands in the doctrine of sanctification.

In this chapter then we want to clarify some points, and to re-express the doctrine in the light of intellectual developments since Wesley's death. Once again, that is a tall order and therefore this can only be a preliminary sketch. But as a prelude to that, it will be useful to think a little more about Wesley's limitations, particularly the limitations of his horizons as a man of his day, an eighteenth-century thinker. That may give some clues about the ways in which his doctrine needs to be reformulated today.

a) Wesley's Limitations

As a man of his time, Wesley lived in a century which had a limited theological vision. While the sixteenth century and even the seventeenth century were periods of new insights and creative thought for Christian theology, as were the nineteenth and twentieth, the eighteenth century was comparatively barren. We may name great eighteenth-century philosophers, Locke, Hume, and Kant particularly, but who (apart from Wesley himself and Jonathan Edwards) are the major theologians of the age? In fact, Christian theology was in danger of being assimilated into Deism, a philosophical kind of theology that wore a Christian veneer, but was in fact another gospel. Christians found themselves facing the new thought of the Enlightenment, and having to wrestle with the question of what was admirable in the new thinking and what was seductive. Since much eighteenth-century church theology was largely stuck in the out-dated scholastic modes of the previous century, it was quite unequal to this new task and the Christian faith lost its intellectual dominance in European culture for the first time in over a thousand years.

In the two centuries since Wesley's death, Christian theology has largely been shaped by the need to re-articulate the faith in the new intellectual environment of "modernity." While many today will rightly reject Schleiermacher's particular way of defending "religion" against its "cultured despisers," the father of liberal theology at least demonstrated the way in which Christian theology ought to be an organic, integrated whole. The problem with Protestant theology before Schleiermacher was the way in which it formulated its confessions in distinct "articles" of faith and, shortly after the Reformation, plunged back into the kind of scholastic Aristotelian method which the Reformers had rejected. Theologians in this era of so-called "Protestant orthodoxy" (such as the scholastic Swiss Calvinist, Francis Turretin) tended to focus in a very rationalistic Aristotelian way on definitions which distinguished different entities, putting them in neat logical categories. There was an apologetic motive for all this, namely to defend the Reformation traditions against the revived theology of the Roman Catholic Church formulated at the Council of Trent (not to mention the fierce in-fighting among themselves!). But this defensive scholastic method tended to compartmentalized thinking, putting each doctrine in its own water-tight compartment, and some evangelical Christians still try to do theology in that analytical kind of way. But that scholastic way of thinking has long ago been left behind by theologians who try to think through their theology in an integrated way as an organic whole. And it has become evident that the greatest of these, whether we agree with him or not, is Barth.

What is clear is that, as a thinker of his time, Wesley, although influenced to some degree by Enlightenment influences such as Locke's empiricism, still thought of his theology in a rather scholastic seventeenth-century way, assuming, for example, the scholastic categories of federal or covenant theology.[2] That is not surprising, since the broad divisions into centuries that we employ to mark different eras are somewhat arbitrary. But the main point is that as a theologian living before Schleiermacher, Wesley tended to think in terms of separate doctrines or "articles," such

2. See Rodes, "From Faith to Faith."

as those in the Thirty-Nine Articles of the Church of England. In his case that was modified in two ways. First, he was a biblical scholar rather than a "systematic" theologian, and therefore he was more shaped by the narratives and practicalities of Scripture than by the dry, scholastic, systematic structure found in seventeenth-century theologians like Arminius or John Owen. Secondly, "systematic" theology was somewhat foreign to the Church of England, and Wesley was not a system-builder, but a practical and pastoral theologian.

As a man of his time then, Wesley did not think through his theology as a whole, connecting his doctrines of the Christian life fully to the central Christian trinitarian dogma in a holistic way. He accepted and taught all the orthodox creedal doctrines of the person of Christ and of the Trinity as well as the doctrine of the atonement as taught by the Reformers, largely following Anselm, and the doctrine of original sin as formulated largely by Augustine. He wrote his longest theological treatise to defend the doctrine of original sin against a Deist. But while the atonement was connected to *justification* in Protestant theology, there was comparatively little reflection on how it provided for our *sanctification*. And while Wesley taught that at the moment of entire sanctification, love "excluded" sin, and defined that as "inbred sin," he did not think through thoroughly the connection between his doctrine of sanctification and his doctrine of original sin. That is clear from a question he tackles in *A Plain Account* as to whether the children of two entirely sanctified parents would be free from original sin. Wesley gives the lame reply that it was not likely to happen![3]

A further way in which Wesley still moved within the conceptuality of seventeenth-century Protestant scholasticism was in his concept of grace. Medieval Augustinianism took the metaphor of grace as a medicine, a force, or substance coming from God, and elaborated that into different kinds or types of "grace" that were "infused" into the Christian through the seven sacraments defined by Peter Lombard. What was a metaphor became a defining model. The Reformers dropped that language of grace as an infused substance, but Protestant scholasticism revived it, differentiating different kinds of grace—common, prevenient, justifying, regenerating, sanctifying, and so on. That scholastic model of grace brings its own problems, particularly a tendency to depersonalize the action of God, replacing the personal action of the Spirit with this impersonal substance called "grace."

---

3. Wesley, *A Plain Account*, 19, "Thoughts on Christian Perfection" (in answer to the fifteenth question).

But in addition to these understandable limitations as a man of his time, there are other problems and limitations in Wesley's thought specifically in the area of his doctrine of sanctification. He not only lived before Schleiermacher, but before the development of the social and human sciences that we associate with names such as Adam Smith, Karl Marx, Max Weber, and Sigmund Freud. The kind of thinking about human motivation and about human society that has been developed by the sciences of economics, sociology, psychology, and psychiatry, all came after Wesley's death. To take only one particularly pertinent example, the whole category of the "unconscious" mind (sometimes called the "subconscious") has become part of the mental furniture even of our popular culture in a way completely foreign to an eighteenth-century thinker. Somehow that needs to be taken into account in any doctrine of sanctification today. Social scientists also have a whole new awareness of societal factors and the possibilities of structural social reform that were not glimpsed in the traditional society of the eighteenth century.

As well as the intellectual limitations in Wesley as a man of his time, there is a further problem in that one cannot easily fit his own pilgrimage neatly into his model as outlined in the last chapter. Methodism went in for "narrative theology" in the shape of the testimonies spoken and written by countless members of the societies. These narratives shaped Wesley's model of the Christian pilgrimage, but they were also shaped by it. Many were the conversion stories which told of conviction, repentance, faith, and regeneration, followed by gradual growth in grace and leading on to "entire sanctification" bringing the pilgrim into the life of "perfect love." But Wesley's own pilgrimage did not fit neatly into the scheme! To begin with, he did not surrender the conviction of the Church of England that regeneration somehow came about at his baptism as an infant in Epworth parish church.[4] But he seemed to hold that, along with the bulk of the population presumably, he had "sinned away" his baptism by the time he was an adolescent and was no longer regenerate.[5]

Then how are we to interpret the total consecration he made to God in 1725 after reading Jeremy Taylor, and confirmed in 1726 after reading Thomas à Kempis, and then again a year or two later when he read William Law? If total consecration brings about entire sanctification (as some later teachers of holiness claimed), then his entire sanctification came before his justification!

4. *Works* (BE) 1:417 (cf. Outler's comment, *John Wesley*, 415).

5. *Works* (BE) 18:242f.

Further, how are we to interpret what happened at Aldersgate Street on 24th May 1738? That has prompted much debate.[6] Should it be regarded as his "conversion," his "regeneration," his "justification," all three, or none of the above?[7] Wesley himself claimed at first that he only became a Christian at this point, but he later modified his view to say that before that he had "the faith of a servant," but only from then did he have "the faith of a son."[8] Reading the famous account in his *Journal*,[9] one notes that his language at the time is that of "assurance" of the forgiveness of his sins through trust in Christ *alone*. This certainly echoes the language of Luther and the Reformation of justification by faith *alone* in Christ *alone*. But was this also his "new birth," or perhaps his "*re*-regeneration"? He does not refer to it as regeneration, but then the later statement that only from then did he have "the faith of a son" may be held to imply that this was the moment of his "new birth" (or possibly its recovery?).

There is the further point that, while Wesley encouraged his Methodists to testify to entire sanctification in a very careful and guarded way,[10] he made no claims himself and never testified to being "entirely sanctified" or made perfect in love. Wesley often linked Christian holiness with humility, and perhaps it was when it came to personal testimony that it came home to him that there is an inherent problem in claiming to be highly holy! But there is also a problem of language here: that so many of the standard terms, both biblical and historic, seem to be absolutes— "perfection," "purity," "entirely sanctified," etc. Any self-aware and sensitive person is going to be very, very, very wary of making claims by applying such words to himself or herself. There is, in fact, an inherent problem in testifying to advanced spirituality, and one only has to put it that way to see that no truly spiritual person could ever make such a claim! The claim immediately invites ridicule precisely because of the paradox at the heart of humility expressed so memorably in the mock book title, "Humility and How I Achieved It." "Holiness and how I achieved it" would be similarly ridiculous. But of course, Wesley would not regard "perfect love" as an "achievement," but as God's gracious gift. It may rather be that

6. See the summary of the discussion in Rack, *Reasonable Enthusiast*, 145–57, and Maddox, *Aldersgate Reconsidered*.

7. See Tyson, "Wesley's Conversion," and Knight, "Transformation of the Heart," in Collins and Tyson, *Conversion*.

8. *Works* (BE) 18:235.

9. *Works* (BE) 18:249f.

10. See Wesley's answer to the eighth question in "Thoughts on Christian Perfection" (*A Plain Account*, 19).

Wesley realized that if he as a public figure testified to "perfection," even in a guarded way that attempted to give all the glory to God, it would still divert any discussion from the biblical basis and truth of the doctrine to focus on himself, and one can imagine the kind of satire and ridicule he would have faced in the age of Swift and Hogarth![11]

Wesley's own biography therefore illustrates that his theological model of the Christian pilgrimage with its "order of salvation" (*ordo salutis*) is only a typical or ideal model, a map or theological analysis of the common features of the journey. But it should not become a straightjacket. Each pilgrim's journey has its own unique features and perhaps only a minority will fit ideally into Wesley's tidy scheme. We need the kind of map for the journey that he supplies from a life-time of experience and thought, but the actual journey of each pilgrim is likely to be much more complicated and messy. At the same time, given all we have said about Wesley's own pilgrimage, it is difficult to believe that he could have analyzed the Christian life so perceptively if he had not himself loved God with all his heart, soul, mind, and strength. Given his life of complete dedication, we scarcely need his verbal testimony.

With those thoughts on Wesley's limitations we may have some clues for the more creative task of sketching an attempt at rearticulating his doctrine of sanctification, and particularly of Christian "perfection," for today. Creative thinking is more open and tentative than the kind of historical study that we have been doing in the last two chapters. It calls for some key concepts and metaphors that may become the defining models helping us to express our insights. These need to be at home in contemporary culture, but they need to get to the heart of the historic doctrine of sanctification, particularly the historic understanding of Christian "perfection" that we have traced through the Christian centuries. The purpose of such an exercise in theology is not to formulate new doctrines, but to communicate the Christian gospel to contemporary people and society. Contemporary culture has developed conceptual tools not available to Paul or Augustine or Luther or Wesley and therefore translating their teaching today requires us to use these creatively but with care. It is therefore not just a matter of

---

11. He presumably felt this particularly once his unwise decision to marry Mrs Vazeille (and the somewhat inflexible interpretation of his commitment to ministry) led to separation after he had been the victim of domestic violence at the hands of his jealous wife. Of course, one outcome of this unhappy story is that Wesley is a witness to the possibility of a life of Christian service even for those who have broken marriages.

flat one-to-one translation, but of employing the theological and psychological insights available today to gain deeper insights.

Among the models or conceptual tools which can help us to get to the heart of this historic and biblical doctrine of sanctification and to express it with deeper insight, we shall concentrate on the twin concepts of motivation and intentionality and on the concept of relationship.[12]

b) Two Key Concepts

Motivation or Intentionality

The key passage in which Wesley tells of his discovery of the vision of Christian perfection from Bishop Jeremy Taylor, Thomas à Kempis, and William Law, contains several key phrases: "purity of intention," "simplicity of intention," "purity of affection," and "religion of the heart."[13] Wesley himself adds the interpretative phrases, "one design in all we speak or do" and "one desire ruling all our tempers." These phrases include some biblical vocabulary, "heart" and "purity," which immediately suggest the biblical phrase "purity of heart." The word "affection" is one of many words for love. Clearly the focus here is not on outward action, moral or pious behavior, but on "the heart," the internal thinking and willing which we see as the origin of outward action. The word "religion" may also be regarded as biblical (despite its rare appearance) if we understand that it is *not* to be taken in its modern meaning of a religious system of belief and practice (as in the modern concept of "world religions"), but in its original meaning as simply piety or devotion (*eusebeia*). Once again, however, since it is "religion of the heart," what we have in view is not the outward actions or institutions of religion, but the internal devotion. The word "desire" (either as a noun, *epithumia*, or as a verb, *epithumeō*) is also biblical and is used for both good and sinful desires. But in this passage from Wesley there are other words which do not appear to be directly biblical, notably "intention" and "design," which in this context are close in meaning, and the word "tempers." This last English word had come to mean a habitual disposition of mind.

Clearly then, Wesley is thinking here of what we should today call "motivation," an area of interest in both ethics and modern scientific

---

12. A third profitable concept, development, could be explored in conversation with developmental psychology.

13. *A Plain Account*, 2. See page 76, note 4.

psychology.[14] Christian holiness, and particularly Christian "perfection," must take account not only of our outward actions but also of our inward motivation. That immediately poses difficulties of course, precisely because what is "internal" or in the "heart" is hidden from observation. In its earliest history, modern psychology initially tried to study inner motivation by Wundt's method of introspection, but then swung to the opposite extreme with Watson's "behaviorism," eventually coming to accept the reality of internal motivation but accepting that it could not be directly observed, and that the study of the mind (or "soul," *psyche*) could only be pursued by experimental observation of outward behavior. Somehow in the study of human motivation, inward intention and outward action have to be correlated.

What is clear from the biblical literature and from twenty centuries of Christian writing is that in formulating teaching on Christian sanctification, both have to be taken into account. In the Pentateuch, the Decalogue includes not only commandments about outward conduct, but also, in the tenth commandment particularly, inner desire or covetousness. In the Wisdom literature, the sages write of "purity of heart." The prophets are aware not only of the necessity for outward justice for the poor, but also of internal personal purity. In the teaching of Jesus, the focus of the Sermon on the Mount is that outward obedience is not enough. Not only must one not murder or commit adultery, but one is not to hate or lust. Paul too wrestles (in Romans 7 and 8, for example) with how we may triumph over "indwelling sin" in the power of the Holy Spirit.

This concern with inner motivation also runs through the historical literature of Christian spirituality. We noted the concern with "purity of heart," for example, in Clement of Alexandria, and we can also refer to the whole literature of monasticism from Antony to Basil, to Benedict and to Bernard, along with many other writers. Of towering significance for that whole tradition as it develops in the West is the thought of Augustine.

The word, "motivation" is not there in this key passage at the beginning of Wesley's *A Plain Account*, nor prevalent anywhere in his writings or in the long tradition of Christian spirituality before him, but the word "intention" is present. This expresses the idea of conscious motivation: what we intend to do is some kind of configuration of motives which gives rise not only to specific actions, but also to the whole tenor of our behavior

14. Clapper, *Religious Affections*, chooses the word "emotion" to discuss this, but that is rather misleading, especially when he defines emotion as something different from "feelings" and also writes of "emotions" being transitive (i.e., attached to an object) and not merely subjective. "Motivation" is a more appropriate term.

r a period of time. The concept of intentionality is therefore part of
:sley's definition of a sinful act, "a voluntary transgression of a known
ν." What is intentional is voluntary: a voluntary or intentional action
is one which we have decided to do, either in a premeditated way or by
sudden impulsive decision, and it is therefore an action for which we bear
responsibility.

Wesley is the heir here of a long tradition of "voluntarism," which
Richard Steele traced from the New Testament through Augustine, Calvin,
and the English Puritans, particularly William Ames.[15] Such a differentiation between a voluntary action and an action that is under some kind
of compulsion is necessary for ethics (even though it is not always easy
to discern the dividing line), and underlies the way in which courts of
law judge degrees of innocence and guilt. But intentionality is not just a
feature of isolated acts: it is also a feature of "tempers," habitual patterns
of motivation that build up over time until they come to shape our character. For Wesley, as we have seen, even the newly regenerate Christian
has reached the basic level of Christian "perfection" at which he or she
does not deliberately flout the law of God. The temptation may still be
there, either weak or strong, but characteristically and in the power of the
Spirit, the intention to obey God carries the regenerate Christian through
times of testing until a habitual pattern builds up and obedience to God
in small and great matters becomes the settled disposition of his or her
motivation.[16]

Eventually, according to Wesley's depiction of the Christian pilgrimage, the Christian comes to the point where the heart is purified from
intentions contrary to God's will, and so is no longer "double-minded," but
has an integrity of intention. Here Wesley is presenting what is essentially
Clement's understanding of the "higher" level of Christian "perfection" or
"purity of heart."

But developments in modern psychology since Wesley help us here
to express an important qualification more clearly. Popular thinking today,
particularly in the church, still tends to be shaped by an anthropology
that divides the human being into distinct parts—body and soul, or body,
soul, and spirit—and to read that into the Bible. This way of thinking is, in
fact, influenced by the Platonist division of the human being into two substances, body and soul, and the later medieval "faculty" psychology that
divided the soul into various "faculties," the intellect, the emotions, and

15. Steele, *"Gracious Affection,"* 34–64.

16. See the full discussion of Wesley's moral theology in Long, *Moral Theology.*

the will. But biblical anthropology is much more holistic, seeing the human being as a psychosomatic unity, and modern scientific psychology is much more in line with that. This is particularly relevant to us at this point for the implications it carries for our understanding of human motivation. Within the psychosomatic unity in biblical anthropology, there are two interrelated "levels" of motivation. In Old Testament anthropology there is no differentiation between the "heart" and the "mind." Both are included in the term, "heart," which was the inner thinking/willing person. But it was significant that that was an anatomical word, for the thinking/willing heart was intimately related in Hebrew thinking to the "flesh," and particularly to the liver, the bowels, and the blood. The visceral organs were the basis of emotion and motivation, as the old, literal translation, "bowels of mercy" makes clear! This was a very concrete, down-to-earth, realistic way of thinking about the human being. The two "levels" of motivation are even more clearly seen in New Testament language where the words "mind" and "conscience" are added to explain further what was meant by the "heart."

Modern scientific psychology operates similarly with the human being as a psychosomatic unity.[17] It was the psychoanalytic school of Freud that first introduced the terminology of the "conscious" and "unconscious" (sometimes called the "subconscious") mind into our popular vocabulary, but experimental psychology (which regards itself as more scientific than psychoanalysis) similarly works with a psychosomatic model in which one can differentiate two levels of motivation. There is the conscious level of deliberate, voluntary choice, and there is the physiological level where our motivation is based in the visceral organs and the nervous system and brain, and where psychologists identify basic "drives" such as hunger, sex, and aggression. We must neither discount the physical "unconscious" basis of our conscious motivation, nor fall into the materialistic reductionism embraced by B. F. Skinner which dismisses conscious thinking and decision-making as "nothing but" physiological and chemical events.[18]

The important qualification for the doctrine of sanctification therefore is that when Wesley speaks of loving God with all the heart, soul, mind, and strength, he is interpreting that biblical phrase *holistically*. Such whole-hearted, undivided love for God comes about as a consequence of

17. See for example Nolen-Hoeksema et al., eds, *Atkinson and Hilgard's Introduction to Psychology*.

18. See Brown, Murphy, and Maloney, eds., *Whatever Happened*; Murphy, *Bodies and Souls*; Green, *About the Soul?* and Green, *Human Life*.

the work of the Holy Spirit in sanctifying the believer "entirely," that is, as a whole or holistically. And yet Wesley became increasingly clear that since the believer is not yet in the resurrection body, the bodily organs are still "fallen." With the terminology of modern psychology to help us to express this, we may interpret it as meaning that while the believer, in the power of the Spirit, can now love God with all of the *heart*, that is, at the level of conscious, voluntary motivation, yet at the unconscious level, the level of the physiological basis of motivation, the believer is still in the old fallen *flesh*. The believer still lacks (as Wesley put it), "better bodily organs," and suffers particularly from "a disordered brain"![19] W. E. Sangster, the prominent Methodist preacher in London during the Blitz in the Second World War, rightly saw that this was the way to interpret Wesley's position and attempted to rearticulate it in line with twentieth-century thinking.[20] From our contemporary understanding of biblical thought, we have to say that this is not dividing the human being into different parts, but an understanding that the human being as a whole, while a psychosomatic unity, has to be viewed within the paradox that we are "not yet" in the resurrection, but have "already" received the Spirit of the risen Lord.

But in order to explore this further, we must look at another contemporary term that helps us to express another dimension of this.

Relationship

The second key concept to be explored is that of relationship.[21] That word is not present either in the key passage in *A Plain Account*, 2, in which Wesley recounts his first discovery of his concept of Christian "perfection." But the word "affection" is present in the phrase, "purity of affection," and it is a word for love. Therefore, although the word "relationship" is not prevalent in Wesley or the historic literature any more than the word, "motivation," this is simply modern vocabulary for what is called "love" in Scripture and history. Of course there are many words for "love" in the ancient languages and we sometimes think (like C. S. Lewis) of different "kinds" of love.[22] But what actually differentiates them is not that they are different entities or substances, but that they are directed towards different objects. Even

---

19. Wesley, *A Plain Account*, 25 ("Farther Thoughts on Christian Perfection") and Sermon 129, "Heavenly Treasure in Earthen Vessels," *Works* (BE) 4:165.

20. Sangster, *Path to Perfection*; see Cheatle, *Sangster*.

21. See Wynkoop, *Theology of Love*, and Oord and Lodahl, *Relational Holiness*.

22. Lewis, *Four Loves*.

though the language of love is not dominant in Wesley's first expression of his discovery of the concept of Christian perfection, it quickly became so, until his favorite explanation of Christian perfection was by reference to the two great commandments, "You shall love the Lord your God with all your heart, with all your soul, and with all your strength," and, "You shall love your neighbor as yourself." Christian perfection for Wesley was perfection in *one way only*, perfection in *love*.

But this adds a whole new dimension to the concept of motivation. Our analysis of it so far in terms of inner intentionality can seem highly individualistic. But, of course, human beings do not exist as isolated monads: we have our being in society, and our very being and identity, *who* we are, is shaped by our relationships, first in the family then in local community, extending eventually to wider circles. Human motivation cannot, therefore, be understood simply by introspection, nor even by a more scientific psychological study of only the internal motivation of individuals. Human motivation can only be understood as human beings are seen in a social context, emerging from a matrix of relationships both biologically and psychologically, and interacting within community.

It is at this point that we have to see that Augustine was such an influential thinker in the whole development of Christian culture in the West. In the light of his *Confessions*, reckoned to be one of the most formative books of all time, he has been hailed as the first great psychologist. And although modern psychology has tried to refine a more "scientific" method, clearly Augustine's analysis of human motivation in terms of our love has been deeply influential through the centuries in ethics and in what we now call psychology. Augustine's analysis of human motivation has a particular understanding of love as its key concept. We have already examined this in chapter 3,[23] but it is worth reminding ourselves of Augustine's model of love (*amor*) as either directed towards the creature or the Creator. If it is directed towards the creature, it is the desire to have, to possess, to consume, to enjoy in order to satisfy our own desires. That way of "loving" he refers to as *concupiscentia* or *cupiditas*, and it includes not only sexual desire, but the greed for possessions, for fame, for self-glory. It is essentially pride or self-centeredness and it can also be seen to underlie idolatry. What Augustine discusses using the vocabulary of "love," contemporary society discusses using the language of "relationship." That is very helpful, for it makes it clear that we are not just talking about subjective emotions, but about the way we function in the world of people and things.

23. See above, page 59–62.

Matt Jenson points out that Augustine's teaching on the Fall, namely that the soul made the flesh corruptible by an act of will initiated by pride, was presented as the Christian alternative to the view of both Platonism and Gnosticism that it was the flesh which corrupted the soul.[24] But although he was using the Platonist categories of "soul" and "body," Augustine was in fact articulating a *relational* understanding of sin and evil. The willful and inexplicable act of our first parents arose out of pride and an ambition "to be as God," thus breaking their foundational ontological relationship with the Creator who had given them life and being. Consequently, evil was not a "substance" with its own ontological status, but was a defect, a "privation of the good" (*privatio boni*). This deformity in human ontology came about when the human was "turned towards itself" (*inclinatus ad se*).[25]

According to Augustine, only love for God, *caritas*, which is not produced by us, but "poured into our hearts through the Holy Spirit who has been given to us" (Rom 5:5), is capable of breaking the spell of that self-centered way of loving. And only when we love God in this way are we able to love our neighbors, no longer with the old selfish love, but with the love of God. It is that Augustinian model, so dominant in the whole Western tradition, which lies behind Wesley's doctrine of "love excluding sin."

Augustine thinks of love (*amor*) as an essential part of what it is to be human: we cannot be human without loving, that is without having *relationships*—without being attracted to persons and things, both concrete and even abstract. He illustrates love as water pouring into the drain, and tells us that it must flow instead into the garden. He draws another verbal picture of a bird that cannot fly:

> For the soul when bound by the love of the earth, hath as it were birdlime on its wings. It cannot fly. But when purged of the sordid affections of the world, extending as it were its pair of wings, and freeing them from every impediment, flieth upon them, that is to say, upon the two commandments of love unto God and our neighbour. Whither will it fly, but by rising in its flight to God? For it riseth by loving.[26]

We could also add a contemporary illustration of a satellite orbiting a heavenly body that is pulled into a new orbit by the stronger gravitational

---

24. Jenson, *Gravity of Sin*, 6–46.

25. Augustine, *Civ.* XIV, xiii, 572–73, quoted in Jenson, *Gravity of Sin*, 23.

26. In Przywara, *An Augustine Synthesis*, 33–44. Augustine, *Psal. Don.* CXXII, 1 (*NPNF*[1] 8:593).

pull of a larger object. In fact, this alerts us to the fact that the very word, "motivation" is a dead metaphor deriving from the Latin word for motion, *motio*. When we are "moved," that is "emotion," and out of that we are "moved to action": that is "motivation." It is, in fact, a model of gravitational pull determining our movements: but it is the gravitational pull of what we love. It is a matter of our *relationships*. The value of Augustine's model, whichever illustration we use, is that it combines visually these two concepts of *motivation* and *relationship*. It is our relationships, what and whom we love, which determine how we are motivated.

c) A Revolution in our Motivation

Christian sanctification can be expressed then as an inner revolution in our *motivation* as a consequence of a new *relationship*. The consequence of this inner revolution is a change in behavior, that is, in outward action. But it is important to see that the two, inward motivation and outward action, go together; they must not be separated. Otherwise we end up in either some kind of self-absorbed charismatic mysticism, which is all about "blessed experiences" but does not result in practical holiness, or else in some kind of legalism, which is all about self-discipline and obedience. The former is hypocrisy; the latter is self-flagellation. A healthy balance of both aspects of Christian holiness, love from the heart and obedience in the life, can only arise as the product of the new relationship with God. It is, in fact, this new *relationship* that is the secret.

The new filial relationship begins with regeneration, when, born again of the Spirit, we are united to Christ and so adopted as children into the family of God. It is by the Spirit that we say, "Jesus is Lord!" and make him Lord of our lives. And it is by the Spirit, who is the Spirit of the Son, that we cry with Jesus, "Abba! Father!" The new motivational pull in our lives is then our love for God: "We love him because he first loved us" (1 John 4:19). Of course, that is not just the love of the isolated individual believer for God. We know the love of God within the fellowship (*koinōnia*) of the Body of Christ, the church. We share in the fellowship of the church, which is the fellowship the church shares with the Father and the Son (1 John 1:3), and which may also be called the fellowship of the Holy Spirit (2 Cor 13:14). And yet, while we are now guided by this new relationship, this new love for God, it soon becomes apparent to the growing Christian that there is a remaining "double-mindedness." The old love for "the world" (as John puts it), the self-serving, self-centered love, does not disappear; it hangs on stubbornly.[27]

It is at this point that Wesley sees "entire sanctification" as the work of God within us, in the "heart," which deals with that double-mindedness. It is important to see that God is treating us here as persons with real ethical experience and not as puppets who can be magically changed by some mechanical operation. Only once we have set out on our pilgrimage as living, choosing persons in the footsteps of Jesus, and only once we have the necessary self-awareness through personal experience of living with that ethical tension between the new love, centered in God, and the old motivational pattern, centered in the self, are we ready for God to deliver us. Coming back to the key phrases Wesley used in describing his first vision of the goal of this higher level of Christian "perfection," *purity of intention, simplicity of intention, religion of the heart,* and *purity of affection,* we can interpret these in terms of *a revolution in motivation*, begun at the new birth, but brought to a new level of "perfection" by what Wesley called "entire" sanctification. By the "heart" is meant the affections, the intentions, the motives, the centre of motivation; and by "purity" or "simplicity" is meant unity, the unifying or integration of all affections and intentions and motives around one dominating all-consuming love. Kierkegaard was later to state it most succinctly in the title of his book, *Purity of Heart Is to Will One Thing.*[28]

The heart of the idea of "entire" sanctification is thus the idea that the Spirit may so work in our hearts—that is, our internal motivation—that, even within this life, we may become wholly devoted to God. This unity or purity of intention or motivation is, in fact, a "perfection," or completeness; that is to say, a *whole-heartedness* in the *relationship* with God. It is a whole, full, mature, all-embracing love for God: it is loving God with all the heart, soul, mind, and strength; that is to say, with the whole being. This is, in fact, what we mean by the word "spiritual," a word that needs to be cleansed from its Gnostic connotations. When we speak of "spiritual life," "spiritual progress," "spiritual exercises," what we are referring to is

27. Sermon 13, "On Sin in Believers" 1763, II, 3, *Works* (BE) 1:322: "Indeed this grand point, that there are two contrary principles in believers—nature and grace, the flesh and the spirit—runs through all the epistles of St. Paul, yea, through all the Holy Scriptures."

28. Kierkegaard, *Purity of Heart.* Cf. Wesley's use of the phrase "a single eye" in, for example, "The Character of a Methodist," 1742, *Works* (Jackson) 8:344, and Sermon 28 (Sermon on the Mount VIII, 1748), *Works* (BE) 1:612–31.

the realm of *personal relationships* with each other and with God. It is this spiritual or *relational* change (love *for God*), beginning from regeneration, which increasingly effects a *real* change "internally" in our motivation, eventually culminating in purity of heart. The all-consuming love for God thus integrates the whole person and personality and life around this one great dominating love. There is an internal revolution, a re-orientation of the pattern of motivation around a new centre.

This positive statement has a concomitant negative aspect. Kierkegaard's book, *Purity of Heart Is to Will One Thing*, is an exposition of James 4:8: "Draw near to God and he will draw near to you. Cleanse your hands, you sinners, and purify your hearts, you double-minded." The unifying of the motives and intentions of the mind and heart is the ending of double-mindedness. There are no longer divided loyalties, rival affections. Other loyalties and affections and motives continue to exist, but they are subordinated and integrated into the unified pattern centered on this one dominating love. And those that will not be subject to it ("inimical" is Aquinas's word) are extinguished. The unifying of all motivation around this central aim of pleasing God *ipso facto* removes the rival centre of motivation, the sinful kind of self-love. That is the concomitant negative aspect. One is no longer in "two minds," with two "contrary principles" warring within. The old mindset has finally given way to the new.

If we ask what this old mindset is, the answer must be: the "mind set on merely human goals and values," the mindset of self-centered living. This is an interpretation of Paul's phrase in Romans 8:5, which Wesley quotes in Greek, where Paul writes of the *phronēma tēs sarkos*, the "mind of the flesh."[29] *Phronēma* does not mean "mind" in the way "mind" is sometimes used, to mean a part of a human being, the intellectual faculty or organ. A *phronēma* is not an entity at all: it is a disposition of mind, a way of thinking, a habitual pattern of thought or bent of mind; in short, a "mindset." The *phronēma tēs sarkos* is in strict literal translation "the disposition of the flesh." It is a disposition or habitual tendency of the mind, set on the things of "the flesh"; that is, ruled by the values and priorities *of fallen humanity*. It is the motivational pattern characteristic of fallen humanity—self-sufficient, self-interested, self-important, and self-centered. In this pattern of motivation, there may be many honorable motives, but in the last analysis it is centered on self-interest and is the mindset of self-centered living.

29. Sermon 43, "The Scripture Way of Salvation," *Works* (BE) 2:165.

The negative aspect of entire sanctification is that this configuration of motives, this motivational pattern centered on one's own desires or ambitions or glory or comforts, *the self-centered mindset*, is nullified. One of the traditional theological terms for this is "the carnal mind," taken from the translation of *phronēma tēs sarkos* in the Authorized Version. But that is a rather obscure phrase today. For the contemporary person without a classical education and not knowing that "carnal" comes from *caro, carnis*, the Latin for "flesh," it is not evident that "the carnal mind" is literally "the fleshly mind." Even if we know that, we may think of "the fleshly mind" as one obsessed with the life of the body, particularly perhaps sexuality. But since the basic Old Testament meaning of "flesh" is *humanity*, "the mind set on the flesh" (the NRSV's helpful translation of *phronēma tēs sarkos*) is best interpreted as the disposition towards merely human goals and values, or, as we have further interpreted it, *the self-centered mindset*.

d) Sinful Humanity

At this point, our discussion has brought us right into the heart of one of the most complex and elusive areas of Christian doctrine, the doctrine of original sin, and it is necessary therefore to stand back a little and consider this. We have deliberately refused here to make this the basis for a doctrine of Christian sanctification, which would be to try to understand light in terms of darkness. But in order to clarify the doctrine, we must now spend the rest of this chapter trying to shed some light in this dark area.

To begin with we need to note that the phrase "original sin" is used to cover a whole complex of notions, and confusion arises when writers slide from one facet of meaning to another. At this point we are mainly concerned to analyze this complex of ideas, not to evaluate them, and we may identify ten different facets. The phrase may well take its rise from (1) the original act of sin as recounted in Genesis 3, but in fact this is rarely if ever the way it is used today. Sometimes it is used loosely to refer simply to (2) universal sin—that all are guilty of sinning—but it implies more than that. It is often generally equated with (3) fallenness, but in fact it is very important to see that "fallenness" is a wider category. These should not be regarded as synonyms. Rather "fallenness" is better understood as referring more to the *ontological* consequences of the Fall, the idea expressed in Romans 5–8 (interpreting Genesis 3) that we are physically affected by corruption or decay (*phthora*) leading to death. Our bodies are therefore "fallen", but this does not imply that they are "sinful" in the sense that physical life is inherently evil. That would be Gnosticism. Confusion is avoided therefore if the phrase "original sin" is more strictly used to refer to (4) the more specifically Augustinian doctrine of original guilt, that we all share in the guilt for Adam's original act of sin, and (5) his doctrine of original sin as a kind of diseased or depraved *moral* condition. That usually includes (6) his view that this condition is hereditary, but there is no necessary logical connection. 'Disease' is presumably metaphorical here, but not all diseases are hereditary and not all that is hereditary is a disease. We have already thought about Augustine's perceptive analysis of this condition as (7) *concupiscentia*, or misdirected self-centred desire, which should be seen as an interpretation of the Pauline phrase, "the mind of the flesh" (Rom. 8: 6, 7). We have already dismissed (8) Augustine's bizarre theory that this was propagated by paternal lust. But we have to take account of (9) the biblical term "flesh" (to be differentiated from "the mind of the flesh"). This is often seen as simply a synonym for "original sin" in the Augustinian sense, but that is misleading. "Flesh" needs to be understood rather in connection with fallenness (see 3 above) referring to the *ontological* status of humanity as fallen rather than directly to our *moral* condition. Lastly, arising from the biblical term "flesh", there is (10) the notion of the corporate. We too often view sin as merely the sinful acts of individuals. But this whole area of doctrine is necessary in order to wrestle with a deeper enigma. A doctrine of sin has to cope with the mystery of both corporate sin and guilt (the *moral* dimension) and corporate fallenness (the *ontological* dimension). But now, having taken note of how many facets there are to this complex and paradoxical doctrine, and therefore how slippery the phrase "original sin" is, we need to examine the inter-connections of these different facets more fully and attempt to think about this doctrine a little more constructively.

On reflection, it is not surprising that an attempt to understand sin and evil is one of the most intractable areas of theology. There is much to be said for the long theological tradition that evil is an inherently paradoxical and somehow unreal reality. That is not merely a Platonist perspective, but a Christian one. After all, if God the Creator is the source of all created being and all created being is, therefore, by definition good (Gen 1:31), and if God is the only reality that is uncreated (i.e., there are no other eternal gods), then evil is an inherently paradoxical "unreal reality." How can evil be real if God is the source of all that is real? Theodicy is thus a legitimate and necessary area of theology, but yet any attempt to use it as a *basis* for theology is bound to end up in confused frustration and vain self-deceit. There can be no such thing as a "theology of evil" or an ordered Christian "demonology," for evil and "logos" are totally incompatible. We can only think of evil and sin as inherently deceptive and irrational, as indeed "anti-rational."

Here we are not concerned to develop an approach to the wider theological question of the existence of evil, but must restrict ourselves to the somewhat more specific area of "original sin" or human sinfulness. But even here, while we must somehow think of good in contrast to evil and holiness in contrast to sin, it is futile to try to build a doctrine of Christian holiness on a doctrine of sin. To repeat, darkness can only be understood in terms of light, not light in terms of darkness. We cannot first determine our doctrine of sin and then produce a doctrine of salvation to fit. Quite the contrary, we must move as some scholars have argued that Paul's thought moves, from "solution to plight," not from "plight to solution." So having come to this point in trying to reconfigure the doctrine of Christian "perfection" or "wholeness," we must now try to gain some insight into the broken and twisted reality of sinful humanity.[30]

Yet we must not treat "original sin" as a separate topic in itself, for it is not a separate reality in itself (not even an "unreal reality"!): it is an aspect of the human condition. Some kind of understanding of the paradoxical reality of what is traditionally called "original sin" can only be developed *within* an understanding of what it means to be human. So we have first to think a little more about theological anthropology, the doctrine of humanity, and expand just a little on what we have already said about theological anthropology, the doctrine of humanity.

A Biblical View

To do so we need to begin with biblical anthropology, the biblical concept of what it is to be human, beginning with the Old Testament. But rather than starting from the isolated phrase in Genesis 1:27 that has attracted so much attention, "the image of God," but which appears nowhere else in the Old Testament, we shall take our bearings from the common Hebrew word for the human, "flesh" (*basar*).[31] Where we use an abstract noun,

30. Although there is much value and clear thinking in Taylor, *Right Conception*, we are proposing here quite the opposite direction of thought.

31. On this approach to Hebrew anthropology, Brueggemann, *Theology*, 452,

"humanity," or "human nature," Hebrew characteristically uses a concrete one. And where we begin by considering the individual as the basic unit of humanity, Old Testament thinking characteristically starts with the corporate, the family, tribe, or nation. But the point is that this corporate humanity is weak and passing away: "All flesh is grass, and all its beauty is like the flower of the field. The grass withers; the flower fades" (Isa 40:6). Decay and death are the common lot of humanity. "Flesh" is inert without the life and energy and dynamic of "spirit" (*ruach*), which comes from God. Humanity can only be understood in relation to God. In Genesis 3, our condition of weakness and mortality is attributed to the disobedience of our first parents. Human death as we know it is a consequence of a rupture in the relationship with God, who is the source of life.[32] There is a connection therefore between death and sin. There is little explanation of how and why it is that all human beings are so sinful, only a narrative, not an analysis, but "the imagination of the human heart" is said to be wicked (Gen 6:5; 8:21). Also, the grand narrative of the Old Testament can be said to be about the repeated, persistent, and apparently ineradicable sinfulness of even God's chosen and holy people. And yet "flesh" is not evil. It is God's good creation, though now deeply flawed.

But there is another aspect to being "flesh," which we have already begun to think about, that each human being is a psychosomatic unity. In contrast to the Hellenistic anthropology—which separates "soul" (*psyche*) and "body" (*soma*) as two substances, and sees the soul as eternal spiritual reality but the body as a temporary abode—ancient Hebrew thinking had a much more monistic view of the human being. Consequently, there was no hope of the immortality of the soul. That Hellenistic belief has long been read into the Old Testament, but actually for most of the Old Testament, it is accepted that, as "flesh," human beings descend at death into the grave, the "pit," *sheol*, a kind of half-life where they can no longer praise God (Ps 115:17). Only in a few late passages of the Old Testament is there the dawning of the hope of life after death, and that not because there is a human soul that is inherently immortal, but because of the faithfulness of God who will raise up his people. The hope is not then based on the immortality of the soul, but in the hope for the resurrection of the whole person as a soul-body unity.[33]

---

references Wolff, *Anthropology*, among others.

32. Much hangs, of course, on that phrase "as we know it."

33. For a summary of Old Testament views of death and resurrection, see Wright, *Resurrection*, 32–128.

Those two aspects of the Old Testament view of humanity as "flesh" (*basar*) are carried over into the New Testament, but there is further development. First, although the language is now Greek (*sarx*), the underlying concept of "flesh" is still the Hebrew one. That is what is behind the concept of corporate humanity (*anthrōpos*) in Paul's phrase traditionally translated "the old man" (Rom 6:6; Eph 4:22; Col 3:9). That does not mean the old "self" (an interpolation of modern individualistic thinking!), but "the old humanity" (*anthrōpos*), considered *corporately*. When "the Word became flesh" (*sarx*) (John 1:14), he assumed that common, *corporate* humanity, weak and subject to death.

Paul adds some new twists to this. He too writes of "flesh" as the corporate nature of humankind, that way of being which we all share in common, which is weak and mortal, subject to corruption in the sense of "decay" (*phthora*) and resulting in death. But Paul teaches in Romans 5 that that is a consequence of the sin of Adam. He takes seriously the connection in Genesis 3 between sin and death. He also adds a new twist to the idea of humanity as "flesh." As a good student of the Old Testament, a son of Israel and not of Greece, Paul knows that this humanity or flesh (*sarx*), our physical existence, while it is fallen, decaying, and mortal as a result of the sin of Adam, is not evil. Though decaying as a consequence of human disobedience, our psychophysical existence is still God's good creation that he will redeem at the Last Day in the general resurrection. The hope of resurrection shines more bright and clear for the former Pharisee, Paul, because already, in anticipation of the Last Day, God has raised Messiah Jesus from the dead. But while fallen flesh is not inherently evil, and while it does not make sense to call the physical flesh "sinful" except as the instrument of sinners, what *is* sinful, according to Paul, is to live "according to the flesh" (*kata sarka*). That is to have "the mind of the flesh" (*phronēma sarkos*). It is not being human ("flesh") that is sinful: it is living *for the human*, being motivated by merely human goals and values; in short, it is *the self-centered mindset*. That can be so powerful that, in one passage (Gal 5), "flesh" is seen as a power that struggles against the Spirit. But it is not an alien power: it is the power of our own human self-centeredness, which holds us in thrall; in our own strength, given our fallen condition, we cannot break free. And to speak of "sinful flesh" is to speak corporately of "sinful humanity": it is not to say that our physical flesh is inherently sinful or evil. That would be Gnosticism.[34]

34. See Schweitzer, "σάρξ," in *TDNT* 7:98–151; also Thiselton, "Flesh," in *NIDNTT* 1:671–82; also Howard, *Newness of Life*, 17–33.

So far, we have tried to stick closely to a biblical theology of human sinfulness, but now we must try to relate that to the way that was later developed in Christian theology and, once again, we shall have to paint this dark picture in broad strokes.

The Theological Development

The doctrine of original sin is often associated with Augustine, and he did indeed insist on it as part of his counter-argument to the teaching of Pelagius. But in fact, while the phrase *peccatum originale* apparently originated with Augustine, and while he added his own particular twist, there is general agreement among the Fathers. It was the Greek Fathers before Augustine who adopted the term "the Fall" (*to ptōma*) to refer to the events narrated in Genesis 3, and who regarded all human beings as consequently fallen. They particularly fastened on corruption (*phthora*, decay) of the human nature (*physis*) leading to physical death as a consequence of the Fall.[35] They quoted Romans 5 and saw it not just individualistically, that is, that each died because of his or her own sin, but corporately. This was the condition of corporate human "flesh" (*sarx*), the condition of what Paul called "the old humanity" (*anthrōpos*). But they also taught that, as a consequence, each human being was a sinner and subject to decay (*phthora*) and death. The physical flesh may not be evil, and it would be a confusion to speak of the *physical* flesh as *morally* corrupt or itself "sinful." Sin can only be attributed to persons, not to physical flesh, except by extension when it is seen as the instrument of sinful persons. But it is "fallen" in the sense that it is disordered and subject to *physical* corruption or decay. The focus of the Greek Fathers often tends to be on the wider *ontological* consequence of the Fall, death, for which the remedy is the resurrection of Christ, rather than the more strictly *moral* category of sinfulness.

Augustine developed the doctrine of original sin as the obverse of his focus on grace. Against Pelagius, he argued that if salvation is all of grace, then that totality must be reflected in human sinfulness. Humankind must be sinful *in toto* before God so that there is no merit in us. That did not mean that fallen humans could not live moral lives, but it did mean that, while we retained our free will despite the Fall, our free will, whatever moral acts we chose to do, could only make choices that were

---

35. The enormous importance of the physical or ontological dimension of the Fall is clear everywhere in that pivotal text of patristic theology, the *De Incarnatione* of Athanasius (*NPNF*[2] 4:36–67).

tainted by our sinful condition. We did not have the freedom or power to merit salvation: we could only believe and obey God because of the *gratia praeveniens*, the grace of God that went before us, healing our sick wills.[36]

Augustine therefore had a greater concern than the Eastern Fathers for the moral and legal aspects, and deeper insight into the psychological aspect of the doctrine. First, in developing the legal or forensic aspect, he relied on his Latin translation of Romans 5:12, "in whom (*in quo*) all sinned," and taught that, since we were all "in Adam" when he sinned, we all share in the guilt for his sin. But this aspect of original sin, namely original guilt, was washed away in baptism. Secondly, he developed the psychological analysis of this sinful condition as *concupiscentia*, and thus at this point, Augustine's doctrine of original sinfulness connected with his analysis of human motivation. The third development, however, was his teaching, repeated again and again, that this "disease" or "pollution" of *concupiscentia* was passed on sexually in the paternal lust necessary for the birth of each human being. This third development we have already dismissed as a totally unbiblical slur on conjugal relations within marriage, which is regarded positively throughout the Bible. It is a rather bizarre attempt to come up with a technical causal explanation. But we must not let this rather absurd third development distract us from his deeper insights, particularly into the psychological dimension.

Unfortunately, perhaps because of Augustine's negative attitude to human sexuality (foreshadowed in the earlier Latin theologian, Tertullian), *concupiscentia* has come into English as "concupiscence," meaning specifically sexual lust. But as we have already seen, in Latin it refers to *all* forms of self-centered desire. It was an *inclinatus ad se*, a tendency or bent towards pleasing oneself. It is, in fact, a good Latin interpretation of Paul's phrase, *phronēma sarkos*, "the mind of the flesh," or, as we have further interpreted it, the mind set on merely human goals and values, the *self-centered mindset*. Augustine further identified it with pride (*superbia*), and with the egotism or self-deification that isolates by breaking relationships, and demands that everything be subjected to the self.

Matt Jenson has traced the development of this analysis of human sinfulness from Augustine to Luther and up to contemporary theologians.[37]

---

36. See McFadyen, *Bound to Sin*, for an excellent analysis of how a merely moral concept of wrong-doing as simply freely-chosen acts is Pelagian and insufficient to cope with the way individual choices are enmeshed in sin as corporate and societal. Only an Augustinian concept of the bondage of the will apart from the grace of God will do.

37. Jenson, *Gravity of Sin*.

But Luther is the one who develops the analysis most radically, taking it beyond Augustine. The problem of our sinfulness is that fallen humanity is *homo incurvatus in se*, humanity turned in on itself. But where this cuts most deeply is in Luther's insight that the last and deepest refuge of our sinful self-centeredness is *in our religion*. A series of interpreters (Oberman, Nygren, Rupp, and Watson) have spoken of Luther's "Copernican revolution," turning the anthropocentric, egocentric religion so prevalent in the late medieval period into a theocentric faith.[38] He is particularly challenging in his insight that it is *homo religiosis*, the religious man or woman, who is *incurvatus in se*. Connected with that is his criticism of Augustine's concept of love for God as *caritas*, including the *erōs* of spiritual desire for God because he is our *summum bonum*. If we love God because he is good to us and for us, then, according to Luther, that is still a self-centered kind of love. What is more, that we are to love our neighbors "as ourselves" does *not* imply that it is good to love ourselves. In opposition to those who would declare that there is a legitimate self-love, Luther regards all self-love as sinful. What the commandment means then is that this sinful self-love is to be *replaced* by love of neighbor. And instead of "using" (*usus*) God to supply us with good gifts which we then "enjoy" (*frui*) we should use (*usus*) God's gifts as the means to "enjoy" (*frui*) none but God. According to Matt Jenson, Luther is "razor sharp in his suspicion of even psychological egoism," and only allows that we can truly love ourselves indirectly as a consequence, but never a motivation, of loving others "kenotically."[39]

Jenson points out that another development in Luther is his rejection of the view of the medieval theologians that the natural human desires are the occasion for temptation but are not themselves evil. Luther takes a more negative view of human motivation as a whole. Rejecting the differentiation of different parts and treating the human being holistically as *totus homo*, he regards all human desires, the "tinder for desire" (*fomes concupiscentiae*), as themselves sinful.[40] Calvin too pronounces that "all human desires are evil."[41] We have to ask whether the Reformers' position here conflates the different levels of meaning in the Pauline use of the word "flesh" (*sarx*) and interprets "sinful flesh" (*sarkos hamartias*, Rom

---

38. Ibid., 47f. See also, Noble, 'Evangelical Reformers' (2001).

39. Ibid., 91.

40. Ibid., 54.

41. Calvin, *Institutes*, III, 3, 10–12.

8:3) to mean not just "sinful humanity," but that our physical flesh is itself so polluted and diseased as to be evil.

Contemporary feminist theology has rejected the identification of self-centeredness and pride as the root of sin. The post-Christian feminist, Daphne Hampson, pointed to the experience of women who, far from being characterized by pride and self-glory, have on the contrary been too dependent on others, losing themselves in relationships, subordinating themselves to another and so sinking into self-deprecation and even self-hatred and suicidal despair. Focusing on sin as self-centeredness and pride and insisting on self-denial and taking up the cross can, in fact, entrench women in a sinful pattern of living when they really need to assert themselves. For Hampson, that analysis led her to reject the Christian faith.[42] But the Wesleyan theologian, Diane Leclerc, has argued that Christian theology should not always identify sin with self-centeredness and pride, but recognize that with many (particularly women), it can be an idolatrous self-denial by idolizing and subjecting oneself to another human being.[43] Matt Jenson points, however, to Barth's analysis as already anticipating this valid critique by feminists.[44]

For Barth, anthropology and our doctrine of sin should not be worked out independently as a prelude that then determines the shape of the gospel and of our doctrines of Christ and the atonement. Quite the reverse: since sin was so deceitful and humanity so broken, our understanding of them had to be viewed from the perspective of the gospel; that is, from Christology and soteriology. He therefore began from the traditional structure of the threefold office of Christ as our priest, king, and prophet. That Christ humbled himself to become our *priest* indicates that sin does take the form of *pride*. But if his humiliation reveals to us our pride, his exaltation as *king* reveals to us how low we have sunk. Barth refers to this as the sin of sloth, but that does not just mean laziness. It is our refusal to accept our salvation in Christ by insisting on isolating ourselves in our own trivial concerns and comforts and refusing to live for God or for others. Egotism therefore does not only take the form of pride; it also takes the form of a selfish and small-minded refusal of our destiny as the children of God, choosing to sink back into inaction, curling up like a hedgehog

42. See Hampson, "The Challenge of Feminism to Christianity" and Hampson, *Theology and Feminism.*

43. Leclerc, *Singleness of Heart*; see also Coakley, *Powers.*

44. See Jenson, *Gravity of Sin*, for his critique of Hampson (98–129) and his summary of Barth (130–87).

(in Barth's vivid picture) and asking to be left alone. This is the stupidity of the atheist obsessed with his rejection of God; it is selfish and uncaring inhumanity to others; it is dissipating one's gifts; it is refusing to accept one's mortality and responsibility to use the time one has been given. It is misery and slavery in refusing the freedom God offers to relate to him or to others. Then thirdly, that Christ is the *prophet*, the true witness to God, indicates that our sinfulness lies in our embracing of *falsehood* by refusing to accept the gospel of God's gracious act of salvation, denying the truth of God's love by living in futile denial of his revelation in Jesus Christ.

What is of most interest to us at this point is that Barth's analysis demonstrates that self-centeredness is not to be identified with pride alone. That is only one form it takes. It also takes the opposite form of sloth. What we may conclude then, along with Jenson, is that self-centeredness gives a unifying category under which so many other forms of sinful motivation may be grouped. It may take the form of self-glorification, self-sovereignty,[45] self-promotion, self-sufficiency, self-dramatization (!), self-satisfaction. But this self-obsession may also take negative forms such as self-concern, self-pity, and even self-denigration.

We may add to that, that self-centeredness may even present a deep insight into the vast and subtle area of idolatry. Calvin gave a deeply perceptive analysis of idolatry as sinful humanity projecting out of the murky depths of their own sinfulness, gods who reflected their own sinful desires, so that idolatry is actually another form of self-worship.[46] Today the most used tool for idolatry is not the hammer and chisel, but the camera and no society has ever had more idols. This suggests a further dimension to self-centeredness; namely that it should not be considered only individualistically. When it takes corporate form in human society, people in effect worship their group, whether that is family, tribe, or nation. Some sell their souls to a business company or a political party, or even to a football team. At one level that may appear trivial, but it can produce racism, tribalism, extreme nationalism, and xenophobia. It has both crass and more subtle forms. And if we follow the analysis of Walter Wink, it may further be seen as the genesis of the demonic, terrifyingly embodied in the Nazi cult, and many other similar forms of political and cultural idolatry before and since.[47]

45. See Howard, *Newness of Life*, 37–65.

46. Calvin, *Institutes of the Christian Religion* I, 11, 8.

47. Wink, *Naming the Powers*; Wink, *Unmasking the Powers*; and Wink, *Engaging the Powers*. See the chapters by Cook (165–84) and Noble (185–223) in Lane, *Unseen World*.

e) Conclusion

However, rather than pursuing that line of thought, which would take us into the wider question of how we are to think of evil, the "mystery of iniquity" (2 Thess 2:7, AV), we must now try to sum up this chapter. Our thinking here has necessarily been more open-ended and even somewhat tentative. Beginning with some thoughts on Wesley's limitations as a man of his time, we have tried to investigate ways in which we may re-formulate his doctrine of Christian sanctification. We have suggested that the linked concepts of motivation and relationship may help us to reformulate and better communicate the doctrine in the twenty-first century. But this has also brought us to wrestle with the dark complexities of the doctrine of sin, and we have to recognize that we shall never plumb the depths of that mystery. Nor should we want to. But the Augustinian tradition as a whole tries to understand sin in the light of grace, and therefore our sinful condition in the light of salvation, our plight in the light of God's solution. Of the ten aspects we identified in the complex concept of original sin, the seventh is the most directly relevant, misdirected self-centered desire and self-love. The key Augustinian term, *concupiscentia*, has therefore to be seen as a warped distortion of true love, *caritas*. But behind the Augustinian word, *concupiscentia*, lies the Pauline understanding of "indwelling sin" (Rom 7:17, 20) as "the mind set on the flesh" (*phronēma tēs sarkos*), which we have interpreted as the "mind set on human goals and values," or further, as "the self-centered mindset." The only possible remedy for that is "the expulsive power of a new affection," or in Wesley's key phrase "love excluding sin."

But we are not delivered in this life from all the effects of sin. We still live as fallen people in "this present evil age." Being filled with the Holy Spirit who is outgoing Love nullifies the old self-centered mindset, but it is not final salvation. Within the "present evil age" we are not delivered from original sin in its physical and corporate aspect. But it is less confusing, we have suggested, to refer to this not as 'original sin' but as 'fallenness.' It is the corporate *ontological* condition we all share as fallen creatures rather than the *moral* and personal aspect of human life. We always remain fallen creatures with the same physiological drives that, though part of God's good creation, are disordered and can so easily be out of control. The Christian who, at the level of conscious intention, loves God with all her heart, mind, and strength is still a creature of fallen flesh. But she no longer lives "according to the flesh" with a "mind set on the flesh." At the conscious, voluntary level, she loves God with all her heart, but at the unconscious level of motivation, shaped by heredity and upbringing, nature and nurture, there is no sudden magical change. She is still in the fallen mortal flesh with all its physiological drives. In some cases that may even have resulted in some kind of addiction from which there may be no immediate release without years of careful pastoral nurture and care.[48] And in every case, we are still shaped throughout our lives by our up-bringing and nurture within the family and local community, and it is part of the doctrine of corporate original sin that every family, even the most refined and Christian, is to some degree dysfunctional.

Further, even at the level of conscious, voluntary intention, the meta-phor of the "death" or "eradication" of the sinful self-centered mindset, the "mind set on the flesh," must not be taken literally to mean that some kind of thing, or bit, or parasite, or manikin within has been extracted so that the operation is irreversible! The Christian loves God with all his heart precisely as long as he loves God with all his heart. He has not been put on some kind of automatic pilot by some kind of mechanical operation. He is still a moral agent who confirms or denies, strengthens or weakens his consecration by ethical choices every day. And he still has to confess daily his faults and failings and how far he falls short. But the same Holy Spirit who fills his heart with love will sanctify his whole bodily life and his intellectual life, as well as his relationships and his whole life-style. As he grows in grace by the gracious work of the Holy Spirit, his physical life too (including any psychological problem or mental illness) will be included in that sanctifying and even healing work. Holistic sanctification will increasingly purify every aspect of his life—body, soul, and spirit.

This is the sense in which our sanctification may be "entire." The phrase "entire sanctification" can be a misleading one in that it suggests that the believer is "entirely sanctified" in such a way that the work of sanctification is finally complete. In other words, it seems to imply "sinless perfection." But to emphasize again what we have already noted, in the Pauline text of 1 Thessalonians 5:23, the word "entire" (*holoteleis*) is not an adverb modifying the verb, but an adjective qualifying the plural pronoun "you" (*hymas*). It is not that the sanctification is finally complete: that will only be so in the resurrection at the coming (*parousia*) of the Lord. It is rather that the Thessalonian believers are to be sanctified *holistically*. As the Lord makes them "increase and abound in love," he will "strengthen their hearts in holiness" so that they are found blameless when the Lord comes (3:12–13). But since human beings are not an amalgamation of

48. See May, *Addiction and Grace*, and Earle and Laaser, *Pornography Trap*.

different bits and pieces (souls and bodies), as in the Greek way of thinking, but holistic psychosomatic beings, as in the Hebrew way of thinking, this love in the heart must therefore affect them in every dimension of their being—intellectually, personally, relationally, and even spread to the physical dimension, giving life and sanctity and healing even to their fallen, mortal bodies.

It is surely vitally important for the church and for each believer that the reality of our continuing fallenness should not, however, rob us of our birthright in Christ. We must distinguish between the *ontological* level, our continued corporate physical existence as fallen "flesh," and the level of the personal, *moral*, voluntary, intentional level of the "mind" or "heart." Christians continue to live with the fallen physical and physiological desires which need to be disciplined. But it is an enormous tragedy if a failure to distinguish between these two levels of motivation leads us to think that we must live with a divided mind and heart. James tells us (James 4:8) that the double-minded can know purity of "heart." And Paul's prayer that we be sanctified "through and through" or holistically (1 Thess. 5:23) reminds us that we are each a psychosomatic *unity*. Therefore, even though we still live as fallen people, when the Spirit pours the love of God into our hearts, that wholeness and healing begins to affect us even at the level of the fallen, mortal body (Rom. 8:11). Paul's prayer for holistic sanctification is one which we must echo for ourselves and for the whole Church of Christ. Faithful is he who calls us who will surely do it!

Charles Wesley can provide words for our prayer as believers in Christ who continue to pursue the perfecting of our holiness by focusing not on our holiness, but on Christ:

> Jesu, thy boundless love to me
> No thought can reach, no tongue declare;
> O knit my thankful heart to thee,
> And reign without a rival there!
> Thine wholly, thine alone I am;
> Be thou alone my constant flame!
>
> O grant that nothing in my soul
> May dwell, but thy pure love alone!
> O may the love possess me whole,
> My joy, my treasure, and my crown;
> Strange flames far from my heart remove—
> My every act, word, thought, be love.

O Love, how cheering is thy ray!
All pain before thy presence flies!
Care, anguish, sorrow, melt away
Where'er thy healing beams arise;
O Jesus, nothing may I see,
Nothing desire or seek but thee!

Unwearied may I this pursue,
Dauntless to the high prize aspire;
Hourly within my soul renew
This holy flame, this heavenly fire;
And day and night be all my care
To guard this sacred treasure there.

Still let thy love point out the way
(How wondrous things thy love hath wrought!)
Still lead me, lest I go astray,
Direct my word, inspire my thought;
And if I fall, soon may I hear
Thy voice, and know that love is near.

In suffering be thy love my peace,
In weakness be thy love my power;
And when the storms of life shall cease,
Jesus, in that important hour,
In death as life be thou my guide,
And save me, who for me hast died.[49]

At this point, however, having attempted in this chapter to clarify and re-articulate Wesley's doctrine of Christian "perfection," and to clarify our thinking on the connected doctrine of human sinfulness, we must now move on in the following chapters to set this in wider theological context. The most subtle temptation, as Luther saw, is for Christians to become concerned with their own holiness rather than with loving God and neighbor. To save this doctrine from falling into that most subtle snare, we have to turn our attention away from the devoted Christian to the Triune God.

---

49. Selected verses from Hymn 362 in *A Collection of Hymns for the Use of the People Called Methodists, Works* (BE) 7:530f.

6

Christian Holiness and the Atonement

The great revival of trinitarian theology in the late twentieth century helped us to understand that the doctrine of the Trinity is not just one Christian doctrine among others. It is the comprehensive doctrine that gives unity to the whole Christian faith. Without it, the gospel itself collapses into incoherence. Whereas it was pretty much a dead letter in the eighteenth century, rejected by rationalists and Deists as an illogical conundrum, and held by many Christians merely as a badge of orthodoxy, it has become increasingly clear in our day that every area of Christian doctrine is illuminated and held together in unity by our confession of the Triune God.[1]

One reason why it was regarded as unintelligible by rationalists and Deists, and as mere "ivory tower" theory by many believers, was that it had become separated from the story of the gospel.[2] Systematic theology tended to begin by talking about "One God" and the divine attributes as if Christianity were merely a kind of monotheism. It seemed to be of secondary importance that God was three and mere speculation about what was true in heaven rather than about our life on earth. It therefore appeared to be a somewhat irrelevant piece of information about God's eternal being, or what theologians called the "Ontological" or "Immanent"

1. Among Wesleyan theologians who have published monographs on the doctrine of the Trinity, see Leupp, *Knowing the Name*; Leupp, *Trinitarian Theology*; Powell, *Trinity*; Powell, *Participating in God*; and Coppedge, *Triune*. See also the following papers: Wainwright, "Why Wesley"; Wainwright, "Trinitarian Theology"; Keen, "Transgression"; and the collection of papers edited by Meeks, *Trinity*.

2. The problem was well analyzed (though not resolved) in LaCugna, *God for Us*.

Trinity. We had somehow almost lost sight of the fact that the belief in God as eternally Triune was based upon the so-called "Economic" Trinity. We seemed to have forgotten that it was in the "economy" of salvation, the story of God's saving action in the world, that Triunity was revealed.[3]

As we begin to explore the basis for the doctrine of Christian sanctification in the doctrine of the Trinity, this is then another way of referring to the central beliefs of the Christian church. We will return in the final chapter to think more about God as the One who is eternally Triune, but begin here with the so-called "Economic Trinity"; that is, the doctrine that God is revealed to be Father, Son, and Holy Spirit *in the narrative of the gospel*. T. F. Torrance refers to this appropriately as the "evangelical Trinity."[4]

A summary of the story of the gospel appears in its earliest form in one of the earliest books of the New Testament, Paul's first letter to the Corinthians: "that Christ died for our sins according to the Scriptures, that he was buried, that he was raised on the third day according to the Scriptures, and that he appeared to Cephas, then to the twelve, then to more than five hundred brothers at once . . ." (1 Cor 15:3–6). Within the pages of the New Testament we can see this very early version of the message expanded in, for example, the great hymn about Christ in Philippians 2:6–11, but according to Luke it was already in triadic form in Peter's speech on the Day of Pentecost (Acts 2:14–36). There it is already clear in a sermon centering on the death and resurrection of Jesus as the Christ, that he had been sent by the God of Israel, who is identified as the Father (v. 33), and who had also now sent the Holy Spirit. The whole story of salvation is comprehended then within the story of these Three.

As we try to investigate what basis there is for a doctrine of Christian holiness within the trinitarian shape of the gospel, we shall begin as the apostles did with the story of Jesus, particularly his dying for our sins. In this chapter we shall examine the doctrine of the atonement, the "Work" of Christ; in the next chapter we shall look at Christology, the doctrine of the Person of Christ; that will bring us then to focus on the work of the Spirit in the actions of the "Economic" Trinity, and finally in the last chapter, to mount up higher to God's eternal Triune life. But in each chapter we shall be asking the question: what basis is there in this central doctrine of

3. Hence the value of "Rahner's rule" in Rahner, *Trinity*, 22: The "economic" Trinity *is* the "immanent" Trinity, and *vice versa*.

4. T. F. Torrance, *Christian Doctrine of God*, 7. See also Eugenio, "Communion with God," on Torrance's Trinitarian soteriology.

the Christian faith, the atonement, the Person of Christ, and the doctrine of the Spirit and the Trinity, for a doctrine of Christian perfecting?

a) The Doctrine of the Atonement

Salvation (*sotēria*) is at the heart of the Christian gospel. Consequently in Christian theology, soteriology particularly addresses the question: what does it mean to say that Christ died "for our sins"? The earliest preaching of the church, as presented in the Acts of the Apostles, was focused on the resurrection as God's vindication of the unjustly executed Jesus. But the deeper mystery is addressed in Paul's letters: given that this was God's Son, the real marvel is not that he was raised from the dead, but that he was executed in the first place! Why on earth would the very Son of God subject himself to such degradation and agony? The cross then is the deeper mystery.

Thinking on this question is by no means absent from the writing of the Greek or Latin Fathers, but it was only with Anselm in the Latin West in the eleventh century that the question was addressed in a treatise devoted exclusively to this question, *Cur Deus Homo* (Why God Became Man). Anselm sharpened the question: why was it *necessary* for Christ to die? The assumption is that God is not a sadist or a masochist. In some way then and for some reason, and in some sense, the death of Christ had to be "necessary," even for God, if we were to be saved. Why? How are we to understand this? Since Anselm wrote his penetrating work, no one can claim to have gained any understanding of the doctrine of the atonement who has not deeply considered that question.

From there the doctrine was developed by other medieval theologians, particularly Thomas Aquinas, but it was the Reformers and their heirs who particularly linked the doctrine of the atonement to the doctrine of justification by faith. Their doctrine was standard among Protestants (including Wesley) until, in the eighteenth and nineteenth centuries, some "liberal" theologians rejected the entire development of the doctrine in the West and dismissed it as simply one "theory." They then presented an alternative "theory," generally known as the "moral influence" or "exemplarist" theory, claiming that it was originated by Anselm's contemporary, Abelard. In the 1920s, a Swedish Lutheran, Gustaf Aulén, added a third "theory," which he claimed to be the "classic" theory of the Fathers. This saw the atonement as the victory of Christ, *Christus Victor*, over the powers of evil. One minor variation on that is the so-called "ransom theory," but that was never very significant among the Fathers.

All this resulted in the simplistic pedagogical approach of many twentieth-century textbooks that there were three (or more) "theories" and that the student could choose which one he or she preferred. This naive and superficial approach to the doctrine of the atonement, which still persists in some publications, needs to be laid to rest. We have to be clear that Christian theology is not a matter of "theories," and that there is no such thing as a "theory of the atonement." The very word "theory" can be taken to mean some kind of tentative systematic explanation which ties up all the loose ends, but such rationalism is quite out of place in theology and particularly when we come to the doctrine of the atonement. Here we come to one of the deepest mysteries of the Christian faith, and what we have been given in Holy Scripture is not a set of "theories," or even the raw material for "theories," but a narrative and a set of metaphors.

Two things must be made clear about this. First, the narrative of the gospel is not a fiction: Christ truly died and was raised from the dead. But further, *metaphors are not fictions.* Some may react against the idea that we only have "metaphors" to explain the significance of the death of Christ. Does this mean that Christ did not *really* die "for our sins," did not *really* deal with our guilt, or did not *really* defeat the powers of evil? But the answer to that worry is that a metaphor is not a fiction. Colin Gunton deals with this issue in his very helpful book, *The Actuality of the Atonement.*[5] In brief, his response is that even though we can only speak of these mysteries in metaphor, the metaphors refer to what actually happened. When we speak of God, we stretch our language, which is a feature of the human realm, so that it applies analogically or metaphorically to God. Jesus is not literally a lamb, the kingdom of heaven is not literally a mustard seed, and God does not literally sit on a throne several miles above the surface of the earth. But although these are metaphors, Jesus *really did* die for our sins in a way that is illuminated by the way lambs used to be sacrificed, the rule of God *really is* hidden but growing, and God *really does* rule over the universe. So with reference to the atonement, Gunton points out that three of the main metaphors, the battlefield, the law court, and the temple sacrifice, point us to features of the actual atonement by which Christ reconciled us sinners to God. And in fact these metaphors are indispensable because, as biblical metaphors, they are God-given.

5. Gunton, *Actuality of the Atonement.*

That is the second point that we must be clear about, that these various metaphors are not options that we may take or leave. One of the most poisonous implications that was drawn from the notion of "theories" of the atonement was the idea that we were free to choose one and dispense with the others. But once we see that these are metaphors, and particularly biblical metaphors, we have to take them *all* into account. Part of the problem here is the modern rationalist assumption that Christian theology can dispense with metaphor and must have the rational, literal consistency of a system of Aristotelian logic rather like Euclid's geometry. Repeatedly in this area of doctrine one comes across the idea that *a* "logically" implies *b*, or that it is "illogical" to hold two things together. But if we are dealing with metaphors, we are not dealing with a joined-up system in which every part of the system may be logically deduced from every other part, or even from "preceding" parts. That would be like trying to force all the parables of Jesus unto one connected narrative!

The underlying question here is: what is the role of logic in Christian theology, and particularly in the doctrine of the atonement? In the last chapter we thought about this in connection with evil and maintained that since evil is opposed to structure and order, it must be regarded as beyond our powers of logic. This applies more widely, however. The infinite God cannot be contained within the human structures and literal definitions of our traditional, formal, finite logic. And certainly the doctrine of the atonement, where we are thinking of God dealing with evil, is of all doctrines the one where logic is quickly seen to be inadequate to deal with the reality. Logic does have a limited use in drawing out the implications of each model (exemplified, for example, by Anselm), but it cannot join up all the models into one logical system.[6]

But this most certainly does not mean that we are free to talk nonsense and gaily throw contradictory ideas around with the excuse that it is, after all, "just poetry"! We may not understand finally what is going on here, but God does. And poetical language full of imagery, including all the metaphors he has given us, is equal to the task of helping us to understand all we need to know. The atonement is, after all, the victory of the Logos over the "antilogos," and we have to trust that he knows what he is doing.

But more than that, cold deduction never created or discovered anything really new. It can only draw out the implications of what we already know. If we are going to go more deeply into understanding anything,

6. On the role of logic in theology, see T. F. Torrance, *Theological Science*, 203–80.

there has to be a more creative or intuitive movement of the mind. That is not irrational, but the highest rationality. In all areas of knowledge and all sciences, while logic is indispensable when it is appropriate, the greatest discoveries are made and the most insightful hypotheses formulated by the intuitive contact of the mind with reality. The new insight is then expressed in *metaphors*. These become "models," that is, metaphors that are definitive for our understanding and that unite whole areas of research and knowledge: light as a "wave" or a "particle," heredity as a "tree," intelligence as "vision," love as a kind of force of "gravity." The list is endless and there are many "dead" metaphors embedded in our language so that we no longer recognize them to be metaphors.[7]

In the Christian doctrine of the atonement therefore, we have to take into account *all* the metaphors we have been given. John McIntyre, in his sharp analytical style, identified thirteen such models that have been used historically: ransom, redemption, salvation, sacrifice, propitiation, expiation, atonement, reconciliation, conflict and victory, punishment or penalty, satisfaction, example, and liberation.[8] They are *all* to be taken into account, but that does not mean that they are just a ragbag collection in competition with each other. Somehow they indicate an underlying unity. And while some may be more relevant in some cultures and others in others, that still does not mean that we can discard any of them. Rather, they are complementary, like the metaphors of wave and particle in the physics of light. McIntyre refers to his teacher, Daniel Lamont, who suggested that they may be thought of as different "dimensions." Dimensions are independent in the sense that we cannot reduce one to the other (sight to hearing); they may exhibit polarity (up and down, inside and outside, North Pole and South Pole); or they may be paradoxical, rather like a painting in which one cow on the canvas is four times larger than another.[9]

In the brief space we have available, we shall organize our models for the atonement by adopting an ancient structure going back to Eusebius, adapted by Calvin and others, and present in Wesley's thought.[10] This is the *triplex munus*, the "threefold office" of Christ as our Messiah, the One "anointed" as "prophet, priest, and king." Going beyond Calvin and Wesley

7. Necessary reading on these methodological questions and their relevance for theology is T. F. Torrance, *Theological Science*.

8. McIntyre, *Soteriology*.

9. McIntyre references Lamont, *Christ*, 64ff.

10. See Jansen, *Calvin's Doctrine*, and Maddox, *Responsible Grace*, 109–14, and the major treatment in Rainey, "John Wesley" on Wesley.

however, who both attached the prophetic office only to Christ's teaching, we shall try to see that office too in direct connection with the cross and therefore with the atonement.

These are also metaphors. Jesus did not literally rule over an earthly kingdom, and he was not a priest of the tribe of Levi. It is more literal to say that he was a prophet, and he was regarded as such during his ministry, but of course he was not just any prophet, but was the prophet of God in a unique way. But the advantage in taking these metaphors as the organizing structure is that they do not focus our thinking just on what he *did*, but on who he *is*. And, as we shall see, those two—the "Work" of Christ and the Person of Christ—must not be separated. In this chapter we will focus on the Work of Christ, and much of the material that has been wrongly presented as "theories" will give us valuable insights once we recognize that they are "models." In the next chapter we will go more deeply into the whole mystery as we focus on his Person, for only then can we begin to see the depth and coherence of the doctrine of the atonement. But in this chapter we are not just going to study the doctrine of the atonement in and for itself. We have a specific question to explore.[11]

b) Christian Perfecting and the Atonement

The question we have to explore is this: *what is the connection between the doctrine of the atonement and the doctrine of Christian perfecting?* Of course, this is not merely an intellectual question about the relationship between concepts, but a question about the relationship between two realities. Doctrine is only "truth" in a derived way, statements that refer us away to reality. As the Greek word for both (*alētheia*) reminds us, it is the *reality* itself which is the *truth*. "Truth" is not merely an attribute of statements, as rationalism holds, but another word for the *real* as distinct from the illusory. The question we are asking, therefore, is what really happened at the cross that now makes Christian perfecting possible? Or to put that back in a more abstract way, how is the doctrine of Christian sanctification an implication of the doctrine of the atonement? How is the doctrine of the Christian life connected to soteriology, the doctrine of salvation?

This seems to have been a somewhat neglected or at least subsidiary question in Western theology. Perhaps that is because Anselm's doctrine

11. Nor is there space for a diversion into discussion of the currently fashionable atonement theories of René Girard, Darby Kathleen Ray, or J. Denny Weaver, which were effectively critiqued in Boersma, *Violence.*

of the atonement started off defining sin as debt or guilt so that the Reformers also saw the cross in predominantly juridical terms. This is by no means to be dismissed, of course. If the cross did not provide for our pardon, for our *justification*, then we are lost. But the Christian tradition (perhaps particularly Protestant tradition) has worked with an over-tidy separation of justification from sanctification in a way that is not truly biblical. And it does not seem to have given the same thought to how the cross effected our *sanctification*. And if that is true of Protestantism as a whole, it seems to be generally true of the Wesleyan tradition in particular.[12] For all that Wesley is unique as a major figure of Christian history in uniting the Reformation understanding of justification with the ancient catholic concern with sanctification, and particularly "perfection," his doctrine of the atonement tends to be concerned with the former.

Kenneth Collins notes Wesley's endorsement of the Anselmic doctrine of the *Book of Common Prayer*, that Christ on the cross made "a full oblation, sacrifice, and satisfaction for the sins of the whole world."[13] Indeed, Wesley often followed the Reformers' version of the Anselmic doctrine of satisfaction, interpreting it specifically as penal substitution.[14] Randy Maddox's analysis also makes clear Wesley's primarily Anselmic stance.[15] Wesley therefore, as a true Protestant, connects the atonement with justification: it is because Christ bore the penalty of our sins that we are pardoned. But he seems to have made no serious attempt to show the basis of his controversial doctrine of sanctification in the doctrine of the atonement, and in this he is simply a man of his time, following the generally Anselmic tradition of the Western church.

Therefore, this is a question that we need to tackle. Given that Wesley's doctrine of Christian "perfection" remains controversial, can it be seen to be based on the doctrine of the atonement? How did the death of Christ on the cross and his rising again bring about our *sanctification*? It would seem that any Christian theological tradition needs to address that question. After all, if our salvation is by Christ alone (*a solo Christo*), and if it includes our final salvation when we shall be sinless in the presence of a holy God, then we *have* to address the question of how the cross brings

12. One exception to that is the popular but perceptive treatment in Hegre, *Cross and Sanctification*.

13. Collins, *Theology of John Wesley*, referring to Wesley's sermon, "God's Love to Fallen Man," *Works* (BE) 2:427, where he quotes from the Prayer of Consecration at the Lord's Supper.

14. Collins, *Theology of John Wesley*, 99–108.

15. Maddox, *Responsible Grace*, 96–106.

about such complete sanctification. The alternative would be to say that the cross only brings justification or pardon, and that we fit ourselves for heaven by the effort of our own sanctifying self-discipline. That, of course, would be a form of the Pelagian heresy. Whether or not one accepts Wesley's doctrine of Christian "perfection" therefore, *any* Christian doctrine of salvation demands that through the death and rising of Christ we are not only justified *but also sanctified*.

But the question is particularly relevant to the doctrine of "perfection." Perhaps Wesleyans have never really grasped how crucial that question is. It is true, of course, that it has always been recognized that we are sanctified "through the blood of Christ." We have sung about that in various hymns and gospel songs. Wesleyans have preached on Hebrews 13:12, that Jesus died "to sanctify the people through his own blood," and on 1 John 1:7, that "the blood of Jesus Christ his Son cleanses us from all sin." Indeed, in a past day, the powerful scriptural imagery of being "washed in the blood of the Lamb" (Rev 7:14, and 1:5 AV, based on a variant reading) was so over-used throughout evangelical Christianity as to become, sadly, a cliché.

Further, Wesleyans have referred to "entire" sanctification as "dying to sin," and yet have not really understood that Paul used that phrase *not* to refer just to the believer, but to refer to *Christ*. We are to consider ourselves dead to sin, *not* because *we* have died to sin as an action of our own (Paul does not say that!), but because *Christ* "died to sin, once for all" (Rom 6:10), and we have been baptized into *his* death. We have also talked about the "crucifixion of the old man" using the traditional translation of this Pauline phrase from the same chapter (Rom 6:6) somewhat simplistically as an equivalent for the death of the carnal mind.[16] But our focus of concern has been upon the Christian's spiritual experience here and now, the cleansing available *now*.

The question we need to face if we are to base the teaching of "entire" sanctification firmly on the doctrine of the atonement is this: *In what way did Christ die to sin then, thus making it possible for us to die to sin now?* In what sense did "the old man" (or better, "the old humanity," *anthrōpos*) die *then* on the cross? The point is, of course, that the shape of what is sometimes called "subjective soteriology" is determined by "objective

---

16. The "carnal mind" (*phronēma tēs sarkos*) or "mind set on the flesh" is best understood as a personal disposition, whereas "the old man" (*anthrōpos*) (cf. also Eph 4:22 and Col 3:9) is corporate fallen *humanity* as it is in Adam. The two are connected, of course. The "mind set on the flesh" is characteristic of each human being who shares the fallen humanity of Adam.

soteriology." What is possible for us now in our Christian lives was determined by what Christ did for us then on the cross. In other words, what Christ does now, by his Spirit *in us*, is the outworking of what he did once and for all on the cross *for us*. The cross is thus seen to be absolutely central. A gospel that focuses on *my* Christian experience, *my* faith, *my* conversion, *my* sanctification, can only be a false one. It can only ultimately appeal to my self-interest, and so feed the very egocentricity that needs to be destroyed! There can be no other focus for the real gospel other than Christ crucified. And paradoxically, surely only a gospel centered *not* on me and my need, but on Christ and his cross, can promise full deliverance, full salvation from the endlessly subtle snares of that self-centeredness that is the essence of sin. Only by meditating on the doctrine of the cross can we be captivated by the love of God in such a way as to love him with that full and whole-hearted love of mind, soul, and strength, which is the essence of "entire" sanctification. The question, therefore, can be formulated like this: *what happened on the cross that makes it possible for believers to be "entirely" sanctified now in such a way that they love God with an undivided heart?*

c) The Victorious King

That Christ is our king is a theme found throughout the New Testament. During his ministry, there were those who wanted to make him king of Israel, implying a revolutionary struggle against Rome, but he refused to be made the "king" of an earthly kingdom. The passion narrative in John's Gospel seems to connect his kingship particularly with the cross. But perhaps the best place to begin is with the very primitive preaching of the gospel in which the royal psalms seem to have played a key role. In Luke's account, Peter's sermon on the Day of Pentecost includes a reference to Psalm 110, a psalm that is thought to have been used as an oracle in the enthronement of the Davidic kings in ancient Jerusalem: "The LORD [referring to YHWH] said to my lord [referring to the king], 'Sit at my right hand till I make your enemies a stool for your feet.'" Peter's message is that in his exaltation, his resurrection, and ascension, Jesus has been made "Lord" (*kyrios*) and Christ, i.e., Messiah, the anointed king. Charles Wesley was exactly right then when he wrote his hymn for Ascension Day, "Rejoice! The Lord is King!" The exaltation of Jesus in resurrection and ascension is his enthronement and marks his victory over his enemies.

Paul also linked the theme of victory over the principalities and powers with the cross and the resurrection (Col 2:15).

Behind this is another Old Testament theme, that beyond and behind everything, it is YHWH who is the victorious king of Israel, a great theme of the book of Exodus. The Song of Moses, "I will sing to YHWH, for he has triumphed gloriously; the horse and his rider he has cast into the sea" (Exod 15:1–18), presents YHWH as a king and warrior. "YHWH is a man of war: YHWH is his name" (verse 3), uses the actual phrase for "warrior" (*īsh milchamah*), and while the noun "king" (*melek*) does not appear, the cognate verb "reign" (*mālak*) is in the final triumphant shout: "YHWH will reign (*mālak*) forever and ever." In the New Testament, the theme of the enthronement of the king of Israel and the victory of YHWH are brought together in that Jesus as Messiah is not merely exalted to a separate throne at the right hand of God, but is seated on the very throne of God. He is, in the words of John the Seer, "the Lamb in the middle of the throne" (Rev 7:17).

Biblically then, the model of king is inextricably linked to the model of victory. Here that dimension of the atonement, which was highlighted by Gustaf Aulén, is seen to be valid, not as an explanatory "theory," but as one of the essential models. Colin Gunton identified it as the model of the battlefield. One necessary dimension then of the Christian doctrine of the atonement is that throughout his life on earth, but culminating in his death on the cross, Jesus was somehow victorious over the forces of evil. He is (in the title of Aulén's book) *Christus Victor*. This has been called the "dramatic" view of the atonement, which itself suggests that it is a model rather than a theory. The minor variant we referred to, sometimes called the "ransom theory," proposes that the way in which God gained victory was by tricking Satan, putting forward Christ as a ransom paid to the slave owner (Satan), which he could not in fact hold. Like a greedy fish, he swallowed the bait. This was never accepted widely. It was presented by Origen and Gregory of Nyssa, but ignored by Athanasius and Basil and explicitly rejected by Gregory of Nazianzus, and it has been given too much prominence in some textbooks. There is indeed a biblical model of *ransom*, but not as Origen and Gregory Nyssen interpreted it. And it is rather the wider *Christus Victor* theme of the victory of Christ that is widely prevalent in the Greek Fathers.

Aulén emphasized that this theme of victory over evil is not just a drama of *salvation*, the deliverance of humanity from the hostile powers, but also a work of *atonement*; that is to say, of at-one-ment in the original sense of the English word—reconciliation. By defeating the hostile powers of evil that hold his world in thrall, God reconciles the world to himself. But since, paradoxically, the powers of evil execute the judgment of God on the world, their defeat also reconciles God to the world. Thus both sides of the reconciliation, the at-one-ment, are achieved by the victory of Christ on the cross.

The significance of this view of the atonement for the Wesleyan doctrine of entire sanctification was explored by William M. Greathouse.[17] "Here is one view," wrote Greathouse, "which highlights Christ's atonement as the destruction of sin making possible man's true sanctification." He adds that while it does not fully explain the atonement, "it does give Wesleyan theology a significant biblical and historical basis for developing a thoroughgoing christological doctrine of sanctification." Christ's victory for us, Greathouse explains, is not only a victory over Satan, but a victory over the power of sin entrenched *within* us. This means the crucifixion of the old man (*anthrōpos*, humanity), that is, our existence in Adam, the head and representative of fallen humanity. Humanity is bound together in Adam in the solidarity of sin and death.

It is clear from Aulén's exposition of the *Christus Victor* theme, that by the powers of evil he has in mind not only Satan and the demonic forces, which are thought of as external to humanity, but also the inseparable powers of sin and death. These are, in one sense, "powers" holding humanity in captivity, but must also be seen as internal. Aulén expounds the view of Irenaeus, whom he regards as the earliest major exponent of the *Christus Victor* theme after the New Testament writers: "He [Irenaeus] thinks of sin as affecting the whole man. It is from one point of view an objective power, under which men are in bondage, and are not able to set themselves free; but from another point of view it is something voluntary and wilful, which makes men debtors in relation to God."[18] According to Aulén, Christ on the cross wins victory over the power of sin in *both* these senses; both as an objective external power *and as internal and voluntary*. Aulén does not develop this aspect at all, but we can understand this in terms of "the carnal mind" (Rom 8:6 & 7, AV) or "the mind set on the flesh" (NRSV), which we have been interpreting as *the self-centered mind-set*, the disposition or motivational pattern revolving around merely human goals and values.

17. Greathouse, "Sanctification."
18. Aulén, *Christus Victor*, 23.

Greathouse is right, therefore, to see this view of the atonement as a basis for the doctrine of sanctification. First, the victory of the cross is victory over sin as an objective power holding humankind in bondage. With this we may link "the flesh," not in its general Old Testament and Johannine sense of mortal humanity in the weakness and powerlessness of its physical existence, but in the derivative sense developed by Paul in Galatians 5, of "the flesh" as a kind of power which wars against the Spirit.[19]

By "flesh" in this sense we may perhaps understand the corporate dimension of human sin, structural sin in human society, the sinfulness of humanity as a race, humanity's solidarity in sinful Adam. Taking "sin" and "flesh" together then, we see them in this sense as powers of evil—shadowy, enigmatic realities transcending humanity, holding us in thrall. Evil is seen to be something vastly greater and more powerful than individual sin, either voluntary sin at a personal level, or even an individual internal "bent" or disposition towards sinning. It has an existence and a power that can only be described as demonic, the kingdom of Satan. But the victory of Christ tells us that sin, death, and hell in this cosmic sense have been defeated on the cross. An objective event has taken place: a real and actual victory.

But from the other point of view, sin is not only an objective power holding humanity in bondage: it is also, as Aulén puts it, "something voluntary and wilful." Here is the internal reality of sin in each individual human being. As something voluntary, sin is a matter of the will. Aulén does not develop this aspect at all, but this can be seen in terms of the "bent toward sinning," "the carnal mind," *the self-centered mindset,* the disposition or motivational pattern revolving around merely human values, "the mind set on the flesh." Here, indeed, is the link between these two meanings of "the flesh." "The flesh" may be thought of as a tyrannical power of evil controlling us precisely because we have our minds set on the things of "the flesh," that is, on merely human goals. It is our *self-centered mindset* that gives "the flesh" its power over us.

It is because human beings are dominated by the motive of self-love and self-glorification, by purely human goals and aspirations, life in the human sphere, the sphere of "the flesh," that "the flesh" becomes, as it were, a power that holds them in bondage. It is as if a man were to cast a huge and menacing shadow on the wall of a cave, a shadow that took on its own life as a terrifying genie, and held him in captivity. Because we are each self-centered, our will is bound to the powers, and because we are

19. See above, pages 34–35 and 117–18.

bound to the powers, we cannot break free from our self-centeredness. The key to breaking this truly vicious circle, the key to victory over the powers of sin, death and hell, the world, the flesh, and the devil, is the death of the self-centered mindset. Somehow, if that vicious circle is to be broken, the victory over the powers of evil must be won *within* us. Somehow, therefore, the victory of Christ on the cross was not only a victory over external forces. If it was to provide real victory, *it must have been in some sense a victory within.*

Seen in this way, as victory not only over external powers of evil, but of sin *within* humanity, the so-called "classic" or "dramatic" view of the atonement, the *Christus Victor* model, does indeed provide a basis for Wesley's understanding of "entire" sanctification as victory over sin *inwardly* in inward thinking and motivation. Christ "in every respect has been tempted as we are, yet without sin" (Heb 4:15). He is our victorious king, in a victory won not only against evil without, but consistently and perfectly over temptations that arose from being truly one of us in "the flesh." That means that his victory may be shared by his people. As king he is head of his body, the corporate body of the church, so that all who are "in Christ" by faith may know inner victory.

But there is more to be said. We must go on to the other two major models in order to pursue further the question of how the cross dealt definitively "once for all" with sin *within* us.

d) The Self-Sacrificing Priest

In coming to Christ's office as priest, we surely come to the heart of the atonement. The English word, "atonement," was coined by William Tyndale to translate *katallagē*, the Greek word that we now normally translate as "reconciliation." It was "at-one-ment," meaning the reconciling of two who had been hostile to make them "at one." But the English word quickly took on another meaning when a related verb "to atone" was coined and used to translate the Hebrew verb *kipper* or *kaphar*. The original literal meaning of the Hebrew verb was "to cover," but it is mainly used metaphorically in the Old Testament in speaking of sacrifices. Sometimes it means the "covering" of the face of an angry opponent with a compensatory offering, mollifying or propitiating him (Esau, for example, in Gen 32:20). But no one is ever said to "cover the face" of God. Rather, in the sin offerings the sin was "covered" before God, not in the sense of "covering up," but in the sense of "nullifying" or "obliterating." This was the role of the priest in the tabernacle and later the temple. Not all sacrifices were for sin, but some were. And particularly on *yōm kippur*, the Day of Atonement, the high priest offered the sacrifices required by God and laid down in the law (*tōrah*), confessing first his own sins and then the sins of the nation. The high priest was then instructed to enter the Holy of Holies—he alone and only once a year—to sprinkle the blood from the sacrifice on the very throne of God, the *kapporeth*, the place where ultimately atonement (*kippur*) was ratified.

What we need to note here is that these sacrifices were *required* by God. The Israelites did not win God's favor by these sacrifices. In that sense then they were not "propitiating" his wrath as other nations round about propitiated their gods when they were thought to be angry. God had redeemed Israel in *grace* from Egypt, and entered into covenant with them by *grace* at Sinai. Nevertheless, God *required* these sacrifices in the law he had given for the tabernacle and the sacrificial system. He had made them *necessary*: they had to be done, and the priest had to do them. The covenant was established by grace, but sacrifices were part of its inauguration (Exod 24:1–9), and the sacrifices offered on the Day of Atonement, along with the other sin offerings, were the enactment of the existence and maintenance of the covenant *despite* the sins of the people. Israel had to be a holy people to be in covenant with God, and because she was in fact sinful, the sacrifices were a *required* and *necessary* part of that relationship.

Satisfying the Law

It was that requirement of the *law*, that *legal* requirement with its element of *necessity*, which Anselm so brilliantly investigated in the *Cur Deus Homo*, a book described by James Denney as "the truest and greatest book on the atonement that has ever been written."[20] The heart of Anselm's argument begins from his definition of sin as "not to render God his due," and God's due is that our will should be subject to his will. Anselm explains: "A person who does not render God this honour due him takes from God what is his and dishonours God, and this is to commit sin."[21] From this definition of sin Anselm argues that because we have sinned by not honoring God, we must make restitution or compensation for the

20. Denney, *Death*, 188. Anselm uses medieval language (of course!), but the idea that his analysis is based on his cultural context is superficial and trivial. The "necessity" he is investigating is clearly biblical.

21. I, 11: Anselm, *Why God*, 84. See also Fairweather, *Scholastic Miscellany*, 119.

honor due. We must make "satisfaction." The book is cast in the form of a dialogue between Anselm himself and his fellow-monk, Boso. Anselm poses the critical question to him: "Tell me then: what will you pay to God for your sin?"[22] Boso replies: "Repentance, a contrite and humbled heart, fasting, and all sorts of bodily work, mercy in giving and forgiving, and obedience." But Anselm shows that this will not do: "When you render to God what you owe to him, even without having sinned, you ought not to count it as payment for a debt you owe because of sin." Here is a prime example of the right use of logic in drawing out the implications of a model, and the logic here is inescapable. The rent you will pay in the future does not cancel the debt of the arrears of rent you have not paid in the past. Boso is forced to the only possible conclusion: "I have nothing to offer him in compensation for sin."

That is humanity's situation. We ought to make satisfaction to God, but we cannot. That was why it was *necessary*, Anselm continues, for God to become human: "If no one but God can make that satisfaction and no one but man is obliged to make it, then it is necessary that a God-Man make it."[23] The sum of the matter is this: that because God the Son became "Man"—that is, humanity—and because, as "Man," he gave to God the satisfaction humanity owed him, God may consistently set aside the punishment of humanity.

The later forms of this Anselmic view of the atonement highlight the concept of substitution inherent within it. Christ as humanity on our behalf offers satisfaction to God in our place, that is, as our representative-substitute. A further development, in Aquinas and others, brought to its fullest expression by the Reformers and their heirs, was to interpret this as "penal" substitution. It was not just, as Anselm had said, that because Christ made satisfaction to God on the cross, our punishment was remitted. It was rather that the satisfaction given by Christ on the cross was actually the bearing of our punishment. Hence, it was not just a matter of substitution, Christ in our place, but of specifically *penal* substitution, Christ in our place receiving our due *punishment* in our place. By doing what he did not need to do, Christ merited salvation for us, and so we are acquitted or justified. This is pushing the metaphor to its greatest extent, but the Wesleys along with their allies in the evangelical revival were certainly prepared to affirm that.[24]

22. I, 20: Anselm, *Why God*, 106.
23. II, 6: Anselm, *Why God*, 124.
24. See Collins, *Theology*, 104.

This heightening of the paradox to an unbearable degree, even to the idea of the Son bearing our *punishment* from the Father, leads many to reject the whole Anselmic tradition and simultaneously leads others to embrace it as the very heart of the sublime scandal of the cross. But for our purpose now of finding the basis in the atonement for sanctification, it hardly seems to be directly relevant. It is true that the Anselmic view in all its forms shows the seriousness of sin as an objective reality. It is not just our attitude to God that separates us from him. If that were so, perhaps a change of attitude on our part (contrition and repentance) and forgiveness on God's part would be sufficient. Athanasius at least seems to consider the possibility, though without endorsing it.[25] There would then be no need for the cross. But sin is not simply attitude: it is act. And the fact of our sinful acts is an objective barrier between us and God. It is that which we have done and which cannot be undone that stands between us and God. The Anselmic view shows the seriousness of sin as the objective reality of past deeds, which we cannot undo and which only God in Christ can undo, miraculously, on the cross. All that is part of Anselm's valuable insight.

But where the Anselmic view is inadequate is that it fails to take account of the even deeper reality of sin, not just as acts or deeds, but a *condition of sinfulness*. Anselm's definition of sin, the starting point of his argument, is: "not rendering God the honour due to him." But that is to define sin only as something external to us, an act or failure to act, and sin is *more* than that. Sin is attitude and disposition; sin is a *condition of sinfulness*; sin is a power that enslaves us; and sin has brought death. It calls in question our very existence as God's good creatures since he is the very source of our *being*, not only initially but continuously. The problem is, therefore, not only relational and psychological and moral; as the Fathers saw, it is *ontological*. Thus Anselm's view of the atonement—while biblical, valuable, true, and necessary, as far as it goes—is not sufficient. It deals with the atonement entirely in external categories: the commercial model of debt and the legal model of acquittal or justification. Human beings, including Christ, are seen as actors, that is, as agents in a kind of commercial/judicial transaction external to themselves.

The Anselmic model may be of the greatest value, therefore, in understanding how the atonement is the basis for our pardon and acquittal—in short, our *justification*. But, particularly where it takes the form of *penal* substitution, and does not see the death of Christ as anything more than

25. Athanasius, *On the Incarnation*, 7.

penal, the punishment can seem somewhat arbitrary. It does not address the inner connection between death and our repudiation of the Creator who gave us our very being. It focuses on the legal and moral dimension of the atonement, but misses the ontological aspect. And it does not seem to have anything to say about sin as a reality *internal* to us. Or at least, while it may account for the forgiveness of inner *acts* of sin—sins of thought, sins in the heart and mind—it has nothing to say about inner cleansing from *the condition of sinfulness*. In short, it provides no basis for sanctification. It offers no explanation of what Paul meant when he wrote of the cross as a "dying to sin." Unlike the *Christus Victor* view represented by Aulén, the traditional Latin Anselmic view of the cross as satisfaction offered to God does not seem to be of any help in this particular quest. It seems to offer no basis for a doctrine of Christian perfecting, or indeed for *any* doctrine of sanctification.

Sacrificial Worship

But it is at this point that we need to note that the Anselmic tradition, which has dominated Western doctrines of the atonement for the last thousand years, does not sufficiently account for the biblical model of the priesthood of Christ. It certainly expounds *part* of it, namely, that the role of the law has to be taken into account. And the *requirement* of God in the Pentateuch that sacrifices be offered by the priests is what is brought out in the key Anselmic concept of *satisfaction*. But, unfortunately, Western theologians in the Anselmic tradition have tended to see this as the whole of the doctrine of the atonement. Those in the tradition who affirm specifically *penal* substitution (especially those in the Calvinist tradition) have tended to see that as the *heart* of the doctrine of the atonement or even the whole of it. Indeed, all the other biblical models are reduced to the level of the illustrative or metaphorical, but the juridical, legal, forensic model is seen as the definitive and literal doctrine of the atonement. But that would imply that the ultimate revelation of God is not that he is "Our Father," but that he is "Our Judge." He is Judge of all, but only wills to be Father to some.[26] Sadly, this elevation of the juridical or legal model to *the* definitive place in the doctrine of the atonement tends to make it definitive too for the doctrine of election and for the very doctrine of God.

26. See J. B. Torrance's critique of the scheme of federal Calvinism which gave priority to God's justice over his love in his "Introduction" to Campbell, *Nature of the Atonement*.

But despite that over-evaluation of the legal model, it nevertheless has to be affirmed as biblical and necessary. And yet we have to be careful that we do not use our concepts of Roman law to expound it. In the Old Testament, atonement did not take place in the law courts: it took place in the tabernacle or temple. It was not the task of a lawyer or attorney, but a priest. It was not a matter of literally paying a debt in the trading exchange: "debt" is a minor model in Scripture. Rather it was a matter of offering sacrifices in the temple, and sacrifice has to be seen in the context of *worship*. Sacrifices are offered *to God*. The covenantal relationship of God with Israel was thus two-way. God had redeemed Israel and brought them into a unique relationship with him. He had given them the land with all its material blessings to enjoy, along with the law, the *torah* (a word that really means "instruction") as a light to their path, showing them how to live in *shalom*, peace, and prosperity. But since this was a two-way relationship, Israel had to make offerings to God, the best of their flocks and herds. The tabernacle or temple therefore represented all of creation in its orderliness, and the priests were charged with offering the sacrifices, the burnt offering which simply honored God, sometimes called the "thank offering," but also the "sin offering," which dealt with inadvertent sins, and the "guilt offering," offered for deliberate and intentional sins.[27]

This brings us back to the act of atonement (*kipper*). We have noted that this action was *required* by God, not because God was a vindictive and moody deity who would fly into spiteful and uncontrollable rage, but because he steadily insisted that offences against him could not be ignored. As in any relationship where there is mutual respect, they had to be dealt with. They mattered. In this refined sense then, and not in the pagan sense, this was an act of "propitiation."[28] Hence, the offending Israelites had to offer something substantial, an animal from their flock offered as a *kopher*, a ransom. Here, incidentally, is the biblical idea of "ransom," picked up by Jesus himself (Mark 10:45)—not a trick payment made to the slave master, but an offering offered to God as an act of worship. But the sacrifice was ordained and required by God himself *in his mercy* because, while the steady wrath of God against evil was real, it was not the last word. The last word is that he was a God of grace and covenant love or mercy (*hesed*). Therefore, priestly propitiation must *not* be seen in the merely

27. Sanders, *Judaism*, 105f.

28. See the exposition of propitiation as a necessary element in the doctrine of the atonement in Wiley, *Christian Theology*, 2:273–90. See also Greathouse, *Romans 1–8*, 128–30.

negative aspect of satisfying the requirement that the seriousness of the sin be recognized. The *positive* aspect is that propitiation is *the re-establishing of relationship*, and another word for that is *reconciliation*. The miracle of grace is that it is the offended party who has gone all the way and further to provide the propitiation and so reconcile us to himself.

But what we now have to focus on is not this refined element of *propitiation* in the sacrificial act of atonement, but the other aspect of the verb *kipper*, the element of *expiation*. These are not alternative ways of understanding the act of atonement: both are needed and the two cannot be divorced.[29] It was the steady opposition of God to sin and evil that made the atoning sacrifices *necessary*. But it was the fact that the sacrifices were acts of *expiation* that made them *effective*. In the sin offering and guilt offering offered by individual Israelites, and especially in the sacrifices offered on the Day of Atonement for the whole corporate nation of Israel, the sacrifices were held to *expiate*, to nullify, to obliterate Israel's offences. Through those sacrifices the cleansing of Israel from her pollution was enacted.

The Anselmic tradition with its concept of *satisfaction* is insisting on the element of refined *propitiation*, which brings about our *justification*, the restoration of our relationship with our Creator. But it is the element of *expiation* in the Old Testament sacrifices that gives us insight into how the sacrifice of Christ brings about the corporate *sanctification* of humanity. While the sacrifices in the temple were valid in their day by the grace of God, when they were seen from the later perspective of the gospel of Christ, they were seen to be ineffective (Heb 10:4). There was no inherent virtue in them: they were "copies and shadows" (Heb 8:5). But what they prefigured, the destruction of sin, the sacrifice of Christ actually achieved.

In the supreme priestly act of his self-offering on the cross therefore, our great High Priest did not merely deal with our punishment. That in a way is the most superficial level and to see the atonement as only "penal substitution" is to fail to see its true depth. Something deeper was needed: he had to deal not just with our punishment, but with our *guilt*. It was not enough that our just punishment should be set aside: somehow our very *guilt* had to be cancelled. Otherwise there would be no true "justification." But there is a deeper level still. Not only was it necessary that our punishment be set aside and that our guilt be cancelled. It was also necessary that

29. C. H. Dodd was half right: this is not propitiation in the pagan sense, but as Leon Morris argued, we cannot dismiss the biblical doctrine of the wrath of God and so dispense with the concept of propitiation altogether. We have to pay attention to the question: why was sacrificial atonement *necessary*?

sin itself be expiated, nullified, and obliterated. Here we are not thinking just of acts of sin, as Anselm did, sins of omission or commission; we are thinking of our sinful *condition*, our very *being* in sin, our existence in the contradictory condition of those who have denied and tried to cut themselves off from the very Source of their *being*. Human *being* has become *sinful* being, and this old Adamic humanity therefore has to die. It has to be crucified so that up from the grave in resurrection may come the new redeemed humanity.

Christ's role as our High Priest is unique therefore, in that it was not the body of another that he offered—a bull, a goat, or a lamb. It was his own *human* body and his own *human* blood. This priest, unlike all the priests of the old order, *was himself the sacrifice*. The work of Christ was not, therefore, something which he did externally to himself. Somehow his deepest work was done *within his own person*. And he did it not simply as God, but, like the Aaronic priests, as a human being representing the people. He represents and so *is* "humanity." This unique High Priest, *as a living, thinking, choosing human being*, obediently, but voluntarily, and as our representative, embodying all humankind in himself, offered *himself* to God. The necessity, therefore, was not just that the wrath of God be satisfied: it was rather that the *love* of God be satisfied by the only appropriately responding act, an act of *ultimate* and *final* love and sacrificial devotion *from the side of humanity*. At-one-ment or reconciliation has to be a two-way affair.

Further, this *voluntary self-sacrifice* was also necessary in order that we humans should be redeemed, cleansed, purified, and re-created through both his crucifixion and his resurrection. This representative human being therefore offered *himself* to God as a sacrifice, a ransom (*lutron*), in order that in his death, the old, sinful, Adamic humanity might die, and we might be redeemed or liberated from our sinful condition. The thought that such a human self-sacrifice was necessary is, of course, appalling! We naturally shrink from such an idea and instinctively want to reject it. But until we have seen that it was necessary, we have not grasped how appalling and serious is the reality of human sin and evil. But it is that sacrifice, and that alone, which can provide a basis for proclaiming with confidence and joy that the death of Christ provides not only for the remission of our punishment, or for the setting aside of our guilt in *justification*, but for the expiation of our sinfulness, the crucifixion of our sinful being, and hence our real and deep *sanctification*.

In the language drawn from German Pietism, which Charles Wesley uses in his hymns, the key word here is the "blood" of Christ. When Charles draws on this stark and deliberately repulsive metaphor, predominantly Johannine (1 John 1:7; Rev 1:5), of being cleansed by the blood of Christ or "washed" in the blood of the Lamb, he is anchoring our purification from sin in the expiatory work of Christ on the cross. Sometimes in his hymns it is the propitiatory aspect that is to the fore, that we are reconciled to God, justified, or set in right relation to God, by Christ crucified:

> And can it be that I should gain
> An interest in the Saviour's blood?

The death of Christ brings peace with God, so that "No condemnation now I dread," and I can approach the eternal throne with boldness. But Charles Wesley also writes of the blood of Christ bringing inner cleansing or sanctification. Christians are those who are, "Washed in the sanctifying blood,/ Of an expiring Deity."[30] He prays:

> My dying Saviour and my God,
> Fountain for guilt and sin,
> Sprinkle me ever with thy blood,
> And cleanse, and keep me clean.
>
> Wash me, and make me thus thine own;
> Wash me, and mine thou art;
> Wash me, but not my feet alone—
> My hands, my head, my heart.
>
> Th' atonement of thy blood apply
> Till faith to sight improve,
> Till hope in full fruition die,
> And all my soul be love.[31]

If then the kingly aspect of the atonement speaks of Christ's victory over the powers of evil and indeed of his victory over temptation in his own inner life, the priestly aspect speaks of the radical expiation or obliteration of the old, sinful, Adamic humanity. It is only because Christ voluntarily offered himself to God on the cross, that we can know today what it means to be "crucified with Christ" and so be sanctified. We will pursue

30. Hymn 246 in *A Collection of Hymns for the Use of the People Called Methodists*, *Works* (BE) 7:387.

31. Hymn 337 in *A Collection of Hymns for the Use of the People Called Methodists*, *Works* (BE) 7:496. See Berger, *Theology in Hymns?*, 120f.

that further in the next chapter. But first we must turn our attention to the third of the "offices" of Christ, namely that he is the unique Prophet.

e) The Unique Prophet

The office of prophet clearly has to do with the proclamation of the word of God, but it is not so immediately clear that it has to do with atonement. Sacrifices of atonement were offered by the priests, not by prophets, and indeed there seems to be a line of prophecy in the Old Testament that is critical of the priestly sacrifices (e.g., Isa 1:10–17). This lack of a connection between the prophetic office and atonement is reflected in the earlier editions of Calvin's *Institutes*, in which he included only the two offices of priest and king. It was only in the final 1559 edition that the three offices received a full chapter.[32] Even then, Calvin interpreted the prophetic office of Christ as his anointed preaching and teaching.[33] Wesley similarly regards the prophetic office of Christ as referring to his teaching, particularly his teaching of the law. Rejecting the idea that the Old Covenant was a "covenant of works" (that applied only to Adam before the Fall), Wesley saw it as a covenant of grace within which the law was given.[34] Similarly the New Covenant was a covenant of grace, but *not* one that abrogated the law. Rather, in his teaching (particularly in the Sermon on the Mount), Jesus revealed that the moral law reflected the eternal character of God.[35]

Calvin and Wesley are surely right that the teaching of Christ must be seen as part of his prophetic office. But, of course, Hebrew prophets not only spoke but also *acted out* the word of God. The Hebrew word for "word" (*dābār*) also means "act." The word of God is not only *informative*, but also *performative*. So here, Christ exercised his prophetic office not merely in what he said, but in what he *did*. His healing of the sick, rescuing of the deranged, and welcoming of the harlot, the publican, and the sinner, all *demonstrated* the love of God that he spoke about in the Sermon on the Mount (Matt 5:38–48), as well as in parables such as the lost coin, the lost sheep, and the lost son (Luke 15), and throughout his teaching. But the culmination of his revelation of the love of God was surely on the cross: "But God demonstrates (*synistēsi*) his love for us in that while we were still

---

32. Jansen, *Calvin's Doctrine*, 39ff.

33. Calvin, *Institutes*, I, ii, 1–2.

34. See Rodes, "'Faith to Faith,'" 62–90.

35. See Collins, *Theology*, 96–98, and Wesley's series of sermons on the Sermon on the Mount, *Works* (BE) 1.

sinners, Christ died for us" (Rom 5:8). As Luther emphasized in his focus on a *theologia crucis*, it is at the cross that the heart of God is revealed and it is *from* the cross, and not merely from the creation, that we are to take our doctrine of God (*theologia*). Insofar then as the prophet is the one who reveals God by his word, so we must see Christ as the unique prophet giving us the final and definitive revelation of God *by hanging on the cross*. And what the cross reveals is certainly the God of judgment who says "No" to our sin, but above and beyond that, the God of love who says, "Yes" to us. The cross is the supreme demonstration of the love of God.

Moral Influence

It was this insight which lay behind the attempt of some liberal theologians in the nineteenth century such as Horace Bushnell and later, Hastings Rashdall, to make this the one way of understanding the atonement.[36] They were understandably reacting against preaching in the Anselmic tradition, which had so emphasized judgment and hell-fire that it left the picture in many minds of God as a kind of Shylock insisting vindictively on his pound of flesh. They co-opted Abelard to their cause, implying that his whole doctrine of the atonement was represented in his commentary on Romans 5:8. In a nutshell, their view of the atonement was that when we see the love of God in Christ upon the cross, we respond in love, and our responding love thus completes the reconciliation from our side. But the implication of that is that the atonement ("at-one-ment," or "reconciliation") is therefore completed *by each of us individually* when *we* respond in love to God's love. Alister McGrath has shown that Rashdall and the others misrepresented Abelard and were ignorant of the fact that the great Immanuel Kant had demolished a similar "theory" in German theology in the previous century.[37]

The inadequacy of "moral influence" as a *theory* lies essentially in this, that it fails to present the atonement as a "finished work." If this is all that can be said about it, then the cross did not achieve anything objective. Nothing actually happened there to effect and complete salvation. It was only an illustration or example (albeit the supreme example) of what was true all the time, that God loved us. It changed nothing and was not crucial. At best, one could say that half of the at-one-ment or reconciliation took place there, God's movement towards humanity in love. But since there is

36. See Rashdall, *Idea of Atonement*.
37. McGrath, "Moral Theory."

no role for Christ as our representative and high priest acting for us, there is no answering movement *at the cross* from humanity *towards* God in order to complete the at-one-ment. *That* does not come till *the individual believer* responds in love to God. We each complete the at-one-ment for ourselves! The atonement was not completed *corporately* for all humanity on the cross: it is completed *subjectively* in the believing *individual*. That is surely a reflection of the individualistic thinking of "modernity" and is clearly inadequate, for it makes each of us our own priest and our own savior. Christ is no longer understood to be our great high priest representing humanity to God, and the cross does not deal in any way with sin, or with judgment.

Even more damning, as a "theory" of the atonement, this completely fails to show *how* the cross is a revelation of the love of God. This is the bloody and unjust execution of an innocent man, degraded by being hung up naked before the world and dying in agony. How on earth can that reveal the love of God? It can only reveal the love of God if it actually *achieved* something. Unless it changed everything and made a real and objective difference, then it cannot reveal the love of God at all. To adapt James Denney's illustration: if a young man drowns while saving his fiancée from a river, that is clearly an act of self-sacrificial love. But if, while they are walking along the bank, he claims that he is going to demonstrate his love for her and jumps into the river and drowns, that does not demonstrate love at all, but only insanity. In order for the cross to demonstrate the love of God, there must be some other explanation as to how it saves us. "Moral influence" on its own does not work as a way of understanding the atonement.

A "Moral Influence" View of Sanctification

Nor does "moral influence" *as a definitive theory of the atonement* provide us with a basis for the doctrine of Christian "perfection." It was during the nineteenth century, when the "moral influence" *theory* was put forward by those minor liberal theologians, that Wesley's heirs developed the language of "consecration." The danger of this development, seen in Phoebe Palmer's "shorter way" or "altar" theology, was that it could leave the impression that *my* sincere, personal consecration will effect my entire sanctification.[38] The key to entire sanctification then becomes the *subjective* consecration of the *individual* believer. Here the deficiencies of the

---

38. Note that the verb here is "effect," not "affect." The difference is significant.

moral influence *theory* as an explanation of the atonement are echoed in an inadequate understanding of entire sanctification. As a *subjective* doctrine of the atonement, explaining reconciliation by our subjective response to God, it can only strengthen the subjectivist, introspective tendencies of the Pietist and Wesleyan heritage. Rather, what we need to know is that God has done something *objective*, that Christ in his work on the cross has actually dealt with sin in humanity so that it is possible for us in the power of the Spirit to be purified from self-centered sinfulness and to live whole-heartedly devoted to God. The "moral influence" view places enormous weight on the response of the individual believer and is not in fact *gospel* at all. It is the responding love of the individual that, according to the moral influence theory, completes the at-one-ment. But there is no objective dealing with sin on the cross, no priesthood of Christ representing us to the Father, no actual dealing with sin, no expiation, no death of that enigmatic and paradoxical reality, "the old humanity," no justification, no cleansing, no real sanctification. Sin as an objective reality, as a real barrier between God and humanity, as sinfulness entrenched in our very flesh, in our very being, is not taken into account at all. When the *individual* responds in love, thus *meriting* sanctification, sin just seems to be forgotten. It seems to melt away, like a mirage, or an illusion existing only in the mind.

If this is our only understanding of the atonement, then our doctrine of entire sanctification will display similar features. To begin with, it will place enormous weight on the response of the individual believer. It will see his or her total consecration, his or her whole-hearted love for God, as the key factor which produces entire sanctification. It will, therefore, tend to emphasize the *obligation*, the requirement or *duty* that we be more consecrated (the subtlest form of hammering people with the law!) rather than entire sanctification as a gospel of grace, something *God* does in us and not something we achieve. It will focus on the sacrifice of Romans 12:1, individualistically understood as *my* presentation of *myself* as a living sacrifice, to such an extent as to make *my* sacrifice the one by which I am sanctified. But it is the sacrifice of Romans 3:21–26, the sacrifice of Jesus, the one and only sufficient sacrifice, that can effect my cleansing—"the cross of our Lord Jesus Christ," as Paul wrote, "by which the world has been crucified to me, and I to the world" (Gal 6:14). My consecration or offering of myself is only possible as *by the Spirit* I identify with *his* sacrifice, and that is only possible by the grace of God.

Such a view of entire sanctification, focusing on *my* consecration, will quite correctly see the importance of sin in the mind. It will correctly see the need to replace double-mindedness and the self-centered mindset with whole-hearted love for God. It will correctly see that entire sanctification is a relational matter in which the healing of my personal relationship with God through whole-hearted love will heal me spiritually as a person, integrating and unifying my motivation and personality around this love for God, healing me by making me whole. But it will be in danger of seeing this merely as an ethical or psychological change, which can be produced in the individual by ethical persuasion at the human level. And all of that can lead all too easily to manipulative preaching, emotional*ism* resulting eventually in spiritual shipwreck.

To be brief, such a view of entire sanctification will reflect all the shortcomings of the old nineteenth-century liberalism that espoused the moral influence theory. It will emphasize *human* response and moral endeavor. It will tend to interpret spiritual matters in ethical and psychological terms *alone*, in terms of relationship. It will focus on the individual's response to God, entirely missing the cruciality of the cross.[39] It will lose hold of the mystery of justification and its theological priority over sanctification and it will fail to see the objective reality and seriousness of sin and sinfulness. These are shortcomings in a doctrine of the atonement and they are similarly shortcomings in a doctrine of entire sanctification. For sin is not only in the mind; it is not only a psychological bent towards sinning, a self-centered mindset, a disposition towards merely human goals and values. There is also this dimension of human solidarity in sin, of sin entrenched not just in our minds, but affecting our whole "flesh"; that is, our whole humanity, our *corporate* being and existence as a fallen race. There could be no release from the so-called "carnal mind," the disposition of the flesh, the self-centered mindset, the psychological bias towards sin in each of us singly, until the total being of humanity in sin (corporately, physically, ontologically)—the old Adam, or "the old man," or the old humanity—had been dealt with ontologically and radically; that is, crucified and buried, once and for all through the cross of Christ.

In short, deliverance from sin is not just an inner psychological matter for the *individual*, not just a relational matter of the individual's responding love for God: it is an ontological matter affecting the very being of corporate humanity. Humanity has rebelled against the Author and Source of our life. Our very existence is, therefore, sinful; an existence that

39. See Forsyth, *The Cruciality of the Cross.*

is an offence to the glory of God. That does not mean that the physical flesh is sinful in itself or that the God-given natural desires are inherently sinful. That would be Gnosticism. But our physical existence is "fallen" in the wider sense that it is disordered and subject to decay (*phthora*) and death. Sinfulness can only be properly attributed to persons, not to physical flesh. However when the word "flesh" is used in its wider sense to refer to the corporate human race and not just to our physical body, then it speaks of our *corporate* sinfulness. And that means that sin has entrenched itself in our physical existence in such a way that our physical "flesh" has become the *instrument* of our sin. Human existence as a whole is therefore lumped together under the sphere of sin. Only God could deal with a problem of that scale and intensity, and he has done so in the cross. The salvation and personal sanctification of each member of the Body of Christ can only be understood in the context of God's universal act of atonement in the cross of Christ, dealing with the sin and the sinfulness of the entire human race as a *corporate whole*. "Entire" sanctification is *not a human possibility*, nor is it achieved by *my* total consecration as an individual. It is God's gracious activity in the life of each believer, within the context of the Body of Christ, the church, made possible by God's once-for-all act of grace in the crucifixion of the old sinful humanity on the cross.

Perfect Love

Nevertheless, even if "moral influence" is inadequate as a *theory* of the atonement (as all the so-called "theories" are) and cannot give a complete explanation, it is most certainly true as a *model* and *aspect* of the atonement. Given the priestly work of Christ in propitiation and expiation, and his kingly victory on the cross, the cross clearly *does* reveal the love of God. If Almighty God was willing to undergo such humiliation and to stoop so low, then no greater love is conceivable. Here our great prophet, the one who is uniquely the Word of God made flesh, reveals in his self-sacrifice the infinite depth of the love of God for us, a race of rebellious and perverted sinners. This is surely the "perfect love" that John writes about: "In this is love, not that we loved God but that he loved us and sent his Son to be the atoning sacrifice for our sins" (1 John 4:10, NRSV).

And it is further clear that when "Christ crucified" is "placarded" before us (as we could translate Gal 3:1), we are enabled to respond in love. That is the movement of faith that Isaac Watts wrote about in his great hymn, "When I survey the wondrous cross." It is when we contemplate the cross and "see from his head, his hands, his feet, sorrow and love flow mingled down," that we respond in consecration:

> Were the whole realm of Nature mine,
> That were an offering far too small;
> Love so amazing, so divine,
> Demands my soul, my life, my all.

It is surely true then that this aspect of the atonement, the prophetic office of Christ, understood as his revelation of the love of God on the cross, can give us a basis for a doctrine of Christian "perfection" as perfect love. Here is the aspect of Christian holiness as relational, and if Christian perfection is to be understood not just in a negative way as purification from sin, but in a positive way as "perfection in love," then the revelation of the love of God in the atonement must be central. This coheres with Wesley's whole approach, which, as Wynkoop reminded us, was "A Theology of Love."[40]

This is, we might say, the other side of the coin. We have devoted some space in dealing with the offices of king and priest to emphasizing that salvation not only has a relational, personal, subjective aspect, but requires the ontological, corporate, objective, "once-for-all" aspect. It is not simply a matter of our personal faith and love and consecration: it is first of all a matter of the action of God in Jesus Christ, particularly in "Christ crucified." That is the side that Pietistic evangelicals (including Wesleyans) are always in danger of forgetting. But the other side of the coin is that salvation not only has the ontological, corporate, objective, "once-for-all" aspect: it also has the relational, personal, subjective aspect. It is not only true that we have been reconciled: it is also necessary to say, "Be reconciled!" (2 Cor 5:18–21). On the basis of God's love for us, supremely enacted and portrayed on the cross, we are called to love him. And it is the sacrifice of Christ that has made that possible in each of our hearts. It is not only something that the King-Priest has accomplished: but, on the basis of that, it is something that the Prophet proclaims to us, calling for our response. But that proclamation is not merely demand: it is gift. It is not merely law: it is gospel. And it is when, by the Spirit, our gaze is fixed not merely in contemplating the state of our own hearts, or desiring spiritual blessing for ourselves, but on the love of God displayed on the cross, that the Spirit of God can so fill us with God's perfect love that we love him with every fiber of our being.

---

40. Wynkoop, *Theology of Love.*

No wonder that Charles Wesley could sing of the love of God displayed on the cross, employing the powerful and shocking metaphor of his blood, which brings not only pardon, but healing:

> O Love divine, what hast thou done!
> Th'immortal God hath died for me!
> The Father's co-eternal Son
> Bore all my sins upon the tree:
> Th'immortal God for me hath died,
> My Lord, my Love is crucified.
>
> Behold him, all ye that pass by,
> The bleeding Prince of life and peace!
> Come, sinners, see your Maker die,
> And say, was ever grief like his?
> Come, feel with me his blood applied:
> My Lord, my Love is crucified.
>
> Is crucified for me and you,
> To bring us rebels back to God;
> Believe, believe the record true,
> Ye all are bought with Jesus' blood:
> Pardon for all flows from his side:
> My Lord, my Love is crucified.
>
> Then let us sit beneath his cross,
> And gladly catch the healing stream,
> All things for him account but loss,
> And give up all our hearts to him;
> Of nothing think or speak beside,
> "My Lord, my Love is crucified."[41]

But we must go into this more deeply yet. Our sanctification is not only based on the work of Christ, what he *did* for us. But what he *did* for us, and therefore our sanctification, can only be more fully understood if we truly understand *who he became for us*. We must search for the basis of a doctrine of Christian "perfection" not only in the Work, but in the *Person* of Christ.

---

41. Hymn 27 (following a later amendment) in *A Collection of Hymns for the Use of the People Called Methodists*, *Works* (BE) 7:114f.

7

Christian Holiness and the Incarnation

Western Christian theology, at least since Anselm, has focused strongly on the cross. Again following Anselm as well as the Latin Fathers, it has understood the cross in terms of guilt and pardon; that is, mainly in legal or juridical terms. That focus on the cross was strengthened at the Reformation by Luther's insistence that true Christian theology was not a "theology of glory" (*theologia gloriae*), climbing up to the heavens to contemplate the glory of God, but a "theology of the cross" (*theologia crucis*). Luther did not just mean that the atonement was central, but that the very doctrine of God (*theologia* in the strict sense of the word) must be drawn from the cross. It was in "Christ crucified" that God was supremely and indeed uniquely revealed.

a) The Centrality of Christ

Perhaps the focus on the theology of the atonement was not quite so true of the Anabaptist traditions, or of Pietism, or today of the world-wide Pentecostal tradition, as it was of the "magisterial" traditions of the Reformation, Lutherans, Calvinists, and the evangelical Anglicans. But even in these other Protestant traditions, the cross of Christ is still central to Christian devotion. And behind all of those traditions of course, as well as the Roman Catholic tradition, is the deep influence of Augustine. That is multi-faceted. In the Roman tradition it led to a strong focus on the institutional church, and in both Roman and Protestant traditions, it led to a strong focus on holiness as "inwardness," with all the dangers of toppling over into subjectivism and indeed into an egocentric piety. Luther's focus on the cross, as we have seen, deliberately opposed to that an objective focus. In his "Copernican revolution" he attempted to replace egocentric religion with theocentric devotion, which of course could only be theocentric by being christocentric. Being christocentric meant being focused on "Christ crucified." But for many Protestants that has meant that soteriology—the death of Christ or Work of Christ, the doctrine of the atonement—has been the centre of interest *rather than* Christology, the incarnation or the Person of Christ.

Some have argued that that focus is fully biblical. After all, Paul writes much more about the death of Christ than about his birth, and the Four Gospels are dominated by the passion narratives. There has been a tendency in the West therefore to criticize Eastern Christianity, and particularly the Fathers, for devoting too much attention to the incarnation. James Denney, for example, put the criticism like this: "The Incarnation may be the thought round which everything gravitates in the Nicene Creed, and in the theology of the ancient Catholic church which found in that creed its first dogmatic expression. But that only shows how far from doing justice to New Testament conceptions was the first ecclesiastical apprehension of Christianity." Denney sums up his point like this: "Not Bethlehem, but Calvary, is the focus of revelation, and any construction of Christianity which ignores or denies this distorts Christianity by putting it out of focus."[1]

Denney's concern is not to be dismissed. As Luther saw, a theology that is not a *theologia crucis* is not truly Christian at all. But there is something wrong-headed surely in putting Bethlehem and Calvary in competition! Of course we must not de-centralize the cross. But neither should we isolate the cross. The cross makes no sense without the nativity and the resurrection. Indeed, it makes no sense unless it is seen as the turning point of the whole story of salvation, the nadir of the descent in the hymn to Christ in Philippians 2:6–11. Perhaps the point can be put this way: the centre of Paul's gospel was "Christ crucified" (1 Cor 1:23; Gal 3:1), but it was *Christ* crucified. It is not merely the event of the crucifixion that is the heart of the gospel. The crucifixion of anyone else (even had that person been innocent and sinless) would not be gospel at all. Everything depends on *who* it was who was crucified. The key to the Work of Christ is the Person of Christ. The key to the atonement is the incarnation. The necessary undergirding for soteriology is Christology.

1. Denney, *Death of Christ*, 179.

It is the failure to see that which can reduce soteriology to a kind of "technology" of salvation. The pragmatic, technological shaping of our whole way of thinking makes us want to find out *how* God makes salvation *work*. The result is to turn the Lord Jesus Christ into a mere instrument for God's use, a cog in the wheel of the machinery. We are not really interested in him for his own sake, but just for how he *works out* our salvation. The so-called "theories of the atonement" then give us neat technological explanations. We are not interested in what we consider to be all the tiresome "metaphysical" debates of the Fathers about the Person of Christ, which issued in the Chalcedonian Symbol. That is merely ivory tower stuff.

If that is the way we characteristically think (perhaps even unconsciously), then we need to repent. We need to fight against the technological mindset that de-humanizes us and de-personalizes the gospel. Salvation is not a method or a technique, pulling the right levers or answering the right questions correctly to produce the desired effect. It is not (as the Gnostics saw it) learning the right passwords in order to enter the bliss of heaven after we die. Salvation is being personally united to a Person, the Lord Jesus Christ. We can only escape from the depersonalizing of the gospel, if we focus on the *Person* of Christ.

Christology and Sanctification

This is supremely true when we come to sanctification. In our technological way of thinking we think of that as some kind of "process," like metal being refined in the fire or clothes being washed in a machine. But while such metaphors may be helpful to some extent, they are *metaphors*. Sanctification, the being made holy, is not such an impersonal "process." That word is quite inappropriate. Rather, sanctification is coming into personal relationship with a Person in such a way that we increasingly image his scintillating holiness, his compassion, his patience, his self-discipline, his self-denial, his out-going love. All of that means that we cannot possibly come to a truly *Christian* understanding of sanctification unless we anchor it in our understanding of the *Person of Christ*.

In this chapter then in looking at Christian holiness and the incarnation, we want to relate the doctrine of Christian sanctification (particularly "perfection") to Christology, the doctrine of the Person of Christ. We are still pursuing the wider aim of relating Christian holiness to the doctrine of the Trinity, but there is no way into that doctrine which bypasses Christology. "Through him we have access to this grace in which we stand"

(Rom 5:2), writes Paul. And the point is even in a clearer triadic form in Ephesians: "For through him we both [Jews and Gentiles] have access in one Spirit to the Father" (Eph 2:18).

As we come to the doctrine of Christ, our guides shall be those great Fathers of the church who framed the orthodox doctrine of Christology, a tradition that includes particularly Irenaeus, Athanasius, the three Cappadocians, and Cyril of Alexandria. The culmination of this truly apostolic and orthodox succession of the church was the Symbol of the Council of Chalcedon of A.D. 451, declaring that our Lord Jesus Christ was truly God, truly Man, but one Christ. Even though it is couched in the cultural thought-forms of its day, the Chalcedonian Symbol remains the touchstone of christological orthodoxy for the Christian church today.[2] But it is of the highest importance to see that while the Symbol is sometimes called the Chalcedonian "Definition," it does not presume to "define" the Person of Christ. All it does is to define what we must *not* say about him, the misunderstandings or heresies into which we very easily fall. We are speaking here of the great *mystery* of Christ, and we will not be able to produce a "definition" of his Person, or answers that explain the mystery away.

Like Anselm, the Fathers used the language and terminology of their day, particularly the familiar metaphysical language and concepts of Platonism. But that does not mean that their doctrine was derived from the Platonists. As Augustine commented,[3] no Platonist would ever have said that the Word *became flesh!* The Chalcedonian Symbol has also been criticized as representing Christ very statically as two "natures," divine and human, united in one Person. But that is simply a failure to see that historically the Symbol of the Council of Chalcedon of AD 451 was not a replacement for the Nicene Creed as finally formulated at the Council of Constantinople in AD 381. Rather it was a footnote, a further clarification of the second article of the Creed, "And in one Lord Jesus Christ," an article that retells the story of the gospel bearing the same dynamic movement as the christological hymn of Philippians 2:6–11.

Sadly, while among the Reformers Calvin particularly was a student of the Fathers, Protestantism since then has not given them their place. We have tended to take for granted their doctrines of Christ and the Trinity, perhaps initially because neither of these doctrines was involved in the dispute with Rome. We insist, of course, on the deity of Christ, but historically, reacting against nineteenth-century liberalism, we tend to

2. For the text of the Symbol, see Hardy, *Christology*, 371–74.

3. Augustine, *Conf.* 7:14.

neglect the equal emphasis of Chalcedon and the Creed on the *humanity* of Christ. And while we agree with the Fathers on these doctrines, we do not think them "relevant" to our pragmatic concerns. But while that neglect of the Fathers is historically understandable, it is no longer tenable. The demise of "Christendom," in which these doctrines were taken for granted, and the rise of secularism since the eighteenth-century Enlightenment, and now the new religions, give these doctrines a critical relevance again to the mission of the church. As the Fathers wrestled with these issues in their pagan multi-cultural world, so we must do so again in ours. Christology and trinitarian doctrine not only have a new relevance, but to neglect them would simply be to perpetuate the superficiality of much evangelical theology.

Once again, however, as in the last chapter, we are not just examining Christology, the doctrine of the Person of Christ, as a study on its own, but we want to examine how it is the basis for our doctrine of Christian sanctification, particularly Christian perfecting. That more abstract way of putting it, as a relationship between *doctrines*, once again reflects the relationship between two *realities*. Christians can only become truly holy people—that is to say, truly compassionate, truly self-disciplined, truly out-going and redemptively loving—as they are truly in union with the compassionate, self-sacrificing, redemptively loving Christ. But to put it in terms of doctrines, our aim in this chapter is to address this question: *what is the connection between the doctrine of the Person of Christ and the doctrine of Christian sanctification?* Particularly, we are interested in whether there is any basis here specifically for a doctrine of Christian perfecting.

b) "Christ Jesus, whom God made . . . our sanctification"

For us, the area of interest centers in the understanding that the Fathers had of the humanity of Christ. It is true, of course, that the major contribution of Athanasius particularly was the defense of the *deity* of Christ. It is also true that Cyril of Alexandria was engaged in the struggle against the Nestorian division of Christ virtually into two Persons, one human and one divine, and hence he emphasized the *unity* of the one Lord Jesus Christ. But through all the writings of these Fathers of the church there is a particularly significant understanding of the *humanity* of Christ and particularly of the key role of the humanity of Christ in our sanctification. Their line of thought may perhaps be most clearly expounded in three statements:

Christ sanctified our humanity by assuming it.

Christ sanctified our humanity by living in it.

Christ sanctified our humanity by crucifying it.

We shall take these in turn.

Christ Sanctified Our Humanity by Assuming It.

Here we are concerned with the human nature that the Son or Word of God united to himself when he became "flesh" and was born of Mary. For the Fathers, a close connection was to be seen between the birth of Christ in our human nature and his resurrection. Irenaeus explains the connection:

> Now, if He was not born, neither did He die; and if He died not, neither did He rise from the dead; and if He rose not from the dead, neither did He vanquish death and bring its reign to nought; and if death be not vanquished, how can we ascend to life, who from the beginning have fallen under death? So then those who take away redemption from man, and believe not in God that He will raise them from the dead, these also despise the birth of our Lord, which He underwent on our behalf, that the Word of God should be made flesh in order that He might manifest the resurrection of the flesh.[4]

In passage after passage, the key point is repeated, an understanding of the resurrection of Christ in terms of Paul's thought in 1 Cor 15:53: "For this corruptible must put on incorruption and this mortal must put on immortality."

This terminology becomes standard in the Greek Fathers. We who are corruptible and mortal will become incorruptible and immortal in our resurrection bodies. But this will happen to all humanity because Christ was first raised incorruptible and immortal in his resurrection body as the first-fruits (1 Cor 15:20, 23), "the first-born from the dead" (Col 1:18), and because the whole human race is joined to Christ according to the flesh. In his birth from Mary, he took that human nature that was common to all human beings.

---

4. Robinson, *Irenaeus*, 104 (par.39).

But the implication of this was clear: if Christ raised our humanity incorruptible and immortal in his resurrection, then it must have been our corruptible, mortal humanity that Christ assumed from his mother. And here the Fathers took with utmost seriousness the link between the Fall and death made in Genesis 3 and by Paul: "You shall not eat . . . lest you die" (Gen 3:3); "For as in Adam all die, so also in Christ shall all be made alive" (1 Cor 15:22). Mortal humanity was, therefore, mortal because of the Fall. Cyril of Alexandria specifically states that "the fallen body" (*to prospesontos sōmatos*) was "united in an ineffable manner with the Word."[5] But although the actual word "fallen" is hardly ever used elsewhere, the implication everywhere is that, in that the humanity Christ took from his mother was *mortal* and *corruptible*, it was in that sense, "fallen" humanity.[6]

But here we must pause to correct some misapprehensions, for it may appear that the Greek Fathers were saying that the humanity of Christ was sinful. But that would be a total misunderstanding because we simplistically equate "fallenness" with Augustine's idea of the inheritance of original sin as a kind of disease. "Fallenness" and "sinfulness" should not be taken as straight synonyms since "fallenness" is more of an *ontological* than a *moral* category. The idea of human sinfulness was also present in the thought of the Greek Fathers, but not with the particular twists that Augustine added to the doctrine of original sin, and we shall see in a moment how the Greek Fathers dealt with it in such a way as to guard the sinlessness of Christ. That indeed is the key to their understanding of sanctification. But before we come to that, it is essential that we have a firm understanding first of all that they had a wider, more comprehensive understanding of the consequences of the Fall. It not only resulted in human sinfulness, but more to the forefront of their thinking was that it resulted in *mortality*. Sin had brought death, not just spiritual death, but death that was total—spiritual and mental and physical.

Athanasius, perhaps the greatest of the Greek Fathers, took the view that the immortality given to the human race originally was an additional

5. Cyril's Commentary on John, commenting on John 1:14 (PG 73:160C): translation from Russell, *Cyril of Alexandria*, 105. Jerome Van Kuiken brought this reference in Cyril to my attention from his current research in the relationship between the fall and Christ's humanity.

6. William M. Greathouse endorses this patristic perspective: "The eternal Son entered into our *fallen* humanity for the sake of our salvation, so that we might become 'partakers of the divine nature' (2 Peter 1:4, RSV). He assumed our *fallen* humanity without being contaminated by it…" (Greathouse, *Romans 1–8*, 236).

gift consequent upon being made "in the Image," given a share "in his own Word," and placed in the special context of the garden. "But if they transgressed and turned away and became wicked, they would know that they would suffer natural corruption (*kata physin phthoran*) in death, and would no longer remain in paradise, but in future dying outside it, would remain in death and corruption."[7]

The key concept, drawn from Paul (Rom 8:21; 1 Cor 15:42, 50), is *phthora*, corruption, meaning not simply moral corruption, but physical, mental, and spiritual corruption—total corruption, corruption of human *physis*, human "nature" in its material, intellectual, and relational dimensions. Men and women were subject to decay, disease, age, senility, and death. The constitution with which they were born (*natus*) was mortal. They were literally disintegrating in body and mind. They were in bondage to death. The process of decay was at work in each human being even as they lived. Every member of the race was doomed, for human *physis*, human nature itself, was in bondage to decay and death.

Sin had thus *ontological consequences* for humankind. It was not only sin that was the problem, although sin was the heart of it, but there was also the consequence of sin. Because humanity had ruptured its relationship with the very Source and Author of life, it was falling away into "the pit." Humanity's very being and existence were due to the Creator Word of God, and because the human race had damaged their relationship with him, their very *being* and existence were therefore called in question. That was why it was necessary for the Creator Word himself to come, and that was why he, the Source of their life, the Image of God, who created them, could alone save them from this death.

Athanasius expresses it like this:

> If, therefore, there had been only sin and not its consequence of corruption (*phthora*), repentance would have been very well. But if, since transgression had overtaken them, humans were now prisoners to natural corruption (*tēn kata physin phthoran*), what else should have happened? Or who was needed for such grace and recalling except the Word of God, who also in the beginning had created the universe from nothing? For it was his task . . . to bring what was mortal back again to immortality.[8]

---

7. Athanasius, *On the Incarnation* (*De Incarnatione*), 3: from Thomson, tr., *Athanasius*, 141, slightly altered.

8. Athanasius, *De Incarnatione*, 7: from Thomson, tr., *Athanasius*, 151 (slightly altered).

Athanasius explains how God the Word did it: "He submitted to our corruption (*phthora*) . . . And thus taking a body like ours, since all were liable to the corruption of death, and surrendering it to death on behalf of all, He offered it to the Father . . . in order that, as all die in Him, the law concerning corruption in men might be abolished."[9] Athanasius's essential point is that by taking our mortal decaying flesh to the grave, Christ transformed it. He buried it in his tomb and raised it incorruptible and immortal in his resurrection. Therefore, since it was our common humanity, our common flesh, we too shall be raised like him in the resurrection from the dead. We may wish to qualify this by saying that it is human death *as we know it* that is the consequence of the Fall, but since Christ was raised in the resurrection body and not just spiritually (as the Gnostics claimed), the Christian faith is committed to saying that salvation is in some sense salvation from physical death. It is the resurrection of the body, that is to say, of the whole human being.

Here then is the way the Greek Fathers understood the Pauline concept of "the old man." "The old man," that is, the old humanity (*ho palaios anthrōpos*, Rom 6:6, Eph 4:22), was an ontological category. It was humanity as it was in Adam; Adamic human nature that, because of the Fall, was subject to disease, decay, deterioration, disintegration, and death. Since that was the humanity that had to be saved, it was absolutely essential and necessary, indeed vital, that it was *that* mortal, corruptible flesh, fallen into bondage to death and decay—that the Son of God took from Mary. The new humanity was not to be a different race, but the *same* race redeemed. The new humanity was connected to the old humanity like the plant to the seed. Rejecting the Platonist belief in the absolute, natural, independent, and inherent immortality of the soul from eternity to eternity, the Fathers saw that it was only relative. It was dependent on our relationship to the One who alone has immortality. If immortality and resurrection life were to be communicated to the old humanity, then it *must* be that old humanity that the Word of God united to himself in the womb of Mary.

Thus far, this dominating theme of the Christology of the orthodox Fathers, seen in its ontological aspect of salvation from death, seems coherent, biblical, and powerful. But what about the moral aspect? If Christ took the old humanity from Mary, did he then take our sin? Did the Greek Fathers think that he took our *sinful* nature, and, if so, does that not compromise the sinlessness of Christ?

---

9. Athanasius, *De Incarnatione*, 8: from Thomson, tr., *Athanasius*, 153.

We need to be reminded that we are speaking here of the orthodox Greek Fathers, the bishops and theologians who formulated the definitive Christology of the Christian church. These are the doctors of the church—Irenaeus, Athanasius, the three Cappadocians (Basil, Gregory, and Gregory), and Cyril of Alexandria—who have been regarded by all branches of the Christian church ever since, and particularly by the Reformers, as the very foundation stones of doctrinal orthodoxy in Christology and the doctrine of the Trinity. Even Augustine, the dominating influence of Western Christianity, looked to Athanasius and the Cappadocians for his orthodoxy. It would be surprising beyond belief if these men were to compromise the sinlessness of our Lord Jesus Christ. The truth is, of course, that they did not. But we must listen very carefully to what they *did* say, for this is the heart of their understanding of how Christian sanctification is achieved "in Christ," and generally we modern Western Christians (especially Protestants) have not been listening to them or studying their thought as we should have.

In a nutshell, the Greek Fathers taught that the fallen humanity, our humanity, which God the Son took from us through his mother Mary, was indeed *sinful* humanity. What other humanity was there? Where would he get a human nature unaffected by the Fall? Sometimes it is said that since sin is not a necessary part of being human, Jesus took a sinless human nature. But that is missing the point. There is no disputing the fact that he was sinless: the question is whether he was sinless because he *took* an *already* sinless humanity from somewhere, or whether he was sinless because he took our sinful humanity and *sanctified it in assuming it.* The real question is: where would he get a sinless humanity to assume? Only a Platonist could think of ideal, unfallen humanity still existing somewhere in the realm of eternal forms! Or if God created for him a new humanity *ex nihilo*, then he would not be one of us, and his death and resurrection would have nothing to do with us. He would not have been born of a human mother (unless she were merely a surrogate); he could not be our priest representing us to God; and he could not be the sacrifice through which sinful old Adamic humanity was crucified, redeemed, and sanctified. So we have to say that he was truly born of Mary, "born of a woman, born under the law" (Gal 4:4). That is to say that he *took* or *assumed* corporate, sinful, Adamic humanity. If he was only "made sin" for us (2 Cor 5:21) in the sense of being a sin offering and taking the penalty of our sin, then his atoning action can absolve us from suffering our punishment, but it cannot sanctify us. Therefore, having our sin laid upon him as the spotless Lamb of God cannot mean *only* the guilt of our sins: again that would provide justification, but not sanctification.

We have to say then that he took our sin in the sense that he took our sinful, fallen human existence. But we also have to say very clearly that, in the very taking of it into union with his eternal person as the Son, he *sanctified* it by his Holy Spirit so that in his own body, in his own human mind and soul as the man Jesus, it was the *old* humanity—weak, mortal flesh, in bondage to decay and death, *but sinless*. Irenaeus writes of "the pure One opening purely that pure womb which regenerates humanity to God, and which he himself made pure."[10] As the Symbol of Chalcedon (451) expressed it, he was "like us in *everything* except sin" (*chōris hamartias*). Taking our sinfulness in no way polluted him. Our debt was swallowed up in his riches, our pollution cleansed in his purity, our sin burned up in the fire of his holiness.

It is important then to clarify here what is meant by "flesh" in the statement, "The Word became flesh." The brilliant Scottish preacher, Edward Irving, was one of the first in modern times to recapture this doctrine of the Eastern Fathers, but unfortunately, he left himself open to the charge of compromising the sinlessness of Christ by saying that the human flesh of Jesus was "sinful flesh" with sinful propensities.[11] Irving maintained that, while his human nature was sinful, his divine Person was sinless and so, by the Holy Spirit, he sanctified his human nature throughout his life. But that is not the consensus of the Fathers. It appears to arise from the failure to distinguish between "flesh" in the Old Testament and Johannine sense of mortal flesh subject to decay (*phthora*) and death, and living "according to the flesh" or with "the mind set on the flesh." If we fail to make that distinction, we tend to make *physical* flesh sinful in a way that is scarcely distinguishable from Gnosticism. "Flesh" as corporate human physical existence is "fallen" in the sense that it is mortal and disordered and so is within the sphere of sin, this "present evil age." One may even loosely speak of our physical flesh as "sinful" in the sense that it is affected by our sinfulness, polluted in that it is the physical dimension of our life and existence. It is in *that* sense that we have been saying that the Word sanctified our physical human nature ("flesh") in assuming it. But we must be careful not to say that physical existence is inherently sinful or evil in itself. That would be Gnosticism and quite contrary to the

10. Irenaeus, *Haer.* IV.33.11 (*ANF* 1:509, altered).

11. On Irving, see McFarlane, *Christ and the Spirit*, Dorries, *Incarnational Christology*, and Grass, *The Lord's Watchman*.

doctrine of creation. To say that God sent his Son "in the likeness of sinful flesh" (Rom 8:3) must therefore *not* be taken to mean that our physical existence is inherently sinful and that therefore the *physical* flesh of Jesus was sinful. Since "flesh" is the concrete Hebrew term for our more abstract word, "humanity," it means rather that he came in the likeness of sinful *humanity*. He came to share our fallen existence, our mortality and decay, and entered into the *corporate* fallenness and sinfulness of human nature and human society. But even in sharing our fallen state—with a body that was the inheritor of the sinfulness of his ancestors back to Adam (read the genealogies!)—he *sanctified* his physical human existence by his Holy Spirit right from conception and birth so that he was personally *sinless*. The human nature of Christ was "fallen" in the sense of mortal, subject to death, existing within the sinful world, this evil age, but, because it was united to the sinless, eternal Son of God, and sanctified from conception by the Holy Spirit, it was *sinless*.

A century ago, the leading patristics scholar, J. H. Srawley, made it clear that the doctrine of the Fathers did not compromise the sinlessness of Jesus in the way that Irving sometimes seems to do. Srawley defended Gregory of Nyssa against the charge that he held that the human nature of Christ was sinful even after he assumed it. After examining various excerpts from his writings, Srawley concluded: "Not one of the above passages explicitly states that the human nature assumed by Christ retained, subsequent to the conception of the Virgin, any of the disease or sinful promptings of fallen humanity."[12] He summed up Gregory's teaching: "Christ assumed our sinful human nature, but from the very moment of its assumption the union of the divine nature with it cleansed it from its sinful propensities."[13]

We have to insist then that the sanctification of our humanity in Jesus takes place right from the moment of his conception. The sinlessness of Jesus is thus intimately connected with the virginal conception of Jesus. Augustine (as we saw) later developed the theory that sinfulness was transmitted to each child by the lust involved in conception, and therefore he explained the sinlessness of Jesus by the absence of a human father.[14] We have already laid aside this Augustinian theory as a speculation that

12. Srawley, "Sinlessness," 435.

13. Ibid., 438.

14. Augustine was not without precedent on this: it is hinted at in Athanasius, *De Inc.*, 8. Jerome Van Kuiken also draws my attention to Gregory of Nyssa, *The Catechetical Oration* (Address on Religious Instruction), 16, which states the view developed more fully by Augustine.

is not only bizarre, but totally unbiblical. The sinlessness of Jesus is not to be explained *negatively* by the absence of a human father, but *positively* by the presence of the Lord God. It was because it was God the Son who was becoming a man, that this man was sanctified and thus *sinless*. It was, as Luke tells, because the Holy Spirit by a divine creative act created new life in the womb of Mary from her substance that the one to be born was holy. Holiness is not to be explained by an absence: holiness is always due to a presence. Only God is the source of holiness: only the Holy Spirit can sanctify. The Holy Spirit alone, not the absence or presence of any creature, sanctifies. The Son of God thus sanctifies *our* common, corporate humanity by uniting it to his own Person in being born as a human being from Mary by action of the Sanctifying Spirit.[15]

If we are going to insist, however, that the humanity of Jesus was sanctified from conception, we need to listen to the Greek Fathers when they insist on the complementary truth that it is only sinful humanity that needs to be, or indeed can be, sanctified. Only the unclean needs to be cleansed: only the impure can be purified. Gregory of Nyssa expressed the point poetically and powerfully: "[God] with a view to the destruction of sin, was blended with human nature, like a sun as it were making his dwelling in a murky cave and by his presence dissipating the darkness by means of his light. For though he took our filth upon himself, yet he is not himself defiled by the pollution, but in his own self he purifies the filth."[16] The words are staggering, but express a profound conviction that the sanctification of human nature was not an act done by Christ *external* to himself, like some great doctor performing a miracle cure on the flesh of someone else but remaining himself untouched, detached and aloof. Rather the sanctification of human nature takes place *internally* "in Christ"—in the very flesh and soul and mind of the man Jesus. The Son of God literally takes our common sinful humanity and sanctifies it, so that *in him* it has a *sinless perfection*.

Gregory of Nazianzus most famously puts the point in his aphorism: "The unassumed is the unhealed." He was writing a letter to combat the Apollinarian heresy that, because the human mind was the seat of sin, the Word of God assumed a human body, but could not have assumed a human mind. Nazianzen insisted that it was precisely because the human mind was sinful that the Word had to assume a human mind in order to

15. Although Barth uncritically endorses Irving, his own exposition of the Virgin Birth in *CD* I, 2, 15 presents this non-Augustinian interpretation of the doctrine.

16. Gregory of Nyssa, *Antirrhetic adv. Apollinaris*, 26, in Srawley, tr., "Sinlessness."

cleanse us. "If only half Adam fell, then that which Christ assumes and saves may be half also; but if the whole of his nature fell, it must be united to the whole nature of him that was begotten, and so be saved as a whole."[17] Nazianzen explains further in the fourth of his *Theological Orations*: "So he is called man (*anthrōpos*), not only that through his body he may be apprehended by embodied creatures . . . but also that by himself he may sanctify humanity (*kai hagiasē di'heautou ton anthrōpon*), and be as it were a leaven to the whole lump; and by uniting to himself that which was condemned may release it from all condemnation, becoming for all men all things that we are, except sin."[18] Athanasius had previously made the same point: "Our Saviour humbled himself exceedingly when he took upon him our frail unworthy nature. He assumed the form of a servant in making that flesh, which was enslaved to sin, a part of himself."[19] In him, however, it was not sinful, writes Athanasius, for he took it "that by the stability and constancy of that perfect obedience, which he was to perform in our changeable frail nature, he might 'condemn sin' in that nature, and in his Person enable us 'to fulfil the righteousness of the Law.'"[20]

The other Greek Fathers could be quoted to the same effect.[21] Their thought is breath taking. Here indeed we must take our shoes from off our feet, for this is holy ground. These things can only be said with fear and trembling. We instinctively want to reject the idea that the Lord came so close to our sin as to take it upon himself. We want to say with Peter, "God forbid, Lord! This shall never happen to you!" (Matt 16:22). But is there not here the authentic note of the gospel, and hope for the foulest and most degraded sinner? "He took my sins and my sorrows and made them his very own."[22]

Charles Wesley sings of the central significance of the incarnation, "Our God contracted to a span, / Incomprehensibly made man":

> He deigns in flesh t'appear,
> Widest extremes to join,
> To bring our vileness near,

17. Gregory Nazianzen, *Ep.* 101, 32 (*PG* 37, 184A); in Hardy, tr., *Christology*, 218.

18. Gregory Nazianzen, *Or.* 30:21 (*PG* 36, 132B), in Hardy, tr., *Christology*, 192.

19. Athanasius, *C. Ar.* I, 43; Robertson, tr., *NPNF*² 3:331.

20. See also *C. Ar.* II, 55, 56, 61, 66, 69, 73, 76; III, 32, 33, 53.

21. On Cyril of Alexandria, see Siddals, "Logic and Christology"; also Weinandy, *Likeness of Sinful Flesh*; Weinandy, "Mystery of the Incarnation," 25f.; and McGuckin, *Saint Cyril*, 185.

22. From a hymn by Mrs C. H. Morris.

> And make us all divine;
> And we the life of God shall know,
> For God is manifest below.

The consequence follows:

> Made perfect first in love,
> And sanctified by grace,
> We shall from earth remove,
> And see his glorious face;
> His love shall then be fully showed,
> And man shall all be lost in God.[23]

But we must not stop here, for this is not the whole story. If it were, it would suggest that the work of human sanctification was brought to an end at Bethlehem, which is not true. Paradoxically, while in one sense Christ was "entirely" sanctified from conception and birth so that in him there was no sin, yet in another sense the work of sanctification still had to be completed by his obedient life and sacrificial death. This paradox is the only way we have of speaking of the mystery of Christ. So we must leave this first statement, that Christ sanctified our humanity by assuming it, and move on to the second.

Christ Sanctified Our Humanity by Living In It

Here we are reminded that there is a dimension to human existence other than the common human nature we all share. There is humanity, human nature, humanness, which we all share by virtue of being born. That is not, as is sometimes suggested, a Platonist idea of a real universal form that exists somewhere in the transcendent realm. Rather it is a concrete, earthly, and indeed *earthy*, Old Testament concept of the corporate solidarity of the human race as "flesh" (*basar, sarx*). Human beings, to put the obvious somewhat flippantly, do not spring independently from the soil. Nor do they pre-exist, as the Platonists said, as eternally immortal, indestructible souls. Human beings are born from human beings and hence have a common nature. The very word "nature" comes from the Latin word for "born" (*natus*). Our "human nature" is that concrete stuff of humanity we share in solidarity with all human beings by virtue of our birth. It is that humanity, our concrete being, which (we have been saying) Christ took and sanctified in his birth from the Virgin. As such, the ontology of what we are

23. Hymn 5, *Hymns for the Nativity of Our Lord*, 13f.

given at birth, our "nature," circumscribes and limits how we think and how we choose and act as living human beings.

But now we turn to that other dimension of being human. For there is not only concrete, common, corporate human nature that sets limits on what we can do and be and which unites us as one human race: there is also that which is distinct and peculiar to each of us. To be human is also to be a distinct, single human being: to live life as a distinct agent, thinking and acting, knowing and loving, relating and deciding. Here then is the concept of the "person," which is not found in ancient literature, but which developed out of Christian trinitarian theology.

Here too our personal human life is sanctified by Christ *from the inside*. He not only sanctifies our human nature, our common "flesh," by assuming it, but he sanctifies the personal dimension of human existence. He does so by living a human life in our human nature, that is to say, living life as a human being within the limits set by our concrete, physical inheritance. But within those limits set by human "nature" (what we are born with) he lived as a human being with distinct, personal, free human agency—thinking and acting, knowing and loving, relating and deciding.

Perhaps the major figure among the Greek Fathers who can most obviously be quoted here is Irenaeus. Brought up in the churches of Asia Minor, probably within living memory of the Apostle John, Irenaeus is well known for his development of the Pauline idea of the Second Adam. He writes: "And, because in the original formation of Adam all of us were tied and bound up with death through his disobedience, it was right that through the obedience of Him who was made man for us we should be released from death."[24] The point is that where Adam disobeyed, the Second Adam *obeyed*. One of the fascinating facets of Irenaeus's thought is that he views this developmentally. He sees Jesus as a growing, developing human being, following the statement of Luke, it would seem, that Christ "grew in wisdom and stature and in favor with God and man" (Luke 2:52). Irenaeus wrote:

> He came to save all through his own person: all, that is, who through him are re-born to God; infants, children, boys and girls, the young and the old. Therefore he passed through every stage of life. He was made an infant for infants, sanctifying infancy; a child among children, sanctifying childhood, and setting an example of filial affection, of righteousness and of obedience; a youth among youths, becoming an example to

24. Irenaeus, *Epid.*, 31; Robinson, tr., *Irenaeus*, 98.

them, and sanctifying them to the Lord. So he was also a grown man among the older ones that he might be a perfect teacher for all, not merely in respect of revelation of the truth, but also in respect of this stage of life, sanctifying the elderly, and becoming an example to them also. And thus he came also to death.[25]

The obedience of Jesus is thus set in a very realistic human framework. It is the picture of an infant, a child, an adolescent, and an adult being obedient at each stage: indeed he "learned obedience" (Heb 5:8). Jesus thinks and acts, knows and loves and makes decisions as an infant, then as a child, then as a youth, and then as an adult. And at each stage, in every choice, he is obedient to the Father.

Two centuries after Irenaeus, it was the Antiochene theologians based at Antioch in Syria who emphasized this line of thought. Recognizing that our salvation depended on Christ's obedience, they insisted that it must have been *real* obedience. That it is to say, Jesus as a real human being must have had real choice. There must be no thought of his divine nature coercing his human choice. He must have been *free* as a human being to choose if the temptation was to be real and the obedience genuine. If there was no genuine choice, there was no real obedience.[26]

The Fathers at their best saw this genuine obedience as the free choice of a real human being, living exactly where we live, with all the constraints and pressures and frailties of a weak, mortal human body. Athanasius picks up the evidence of Scripture when he writes: "Although he was God, he had his own human body, formed and fashioned like ours since he had become man for us. And on account of this, and because he existed in human nature, the properties of that nature are said to be his, such as hungering, thirsting, suffering, labouring, and such like, of which the flesh is capable."[27]

This clearly implies that in condescending to become a human, our Lord condescended even to experience basic physiological human drives such as hunger and thirst. But at that very point where we fail and sin, he so disciplined his own body that in him, the natural human desires were never misdirected, never became evil desires.

---

25. Irenaeus, *Haer.* II, xxii, 4, based on Bettenson, tr., *Christian Fathers*, 80. See also *ANF* 1:391.

26. For Antiochene Christology, see Kelly, *Christian Doctrines*, 301–9; also Sellers, *Ancient Christologies*.

27. Athanasius, *C. Ar.* III, 31 (also in *NPNF*[2] 4:411).

Athanasius expressed it this way: "For the Son of God, having assumed our flesh, as has often been said, wholly extinguished all the venom of the serpent from it: if anything evil was produced out of the motions of the flesh, it was cut off and sin and consequent death together destroyed."[28] Is this not Paul's meaning when he wrote, "He condemned sin in the flesh" (Rom 8:3)? The natural human desires become the occasion of temptation, and when misdirected become sinfully distorted and so the means of enslaving us. But in Jesus the natural human desires of his mortal human body never led to sins either of deed or of thought, and were never allowed to become sinfully distorted. According to the insight we are given by the wilderness temptations, he was tempted for example through his hunger, but he remained in control (Matt 4:1–11; Luke 4:1–13).

If we are to develop this view of Athanasius, it would be along these lines: that where our desires become self-centered and we allow ourselves to be controlled by merely human goals and ambitions—self-gratification, self-glorification—in Jesus *the self-centered mindset*, the mind shaped by the natural desires of the flesh, never developed. He resisted the devil's temptation to self-glorification just as victoriously as the temptation to self-gratification. He did not live to please himself. He lived to please the Father and gave himself to the service of humanity. In him there was thus no "original sin," no *concupiscentia* (as Augustine called it), no "carnal mind," no *self-centered mindset*.

It was not that the absence of that gave him an advantage over us. On the contrary, he inherited all our disadvantages, all our bodily desires and instincts, our humanity made mortal by the Fall. He was born of a woman, as Paul put it, "born under the law," (Gal 4:4), born "in the likeness of sinful flesh" (Rom 8:3). But it was precisely in that condition, which was bondage and captivity for us, that he broke the bonds and snapped the chains of sin. It was precisely in those conditions, where we are disobedient, that he won the victory by his consistent outward and inward obedience. It was precisely where we are defiled that he purified and sanctified human flesh and human life in the power of his Holy Spirit. Becoming human, he assumed "flesh," that fallen, corporate, concrete humanity that we all share, subject to decay and death. That shapes us into egocentric people governed by our natural and psychological desires so that we develop the *self-centered mindset*, perpetuating the natural egocentricity of infancy into a sinful self-centeredness that then holds us in thrall. But he, receiving the same physical and physiological and psychological inheritance, and

28. Athanasius, *C. Ar.* II, 69 (also in *NPNF*² 4:386).

so subject to the same pressures, consistently chose the right. He did not sail through life and temptation untouched and unaffected. He was "on all points tempted like as we are" (Heb 4:15, AV), so that he fought "the good fight of faith" (1 Tim 6:12), thus becoming the "pioneer" (*archēgos*) in the way of faith for Paul and for us all (Heb 2:10).

Here surely is how Christ sanctified our humanity: by living a human life with all the practical choices and decisions of every day, and with all the outer demands and all the inner pressures and weakness of mortal humanity living in a fallen world in this present evil age. He took our sin, but in no way was he sinful. He entered into our slavery, but in no way was he enslaved. He entered into our pollution, but in no way was he defiled. Rather he sanctified not only our human nature in his nativity but also our human life by his consistent and continuously holy living. Having become one of us, a member of our sinful human race, "sinful flesh" (Rom 8:3), he not only sanctified our human nature in his own Person, but so sanctified human personal life that it became possible for us too to live as he did as genuinely compassionate and holy persons. It was under these conditions, we must conceive, that he sanctified our human life by consistently self-less, God-centered choices, which ultimately were to lead him inevitably to the cross.

Charles Wesley sings of following the one who sanctified our human life by living it, and prays that we may follow in his footsteps:

> Holy Lamb, who thee confess,
> Followers of thy holiness,
> Thee they ever keep in view,
> Ever ask, "What shall we do?"
>
> Governed by thy only will,
> All thy words we would fulfil,
> Would in all thy footsteps go,
> Walk as Jesus walked below.
>
> While thou didst on earth appear,
> Servant to thy servants here,
> Mindful of thy place above,
> All thy life was prayer and love.

Such our whole employment be:
Works of faith and charity,
Works of love on man bestowed,
Secret intercourse with God.[29]

So we come to our third statement.

Christ Sanctified Our Humanity by Crucifying It

We have already given attention in the last chapter to the basis for our sanctification in the death of Christ. But here we want to indicate how his death on the cross is integral to the whole movement from his descent to his ascent, from his birth to his ascension. We need to see more fully how his death is the culmination of his incarnate life and how his priestly office is closely connected to his true and full humanity.

It was, we have been saying, the consistently selfless life of Christ that led him to the cross. Indeed, his whole life was a death—a death to sinful self-interest. The cross cannot be artificially separated from his birth, his life, and his ministry, as if his sacrifice and bearing of our sins and sorrows only began at Golgotha. His *whole life* beginning from birth, and especially his ministry, was a self-sacrificial bearing of the sins and sorrows of humanity. Our sins were laid on him not just when the nails were driven through his hands and feet and he was lifted up on the cross. As we see from the accounts of his deep compassion for the sick, his angry sorrow at the hard-heartedness of the religious, and his deep grief at the tomb of Lazarus, he felt the weight of our sins upon himself throughout his life. His whole life was an at-one-ment of God and humanity. God and humanity were "at one," fully reconciled, uniquely in the Person and life of the God-Man. Long before he came to the cross, John the Baptist said to his disciples, "Behold the Lamb of God." That pointed forward to the cross, but it also indicated that *already*, in his human life, he was "the Lamb of God." Two sides of this need to be held together here. On the one hand, the One who bore our sin was truly the *spotless* Lamb of God. But on the other, the spotless Lamb of God truly took not just our punishment, not just our guilt, but sinlessly, in some sense which is beyond our ability to express, he took our very *sin*. This is the mystery of "Christ crucified."

But while we need to think of his sin-bearing as beginning at birth and continuing throughout his life, nevertheless the climax, the culmination

29. Hymn 545 in *A Collection of Hymns for the People Called Methodists*, John Wesley, Works [BE], 7:707.

and the completion of that self-sacrifice took place on the cross. The cross remains the unique centre of the story. There he denied himself finally and definitively. At any point up to death, he could have withdrawn: his obedience and self-sacrifice were not yet completed or "perfected." It was carrying it all the way through to death that "finished" or perfected it. But there on the cross, as our representative, he finally and fully denied that he had human rights to life, to liberty, and to the pursuit of happiness. He recognized that before God sinful humanity could claim no rights, and so, embodying humanity in his own Person, he claimed none: no right to the pursuit of happiness, for he gave himself to sorrow; no right to liberty, for he gave himself into captivity; no right to life, for he gave himself up to death. He was tempted to live for himself, for he was tempted on all points as we are (Heb 4:15). But there at the cross, the temptation to live according to the old Adamic self-interest, which he had denied and mortified within himself consistently and perfectly in his obedience to the Father at every moment of his life, finally and definitively died. That is surely what it means to say that "the death he died he died to sin" (Rom 6:10). The "old man"—that is, the old fallen Adamic humanity—was crucified with him and in him there on his cross and was buried in his tomb.

It is surely no accident that the word we find rising to our lips to express this is "sacrifice."[30] The worship of the temple provides the language of sacrifice: priest, altar, blood, and expiation. But while animal sacrifice was commanded by God, and given validity within the Old Covenant for dealing with sin, we come back to the point that, from the perspective of the New Covenant, it was seen that "it was impossible that the blood of bulls and goats should take away sin" (Heb 10:4). The Old Testament sacrifices were only types and models. They depicted the expiation, the obliteration of sin, but they did not actually in themselves achieve it. They only had provisional value because they were ordained by God to point forward to that one "full, perfect, and sufficient sacrifice, oblation and satisfaction for the sins of the whole world."

What they pictured or represented, the sacrifice of Christ in some way really achieved. For this priest did not sacrifice an animal: he sacrificed himself, his own *human* body and soul, born sinlessly but from the sinful, fallen human race of Adam. The Old Testament sacrifices symbolized the death of sin: but *somehow* the death of Christ *was* the death of sin—the expiation, the obliteration, the crucifixion of the old sinful, Adamic humanity. It is only when we give deep consideration to Christology—the

30. See Sarah Coakley's inaugural lecture at Cambridge, "Sacrifice Regained."

doctrine of the Person of Christ—in this way that we can begin to grasp the enormity of what happened in the atonement, the Work of Christ. It is only when we consider the reality of the true human nature of Christ, "the son of Adam" (Luke 3:38), that we can understand the deepest significance of the expiation of our sin effected on the cross.

If Christ did not "bear our sins in his body on the tree" (1 Pet 2:24), and if he was not sinlessly "made sin for us" (2 Cor 5:21), then we can never stand before God purified from sin at the Last Day. From any theological perspective, the cross must have not only set aside our punishment, but dealt totally not only with our guilt, but with our *sin*—sinful thoughts, words and actions, but also sin at the deeper level, sin as attitude, sin as condition, and sin as being—ethical, relational, and ontological.

It is the fact that Christ on his cross accomplished a finished, perfect work for us, a complete cleansing of corporate humanity from sin, a definitive and final crucifixion of the "old humanity," which is the only foundation for our hope of standing before the throne sinless in the hereafter. And it is this same perfect, finished work, perfected on the cross for us, that is the foundation for the hope that he will purify our hearts here and now, filling us with *his* perfect love for his Father, so that the self-centered mindset that makes us double-minded people is extinguished. How this perfect love is given to us through entire sanctification we will examine in the next chapter as we think of the work of the Holy Spirit. In the last chapter we will try to relate perfect love to the eternal Trinity.

8

Christian Holiness and the Holy Trinity

Our exploration into the foundation of Christian holiness has so far taken us into the doctrines of the atonement and the incarnation. It is not just that at the conceptual level, the *doctrine* of Christian holiness has its basis in the *doctrines* of soteriology and Christology. It is not just a matter of a system of ideas, or the systematic relationship of doctrines or abstract truths. It is a matter of objective realities. Wherever we may encounter the reality of a genuinely holy Christian, a genuinely selfless person whose life is centered on God and so lives with compassion for others, then that is because that person has learned what it means in his or her own experience to die with Christ to self-centered living. But that is only possible for him or her because Christ first died to self-centered living, because throughout his life from beginning to end he not only lived in whole-hearted obedience to his Father, but took that obedience to its ultimate and final completion by *dying* in whole-hearted obedience to his Father, accepting the righteous judgment of the Father upon humanity, corporately represented in his own person.

Thus definitively the old self-seeking, self-centered humanity, subject to disintegration, decay, and death, finally died *in him*, and the new humanity was raised in the power of the Spirit in the resurrection body of the risen Lord. The one and only foundation for Christian holiness is to be found then in the Christ who died and rose again. That is surely what we mean when we employ the sacrificial imagery of the old temple worship as developed in John's Apocalypse, and speak of being "washed in the blood of the Lamb" (Rev 7:14).[1] The provision for Christian holiness is to be found in the cross of Christ, "by which," as Paul wrote, "the world has been crucified to me, and I to the world" (Gal 6:14). In his flesh, sin was condemned, and in his death, sin died. But we noted that two sides of a paradox have to be held together here. If it was not the *sinless* Lamb who bore our sin, then we are not saved from sin. But if the sinless Lamb did not in some way *really bear our sin*, then equally, sin is not dealt with, and we are not saved. In some way, when Christ was crucified, sin died.

But it is not just the mere event of the crucifixion that is the foundation of Christian holiness. What we mean is that *Christ himself* is the foundation—Christ, incarnate, crucified, risen, and ascended. In him, "the first-born from the dead" (Col 1:18; Rev 1:5), the old humanity has died and the new humanity, the new creation (2 Cor 5:17), has begun. Christian holiness is founded upon—is a participation in—what he has done for us, once for all time in his death and resurrection. It is a participation *in him.*

But having looked at what Christ has done *for us* on his cross, we must now look in this chapter at the consequence of that: what Christ does *in us* by his Spirit. The atonement is complete: but we must enter in. We, the human race, *have been* reconciled corporately: therefore we are each called *to be* reconciled personally. We come to speak, therefore, of the work of Christ in and through his Spirit. That will lead us to see that we cannot speak about Christ and the Spirit without speaking too of their unity with the Father. As Peter's first declaration of the Christian gospel on the day of Pentecost demonstrates, a Christ-centered gospel that proclaims his death and resurrection has to be seen in trinitarian context. The expanded form of the gospel that Christ died and rose for our sins is that God so loved the world that he sent his only Son, and that the Son came in the power of the Spirit and then sent the Spirit from the Father to empower the mission of the church. All through the last two chapters therefore, we have really been trying to base our understanding of Christian holiness on the saving *economy* of God the Holy Trinity. But we must now think more in this chapter about the roles played in this story of salvation by the Spirit and the Father.

To explain that further, we must think in this chapter about the work of the Spirit in the incarnate Son, and then the work of the Spirit sent by the Son from the Father. That means thinking about the work of the "economic" Trinity, or, to put that better, the work of the Triune God

---

1. A.V., based on a variant reading; cf. also Rev 1:5.

in the "economy" (*oikonomia*) of salvation. Then in the next chapter we shall get so far as to think in a very preliminary way about holiness in the "Immanent" or "Ontological" Trinity. That is to say, we shall give some thought to the eternal holiness of the Triune God that we are being called to reflect. What is too often forgotten is that the formal doctrine of the Trinity, what is technically called the "Ontological" or "Immanent" Trinity, that God is eternally three Persons in one Being, arose historically out of what is technically called the doctrine of the "Economic" Trinity (God's revelation in salvation history as Father, Son, and Holy Spirit). It is in the *oikonomia*, that is to say, in the narrative of the salvation of the world, that God is seen to be Triune. The doctrine of the Trinity is, in fact, based on Christian experience, but not merely the experience of the individual believer. Primarily it is based on the historic corporate experience of the church as the community of faith.

It was because (a) the apostles of Christ came to believe that in Jesus they had encountered the Lord God himself, the Word made flesh; and because (b) through him they came to know God as "Father"; and because (c) they recognized that the Spirit within them—who enabled them to preach, and bound them together in unity, and mediated to them the presence of Christ—was both the Spirit of Christ and the Spirit of God; that they could speak of the Three as One. In one of the many triadic passages in the New Testament, Paul writes to the Galatians: "God has sent the Spirit of his Son into our hearts, crying 'Abba! Father!'" (Gal 4:6). Here is no formalized doctrine of the Trinity, but rather a sense that the experience of God as Spirit, shared by all Christians, was in fact a sharing in the divine Son's living relationship with his Father. There is thus in Paul's thought a distinction of the Son from the Father, and a distinction of the Spirit from both the Son and the Father, but at the same time an indivisibility and profound unity.

We continue to think about the "Economic" Trinity then, by moving on first from Christology in the last chapter to pneumatology, the doctrine of the Spirit, who is the Spirit of the Father and the Son.

a) The Spirit and the Last Days

It is not an exaggeration to say that a fully biblical doctrine of the Spirit can only be gained if it is approached from eschatology, the doctrine of the "End" or the "Last Things." Here we still suffer perhaps from the old scholastic approach that tries to dissect Christian theology into separate articles of faith. The Holy Spirit is placed in one article and eschatology in another. This whole way of setting out doctrine, which we have inherited from the Reformation and from the post-Reformation period of scholastic Protestant orthodoxy, encourages a scholastic mindset. It encourages us to parcel out Christian theology into tidy boxes and to elaborate fussy distinctions and rigid categories of thought that perhaps have more to do with tidy lecture notes than with real theology! This failure to grasp Christian theology as a whole is also due to the structure of contemporary theological education where the study of theology is typically parceled out into short courses lasting only for one semester and devoted to one doctrine. Nowhere is this analytical bent of mind more likely to distort than when it separates the doctrine of the Spirit from eschatology, the doctrine of the Last Things.

It is true, of course, strange as it may seem, that the framework of eschatological belief in the first century was only recovered by the scholarly research of the twentieth century, the historical and literary criticism associated particularly with the names of Albert Schweitzer, C. H. Dodd, Oscar Cullman, Werner Kümmel, and G. Eldon Ladd. Since that rediscovery of the eschatology of Judaism and of New Testament Christianity, eschatology is no longer merely the last chapter of theology as it was in the traditional shape of systematic theology. It now is seen to shape the whole book. This is particularly so with the doctrine of the Spirit. It is really no longer possible to speak of, say, "the baptism of the Spirit" or being "filled with the Spirit" purely in terms of the *ordo salutis* in the life of the individual Christian of today. These terms must first be understood in the historic, first-century context; that is to say, within an eschatological framework. Here the Fathers are not particularly helpful. By the time they wrote, the apocalyptic framework of thought of first-century Judaism was passing away in the church and being replaced by Hellenistic ways of thinking.[2]

Perhaps the best starting point is the prophet Joel, and particularly the words quoted by Peter on the day of Pentecost: "'And in the Last Days it shall be,' God declares, 'that I will pour out my Spirit upon all flesh, and your sons and your daughters shall prophesy, and your young men shall see visions, and your old men shall dream dreams'" (Acts 2:17). The crucial point about this oracle is that the expected outpouring of the Spirit will be "in the Last Days." The phrase is made more specific in Acts to emphasize that the prophet Joel was speaking about the Day of the Lord.

2. See Noble, "Eschatology."

In the prophets, the Spirit was associated with eschatological renewal, that renewal of Israel that would come at the *eschaton*, the Last Day. In the oracle of salvation in Isaiah 44:1–5, the promise is given: "I will pour my Spirit upon your descendants, and my blessing on your offspring" (Isa 44:3). In Ezekiel's vision of a renewed, revived Israel, it is the Spirit of the Lord "which is to be breathed into the corpse of the present nation."[3]

In the New Testament, the Spirit is primarily associated with the dawning of the New Age. The early church shared with many other groups in contemporary Judaism this eschatological hope and expectation. The Last Days were upon us, and the age to come, the kingdom of God, was expected imminently. But for the followers of Jesus there was an extra dimension to this hope, namely, the belief that although the age to come was yet to dawn, in some sense it had *already* come. New Testament eschatology is therefore distinctively characterized by the tension between the "not yet" and the "already." The Last Day was "not yet"; the return of the Lord Jesus was "not yet"; the general resurrection was "not yet." But "already," in anticipation of the Last Day, the Lord was risen and exalted and the Spirit had been given.

Marie Isaacs writes: "For Paul, *pneuma* is essentially an eschatological gift; the power of the future operative in the present. That is why he regards it as an anticipation, pledge or down-payment—the *arrabōn* of the final *eschaton*."[4] The Spirit is thus the "already." Although we still live in our mortal bodies, doomed to die, the Spirit is given to us so that "already"—because we have become partakers of the Holy Spirit, who will "give life to our mortal bodies" (Rom 8:11)—we have tasted "the powers of the age to come" (Heb 6:5). The Christian experience of the Spirit cannot be understood, however, apart from Christ. Experience of the Spirit was never something different from knowledge of Christ.

b) The Spirit and Christ

Here we need to look again at the events of the life of Jesus, but this time to see the role of the Spirit at each point. We have already seen in the previous chapter how the Holy Spirit was active in the sanctification of Jesus in his conception and birth: only God is the source of holiness and only the Holy Spirit can sanctify. But we must think here of God as inseparably Father, Son, and Holy Spirit. The Holy Spirit sanctifies the flesh of the

3. Isaacs, *Concept of Spirit*, 83.
4. Ibid., 86–87. Cf. Rom 8:23f.; 2 Cor 1:22; 5:5; Eph 1:13; 4:30; Gal 3:14.

unborn babe in his mother Mary, so that the God-Man is holy and sinless. But the Son is not passive, for we could equally put it this way: that the Son sanctifies the flesh by his Spirit in assuming it and in uniting it to himself. And indeed it is from the Father that both Son and Spirit come, acting (in the beautiful imagery of Irenaeus) as the two "hands of God."[5] Thus it is by action of the Triune God that the man Jesus is born, not by "the will of the flesh," that is, by human initiative, but born by the Spirit, born "from above." Athanasius comments: "He is declared to be and is, the First-born of us in this respect, because all men being lost by the sin of Adam, his flesh was first saved and freed in becoming the body of the Word himself, and the rest of us were saved through him as those who were united in the one body."[6]

Once again at his baptism the Father, the Son, and the Spirit are revealed. The Incarnate Son, to the perplexity of John (and to our perplexity!) takes his place in the line of *sinners* awaiting a baptism of *repentance*. He descends into the waters and as he rises out of the waters, the heavens open, the Spirit descends upon the One who is then to baptize with the Holy Spirit, and the voice declares him to be "my beloved Son" (Luke 3:22). It is Luke who tells us that, when he returned from the Jordan, Jesus was "full of the Holy Spirit" (Luke 4:1). He is "led by the Spirit" into the wilderness to battle with the temptations of the devil and returns "in the power of the Spirit" to begin his servant ministry in Galilee.

There he claims for himself the testimony of the mysterious Servant of the Lord in the book of Isaiah: "The Spirit of the Lord is upon me, because he has anointed me to preach good news to the poor" (Luke 4:18). The battle continues against evil entrenched in human flesh. The exorcisms of the evil spirits are done in the power of the Spirit, and are an eschatological sign: "If it is by the Spirit of God that I cast out demons, then the kingdom of God has come upon you" (Matt 12:28). The healing Jesus brings, however, is not brought in a clinical detached way. He is personally involved. He is personally tempted to self-gratification and self-glorification, but is victorious over the temptation by choosing the way of the cross in obedience to the Father (Matt 4:1–11; Luke 4:1–13). His victory is won not only against external forces of evil, but internally in his own mind and heart.

We have already considered Jesus' sanctification of our humanity by living a human life of obedience. But what we need to add and emphasize

---

5. Irenaeus, *Haer.* V, 6, 1; V, 28, 4 (*ANF* 1:531, 557).

6. Athanasius, *C. Ar.* II, 61 (author's translation; but see *NPNF*[2] 4:381).

here is that his obedience was *in the power of the sanctifying Spirit*. So as a human being—a *free* human being—it is *in the power of the Spirit* that he goes obediently to the cross to perfect his self-sacrifice, his offering of himself to the Father in love and obedience. Thus the writer to the Hebrews, in a phrase unique in the New Testament in linking the Spirit to the cross, writes of Christ "who through the eternal Spirit offered himself without blemish to God" (Heb 9:14).

Thus, to summarize, Jesus is *born of the Spirit* and, from his birth, *sanctified by the Spirit*. But sanctification is not something that happens to a completely passive Jesus and which is finally completed at his birth. This truly human man actively sanctifies not just human *flesh*, our concrete, corporate physical existence, but, as we have seen, human *living*. What we are emphasizing here however is that it is *in the power of the Spirit* that he is victorious over evil—not only over evil entrenched in the minds and hearts and bodies of other human beings, but even when evil seeks to gain an entrance internally by means of his natural desires. Thus he sanctifies our life as a free human being, living always *in the power of the Spirit*. He completes our sanctification by his self-sacrifice on the cross, his offering of himself *to the Father through the Spirit*. The whole movement from conception and birth, through his life of selfless service to his sacrifice on the cross is a sanctifying of human flesh and human life. It is a sanctifying of *our* humanity. Indeed it is *our* sanctifying. He does it to sanctify *us* as the pioneer of faith (Heb 2:10; 12:2), the first (and in one sense, the *only*) entirely sanctified human being. But he does it as a free human being *in the power of the Spirit*.

What we want to stress here then is that the inner secret of this life, entirely sanctified from conception to death, is not his victory over evil. That is the consequence. The inner secret is his relationship *with the Father*, and that relationship is a relationship *in the Spirit*. The word, "Abba," as Jeremias showed, reveals the inner mystery of this relationship.[7] Although James Barr argued that too much weight should not be placed on the word itself, nevertheless he agreed that the importance of the fatherhood of God for Jesus is amply demonstrated in the Gospels.[8] The relationship of Jesus to God is a relationship characterized by a total devotion, a whole-hearted zeal *in the Spirit* for *the glory of the Father* and a whole-hearted consecration to *the will of the Father*. The sanctifying life of Jesus has to be seen in

7. Jeremias, *Prayers*.

8. Barr, "Abba, Father."

trinitarian context as the concerted work of the three Persons of the Holy Trinity.

Here indeed in this man there is no double-mindedness and no sign of a self-centered mindset. But it is not the automatic compliance of an automaton, for there is a counting of the cost and a natural shrinking from self-sacrifice: "Abba Father, all things are possible to you, let this cup pass from me."[9] But at the level of conscious ethical choice, there is *purity of intention, a single eye*, that *purity of heart*, which is to will one thing: "Nevertheless, not my will, but yours be done" (Mark 14:36). And this "entire sanctification" is at its heart *relational*: it is pure love, perfect love *in the Spirit for the Father*. And it is because of this "perfect love" for the Father that there is purity of heart, singleness of purpose and no place for the self-centered mindset.

Matthew and Luke both have the saying in which Jesus speaks of this mutual and exclusive relationship of the Father and the Son: "No one knows the Son except the Father, and no one knows the Father except the Son . . ." (Matt 11:27; Luke 10:22). Luke places the saying moreover in the context of Jesus' thanksgiving to the Father *in the Spirit*: "In that same hour he rejoiced in the Holy Spirit and said, 'I thank you, Father, Lord of heaven and earth'" (v. 21). But it is perhaps Paul who most concisely expresses our inclusion within this intimate trinitarian relationship when he writes, "God has sent the Spirit of his Son into our hearts, crying, 'Abba! Father!'" (Gal 4:6).

The point to note here is that before the Spirit is ever sent into *our* hearts, before *we* are ever adopted and (whether we are male or female) given the privileges traditionally given to sons, it is the role and nature of the Spirit of the Son, the "Spirit of sonship" (*huiothesias*) (Rom 8:15) within the Godhead to cry "Abba!" Here is the root of Augustine's profound and beautiful thought that the Holy Spirit is the *vinculum caritatis*, the bond or communion of love in the Holy Trinity between the Father and the Son.[10] The Father gives himself in love in his Spirit to the Son, and the Son gives himself in love in his Spirit—the same Spirit—to the Father. Here is "perfect love" indeed, for within the Trinity, in the intimate relationship between the Father and the Son in the Spirit, God is love— "*perfect* love" (1 John 4:8, 16ff.). When the Son became human, that divine and eternal but intimate relationship of "perfect love" became grounded in our humanity and so open to us. It became possible for us to share in it.

---

9. See the exposition of this by Athanasius in *C. Ar.* IV, 57 (*NPNF*[2] 4:424).

10. Augustine, *Trin.* V, 11; VI, 5; XV, 17 (*NPNF*[1] 3:93, 100, 215).

That "perfect love" which the man Jesus had for the Father was love *in the Spirit.* As a human being, he was filled with the Holy Spirit and so was *the* entirely sanctified man, filled with "perfect love" toward the Father. The Holy Spirit who is the *vinculum caritatis,* the bond of love in eternity between the Father and the Son, now continues to fill the Son even when incarnate, so that in Jesus, *a human being* loves the Father with all his heart, soul, mind, and strength.

So it is that this whole-hearted and truly *human* love for the Father was brought to its culmination and completion, the most extreme and ultimate expression possible, in his obedience even to death. And it was after the sacrifice was completed, after the perfect, utter, self-sacrifice of this human being, "who *through the eternal Spirit* offered himself without blemish to God" (Heb 9:14), that the Father demonstrated his acceptance of this perfected sacrifice, which he himself had initiated, by raising Jesus from the dead. Here once again the Spirit was active, for Jesus is "designated Son of God in power *according to the Spirit of holiness* by his resurrection from the dead" (Rom 1:3–4). Jesus was raised from the dead *in the power of the Spirit.* Now he is no longer "in the flesh." That is to say, he is no longer in the old mortal, corruptible flesh, subject to *phthora*—decay, deterioration, disease, disintegration, senility, and death. He is now in the "spiritual body" (1 Cor 15:44), not a spirit or ghost, but a spiritual *body*—an immortal, incorruptible, resurrection body, no longer in the realm of "the flesh" and this "present evil age" (Gal 1:4), but fit for the realm of the Spirit, the "age to come," the new creation.

And so it is that he, who was the first human being to be born of the Spirit, and who received the Spirit *as a human being* at the Jordan to empower him for his ministry, becomes the source of the Spirit for all other human beings. Having been raised from the dead in the power of the Spirit, he now becomes "life-giving Spirit" (1 Cor 15:45). The Risen Lord breathes the Holy Spirit upon his disciples, signifying that he is the source of the Holy Spirit for them (John 20:22). On the Day of Pentecost, that acted parable recounted in John 20 was fulfilled in the descent of the Spirit, and it was Jesus, the risen, ascended Lord, who baptized his church in his Holy Spirit. He who received the Spirit that he might live in "perfect love" and communion with the Father poured out that same Spirit, *his* Spirit, on the gathered body of the apostles. All the benefits of his sacrificial, sanctifying life and death, all the benefits of his atonement, were now theirs.

How then does this sanctification of our humanity in Jesus by the Spirit *for us*, become his work of sanctification by his Spirit *in us*?

c) The Spirit and the Apostles

The apostles must be recognized as a unique generation spanning the ages. We must be very careful therefore about the way we extrapolate from their experience to ours. They were born into the old age, "this present evil age." As good Jews of that era, they expected "the age to come," the kingdom or kingly rule of God, but as yet, it had not come in any sense as far as they were aware. Then they met Jesus and became aware that the Spirit of God had descended on him and rested or remained upon him uniquely. They also became aware of his intimate relationship with God, whom he called "Father." The deeper truth as to his Person dawned on them later. But right from their first acquaintance with him, they realized that here was a man totally devoted to the one he called "Father," an entirely dedicated, entirely sanctified man. Because the Spirit rested upon Jesus and filled him, all he did was done in the Spirit.

Insofar as the disciples entered into a relationship with Jesus therefore, we must say that they entered into a relationship with the Spirit, for the Spirit rested upon him. All his relationships were relationships in the Spirit. That does not mean that the disciples had conceptualized the Holy Spirit as a *hypostasis* or *persona*, far less as the third Person of the Trinity. No such concept needed to be in their minds. But it must be true to say that they were aware of the Spirit in that they were aware of the *charisma* or aura of Jesus. Thus, in fact, their relationships with Jesus were relationships in the Spirit, and their dim recognition, not yet fully conceptualized, as to who Jesus really was, was revealed to them by the Spirit. But the Spirit did not yet rest upon them. The Spirit was "not yet given" (John 7:39). He was not yet "in" them, although he was "with" them (John 14:17) in that they were in relationship with Jesus. But the presence of the Spirit with them was limited and provisional. It was physically limited by the number of people who could meet and know this one man personally, and it was provisional in the sense that it depended on the presence of this one man on earth as a living human being in relationship to them.

Then Jesus went to the cross, crucified the old dying humanity, and was raised in the new glorified humanity, not only dead to sin (Rom 6:10), but now forever freed from its physical effects. The old fallen humanity, sentenced to mortality and death in Adam, "the old man," the old humanity (*anthrōpos*), was dead and gone, and from the tomb came the "first-born from the dead" (Col 1:18), the Last Adam (1 Cor 15:45), the "New Human Being," the prototype of the new humanity. He is already the first-fruits of the new creation: he is already in the new age, the age of the Spirit. Then, having ascended in the resurrection body into the very presence and glory of the Father, he sends upon his *disciples the same Holy Spirit in whose power he had lived a life of holiness*, baptizing them "with the Holy Spirit and with fire" (Luke 3:16).

Pentecost must therefore be seen as primarily a once-for-all unrepeatable event. It is the final event in the series of the mighty acts of God in Jesus. In that sense it is as unique and unrepeatable as the incarnation, the crucifixion, the resurrection, and the ascension. And what it means is that now that the work of Christ has been completed on the cross, it is possible for the first time for men and women to receive the benefits of his atonement. True, men and women received the forgiveness of God before then, but only provisionally in the light of the sacrificial death that was still to come. Even the word of forgiveness spoken by Jesus to individuals during his life on earth was provisional in the sense that the one "full, perfect, and sufficient sacrifice, oblation and satisfaction, for the sins of the whole world" had not yet been completed. But now it had been completed on the cross, the perfect and finished work of atonement. Therefore at Pentecost, now that the atonement was complete, the ascended Christ was able to pour out his Spirit upon "all flesh," all humankind. That universal "pouring out" of the Spirit was what was to condition and energize the mission of the church to the ends of the earth. It was not, of course, that all human beings received the Spirit on the Day of Pentecost in the same way as the apostles. They, as the foundation stones of the church, built on the cornerstone (Eph 2:20), now for the first time each received the Spirit, who was now to remain on each of them as he had remained upon Jesus during his earthly life. And in receiving the Spirit "in" them, they received the full salvation won on the cross—forgiveness, his intimate relationship with the Father ("Abba!"), and the resurrection life of Jesus.

Only now that Jesus had died could they fully receive the benefits of his atonement. Only now that Jesus was risen and exalted could they receive his resurrection life, life in the Spirit. Only now, when the Spirit was given, poured out once and for all upon "all flesh," could they each receive the Spirit, be born of the Spirit, and, indeed, be filled with the Spirit. Because the ascended Lord sent down his Spirit once for all on that day upon the apostles, and because the Spirit has never since been withdrawn, ever since it has been possible for "all flesh"—that is, all humankind—to receive the Spirit, to be born of the Spirit and, as they are enabled by his leading and enlightening, to be filled with the Spirit.

But in order to understand what is true for "all flesh," which includes ourselves, it is necessary to make one important clarification about the apostles. It is this: that although at Pentecost they received the resurrection life of the Spirit, and indeed received the Spirit in all his fullness, they were not yet in their resurrection bodies. Hymenaeus and Philetus were later condemned because they "swerved from the truth by holding that the resurrection is past already" (2 Tim 2:17–18). Clearly then, although the Spirit had been poured out, the age to come had not yet *fully* come, for the return of Christ and the resurrection of the dead were still awaited. Even after Pentecost therefore the disciples and all the New Testament church lived in this paradox we described earlier, the tension in New Testament eschatology between the "already" and the "not yet." The *not yet* aspect was that they were not yet in their resurrection bodies. Final salvation of the whole human being—body, soul, and spirit—still lay in the future.

d) The Spirit and the Disciple Today

And what was true of the apostles, even after Pentecost, has been true of all believers ever since, and is true of us. The general resurrection is not yet past; it has still to come. Therefore, until that day, we shall always be fallen men and women living in the old mortal bodies, the old fallen flesh, subject to disease and death, subject to disorientation of the physically-based, physiological desires of the flesh, seeing the weakness and decay at work in our human *physis*, our nature. This is the point strongly emphasized by Wesley in one of his last sermons, "Heavenly Treasure in Earthen Vessels."[11]

William Burt Pope, the nineteenth-century Methodist theologian of Didsbury College in Manchester, made the same point by distinguishing between two meanings of "original sin." He wrote: "There is first the individual portion of the common heritage" from Adam, and there is secondly "the common sin that infects the race of man." Pope continued: "As to the latter, it is not to be doubted that original sin, or sin as generic and belonging to the race in its federal constitution on earth, is not abolished till the time of which it is said, 'Behold, I make all things new.'"[12] H. Orton Wiley,

11. Sermon 129, *Works* (BE) 4:161–67. See above, page 92.

12. Pope, *Compendium*, 3:47.

the authoritative twentieth-century Nazarene theologian, reproduced this sentence almost *verbatim*.[13] Perhaps since the phrase "original sin" has so many subtly different and inter-connected meanings, it would be less confusing to refer to this as "fallenness." What it means is this: that as long as we live in the fallen environment of "this present evil age," in fallen bodies with fallen minds, it is always possible to fall into sin. But more than that, there are always the natural desires—physiological and psychological, perfectly legitimate in themselves and part of God's good creation, yet so affected by the Fall—that, if not subject to temperance or self-control (*egkrateia*, Gal 5:23), may pull us at any moment into sin. Full understanding of this point means that the historic tradition on Christian "perfection," held by the Eastern Fathers, Bernard, Aquinas, and Wesley, and, on the other hand, the Reformation traditions of Luther and Calvin, are perhaps not so far apart as has been thought.

The Christian never gets beyond the Apostle Paul, who had to buffet his body (1 Cor 9:27) and bring every thought into captivity to Christ (2 Cor 10:5). The very fact that we are fallen makes sin—even conscious, deliberate sin; sins of the flesh or sins of the spirit—a daily, hourly possibility. To go further than that: to the extent that we do not fully know ourselves and our motivation, and may do things with mixed motives, and since we have a great capacity for self-deception, we may err daily unconsciously or semi-consciously, on the borderline of our awareness. Even when we are aware of our motives and consciously reject the wrong and choose the right, we are conscious that we do not do it as perfectly as we could, and therefore must always fall short of that absolute perfection. We are conscious that no matter how well we do, we could always do better, and we could always do more. And therefore, although we no longer live in condemnation but rejoice in the forgiveness of our sins, and although we do not deliberately and flagrantly transgress the laws of God, yet at the same time we need a life-long attitude of confession and penitence towards God, not only for what we used to be, but also for our present short-comings and faults. As William Burt Pope wrote: "There is no man who must not join in the prayer: 'Forgive us our trespasses.'"[14] Or, as Charles Wesley adjured us: "Day by day your sins confess, Ye that walk in righteousness."[15]

---

13. Wiley, *Christian Theology*, 2:488.

14. Pope, *Compendium*, 3:47.

15. Wesley, *Short Hymns*.

There indeed is the paradox, with the *not yet* aspect fully recognized. We are not yet in the resurrection body: we are still fallen creatures living in mortal bodies with fallen minds weakened by sin and subject to decay. We still fall short of absolute perfection, and so the *not yet* aspect must be put as strongly as that. The Lutheran and Reformed theologians have a full grasp of that in the *simul iustus et peccator*, and have legitimately criticized Wesleyans, particularly some in the Wesleyan holiness tradition, for being unrealistic at this point. And yet the realism is there in Wesley himself and in some contemporary Wesleyan theologians. The New Testament scholar Richard Howard put the point powerfully, beginning with his struggles as a young pastor, in his popularly written book, *So Who's Perfect?*[16] Indeed at the popular level, all this suggests that the word "perfection" in modern English is a stumbling block that should be avoided. In popular speech, it inevitably conveys the impression that those who speak of Christian "perfection" are claiming to be sinless paragons. That leads to disastrous disillusionment when they demonstrate their fallible humanity.

But, having said all that, the strength of the Wesleyan understanding of Christian holiness is that, in line with the Eastern Fathers, Bernard, and Aquinas, it does justice to the paradox by emphasizing the other side of the eschatological tension: the *already*, the "optimism of grace."[17] *Already* Christ is risen and sits at the right hand of the Father as the New Man, the Second Adam, the prototype of the redeemed race, "perfected through suffering" (Heb 2:10). He is not only perfect in love towards the Father, but now also perfected in body: no longer in the fallen, mortal body, but in the resurrection body, the Head of the redeemed race, perfected, incorruptible, and immortal.

That is what we shall one day be in the age to come when we shall be like him and see him as he is (1 John 3:2). But *already*, because Christ is our brother and the new Head of the race, we are raised up with him and made to "sit with him in the heavenly places" (Eph 2:6). We may take that to mean that, because he is there, our representative and forerunner, we too, as it were, are included. Because of his incarnation, the whole human race is corporately joined to him "according to the flesh" (*kata sarka*), and it is that common flesh or humanity that we share with him, which has been redeemed and perfected by crucifixion and resurrection in him, and which is now with the Father. Not only so, but being the perfect human in the glory of the Father, he has sent down his Spirit so that *already*, in

16. See also Richard Howard, *Newness of Life*.

17. Rupp, *Principalities*, 90.

anticipation of the Last Day, even while we are still in the fallen world in our mortal bodies, we may be united to him and so share in his perfected humanity. Christians are those who are united to Christ not only "according to the flesh" (*kata sarka*)—that is, our common humanity—but also "*by the Spirit*" (*kata pneuma*). *Already* he has poured out his Spirit to give life to our mortal bodies through his Spirit who dwells in us (Rom 8:11).

Every Christian has received his Spirit, and so is incorporated into the church, the body of Christ. Every Christian, being baptized into Christ and being "in Christ," is therefore given to share by the Spirit in the perfected humanity of Christ. Athanasius put it like this: "But if on our account he sanctifies himself and did this when he became man, it is very obvious that the descent of the Spirit on him in the Jordan was a descent on us because of his bearing our body . . . when the Lord, as a man, was washed in the Jordan, we were the ones washed in him and by him. And when he received the Spirit, we were the ones who became recipients of the Spirit through him."[18]

In one sense therefore, since all Christians are "in Christ" and have received his Spirit, they are "sanctified." Wesleyan theologians have sometimes called that "initial sanctification" and rightly insisted, against antinomian tendencies, that there is a sense in which even the newly born-again Christian is *not* a sinner and does not deliberately transgress God's laws. But in another sense, sanctification cannot be automatic and immediate. We are not puppets: we are thinking, growing, choosing, developing, human beings, living in the real world of time and history. Therefore, there must be an ethical, developmental aspect to sanctification. It is as Christians wrestle with the ethical choices of every day that we each realize what allegiance to Christ implies in practice. Before setting out to follow Christ, it is impossible for the Christian to know experientially from the inside what consecration actually implies. But it does not take long to discover that although she has given her life to Christ, there is within the new Christian a motivational pattern, a *self-centered mindset* that resists the Spirit.

This disposition toward "the flesh," or "mind set on human goals and values," wrestles against the Spirit and the Spirit, as it were, against it. The Christian had never been so aware of it before, for it had never been challenged so radically. Only now, when she tries to live for Christ, does she become aware of this self-centered mindset, which now makes "the flesh" appear as a dominating power within. Whenever and however that may

18. Athanasius, *C. Ar.* I, 47 (*NPNF*² 4:333).

happen, the Christian then faces the need to deal with this, if the determination to follow Christ is to continue to be a reality. But we discover that we cannot deal with it by a re-consecration, or a deeper consecration, or even total consecration. *We* cannot deal with it at all. Only Christ can deal with it, the High Priest who is "touched with the feelings of our infirmities" (Heb 4:15). For Christ, living exactly where we do, lived in total consecration to the *Father* by the *Spirit* throughout his earthly life so that the self-centered mindset was never even formed in him.

So it is that when the double-minded Christian, aware of this inner struggle, comes to him for rest, Christ will fill him or her with his Spirit, his full and whole-hearted love for the Father. To speak of being "filled" with the Spirit is, of course, a metaphor. The Spirit is not literally water: that is simply one of the significant biblical metaphors for the Spirit, indicating the cleansing and life-giving role of this divine Person. Nor is this the Christian's first reception of the Spirit, for, as baptism signifies, the Spirit's cleansing and life-giving work of sanctification begins right from the new birth, if not before.[19] But the consecration made at the beginning of each believer's pilgrimage is now brought to a "fullness" or a level of completion in such a way that the total commitment made in principle at the beginning is now fully actualized. At this point in his or her spiritual development then, the Christian is able—not merely by effort or moral energy or discipline alone, but by the grace or gift of God—to make his or her consecration fully actual, and to love God and his perfect will wholeheartedly. While still in the fallen body as part of a fallen human race ("flesh") and liable therefore to daily temptation, this mature Christian is no longer of a divided mind or heart. The whole thought-life is then "integrated," that is to say, has *integrity* or *unity*, around this one dominating desire: to please God. This is not final "perfection," but it is a new level in the believer's "perfecting." It may be called "perfect love," not in the sense that it is the kind of perfect love we shall know hereafter (Aquinas and Bernard can help us here), but in the sense that it is all-consuming love for God and neighbor with an undivided heart. And it is surely characteristic, not only of those who affirm the historic patristic and Wesleyan doctrine of "perfect love," but, whether they realize it or not, of mature Christians in every branch of the Christian church.

It is true that other desires, other motives, remain. Some, such as the desire to eat well, or to take exercise or relax, are directly based in our

---

19. On the relation between baptism and "baptism of the Spirit," see Deasley, "Entire Sanctification."

physiology. Others are more complex, such as the legitimate and appropriate desire to have fulfilling work to do. Or they may be more complex still: for example, the motive, or desire, or need to have an attractive, intelligent, loving marriage partner. Such motives and desires as these do not disappear; nor are they *automatically* integrated into the one dominant motive of serving God. There is still the need for discernment and discipline, and room for growth. There is still temptation to be faced, and the Christian needs to work at the ethical choices of every day, and may not always be sure what the right choice is. He may not even know himself well enough to know what his real motives are, and may frequently appear a pretty imperfect fellow to those around him! But one thing is clear: the Christian filled with the Spirit of Christ is not a person torn in two. Being filled with the Spirit of Christ the Son (the "Spirit of sonship") and loving the Father whole-heartedly, the Spirit-filled Christian daily works at the business of reconciling every other desire and motive to the one dominating, overriding, all-embracing passion of life, to serve God with all the heart, soul, mind, and strength.

Charles Wesley expresses for us the constant daily prayer that Christ, who is Love incarnate, crucified, and ascended, may breathe into us too his own Spirit that we may be filled with his love:

> Love divine, all loves excelling,
> Joy of heaven, to earth come down,
> Fix in us thy humble dwelling,
> All thy faithful mercies crown!
> Jesu, thou art all compassion,
> Pure unbounded love thou art;
> Visit us with thy salvation!
> Enter every trembling heart.
>
> Breathe, oh, breathe thy loving Spirit
> Into every troubled breast!
> Let us all in thee inherit;
> Let us find that second rest:
> Take away the bent to sinning,
> Alpha and Omega be,
> End of faith as its beginning,
> Set our hearts at liberty.
>
> Come, almighty to deliver,
> Let us all thy grace receive;
> Suddenly return, and never,

Never more thy temples leave.
Thee we would be always blessing,
Serve thee as they hosts above,
Pray and praise thee without ceasing,
Glory in thy perfect love.

Finish then thy new creation,
Pure and spotless let us be;
Let us see they great salvation
Perfectly restored in thee;
Changed from glory into glory,
Till in heaven we take our place,
Till we cast our crowns before thee,
Lost in wonder, love, and praise.[20]

As one of the most popular hymns in the language (perhaps because of the incomparable tune, Blaenwern, to which it should always be sung!), this is perhaps also Charles Wesley's greatest hymn on Christian "perfection." But in Charles's hymns, Christian perfection is always a prayer, never a claim. We are never to rest on our laurels, but always to pray that God will fill us afresh with the Spirit of Love who is the Spirit of Christ.[21] And the last verse makes it clear that while we may be daily filled with the perfect love of Christ here and now, *final* spotless perfection only comes in the life to come.

If this very practical picture, this view of Christian *praxis* that we have tried to sketch in this chapter, is a true understanding of Christian holiness, and, specifically, of that Christian maturity or "perfecting" that has been taught and lived down through all the centuries of the church, then it is not an unrealistic kind of perfection*ism*. It is not merely revivalistic emotionalism, or some illusionary, quick-fix, instant holiness, nor some superficial, simplistic, sectarian "distinctive" or hobby-horse. That we may be filled with the perfect love of Christ by the in-breathing of his Spirit, and so come to love him with all our hearts and to love others, is a doctrine firmly based in Holy Scripture and in the central doctrines of the Christian church: the atonement, the incarnation, and the doctrine of

20. Originally published as Hymn 9 in *Redemption Hymns* (1747), the second verse was omitted by John when he included it in *A Collection of Hymns for the Use of the People Called Methodists, Works* (BE) 7:545, because he thought that the line which originally read, "Take away the power of sinning," was too strong.

21. On Charles Wesley's theology, see Tyson, *Charles Wesley;* Kimborough, *Charles Wesley;* and Lloyd, *Charles Wesley.*

the Trinity. It is a spiritual, experiential reality with a firm foundation in the cross, in Christ, and indeed in the Triune God, Father, Son, and Holy Spirit.

9

Reflecting the Holy Trinity

Our aim in this book has been to address the theological question: what basis is there for the historic view of Christian holiness, embraced in the Wesleyan tradition, particularly Christian "perfection," in the central Christian doctrines—atonement, incarnation, and Trinity? We have tried to see that the most comprehensive Christian doctrine, embracing all the others, is the doctrine of the Holy Trinity, and in the last chapter we tried to see the gospel story, the story of salvation in Christ, as the story of God the Holy Trinity. Some theologians have argued that that is all we can do. Reacting against the way in which the doctrine of the Trinity had been made irrelevant to Christians and the church because theologians had concentrated on the mysteries of the Immanent Trinity, the Triune God in eternity, some have suggested we need to limit ourselves to speaking of the "Economic" Trinity, the story of God in the world. But the danger of that solution is that it becomes too easy to tip over again into the anthropocentric theology against which Luther prophesied and that became once again the trap into which so-called "liberal" theology fell. Feuerbach analyzed such theology acutely as merely anthropology in disguise. That then is the recurring danger of our sinful condition. We do not really want to speak of God; we really want to speak about ourselves! What really interests us is not genuine *theo*logy, the truth of *God*, but our own religion. Beneath it all, we are really religious humanists whose absorbing interest is our own human story!

That danger is never greater than when we make our own holiness the centre of our interest. "It is a dangerous thing to do," wrote P. T. Forsyth, "to work at your own holiness."[1] Surely, as Luther saw, the last and most subtly hidden bastion of our sinful self-centeredness is self-centered religion. As Paul makes clear in Philippians 3, the aim of the "perfect" is not their own perfection, but that they may know Christ. *He* is the goal. Christian "perfection" is only a by-product. Only as we are Christ-centered and being conformed to his image—that is, coming increasingly to reflect him—can we cry, "Abba!" and grow by his Spirit in deep personal knowledge of the Father. We are to love God for his own sake, not merely for our own. And since Christ is exalted, we are called to lift up our hearts and thoughts to "things above" (Col 3:1–2). It is, therefore, appropriate for us to devote our attention, so far as God's revelation in Christ has made it possible, to meditate on the eternal or "Immanent" or "Ontological" Trinity. To fail to do so is to run the danger yet again of losing our hold on the truth of the *transcendence* of God, and to imagine a god who is "too small,"[2] an idol that is tailored to our needs.

We come finally to think therefore, at least in a very introductory way (so much more could be said!), about the holiness of God in his transcendence as the eternal Trinity. Looking back through these chapters, the route we have followed began with the doctrine of Christian holiness and tried to trace that back to its source in God. That is to say, rather than presuming that we know all about God and beginning with our own articulation of the doctrine of God, we have asked how we can ascend from where we are in our creaturely weakness and sin to God. The answer we discovered is that "the road to up is down."[3] The only way for sinful humanity to come to God is through the cross and the resurrection. And yet the suffering of the cross is not the final goal. That would be masochism. It is rather the gateway to glory. And to gain some understanding of the atonement, we must therefore see not only what we have been saved *from*, but also what we are saved *to*. We must reflect, as John McLeod Campbell put it, not only on the *retrospective* aspect, but also on the *prospective* aspect of salvation.[4] We are redeemed to become the children of God, embraced within the communion of the Holy Trinity.

What then does all this tell us about the God whose presence is our destiny and goal? Who is this God revealed in the story of the gospel,

1. Forsyth, *Work of Christ*, 71.

2. Phillips, *Your God*.

3. The theme of a powerful sermon by the late Alan Redpath on Philippians 2:6–11 preached at a Spring Harvest conference on "The Servant King" (1984).

4. Campbell, *Atonement*.

indeed in the grand narrative of Holy Scripture? In particular, why do we speak of God not only as the Trinity, but as the *Holy* Trinity? This is a vast subject, but at least in this final chapter we can make a beginning.

a) Trinitarian Debates

Before we tackle the question of how we as Christians can reflect the perfect life of the Holy Trinity, we need to attempt a brief preliminary orientation to the current trinitarian debates. This can only be the briefest sketch of a large and complex theological discussion.[5]

Briefly, then, it is generally held that in the era of modernity, the doctrine of the Trinity suffered an eclipse. The rise of Deism with the Enlightenment meant that great value was placed on those elements of "religion" that were thought to be common notions across world religions and cultures: that there is one supreme deity, that this deity is to be worshipped, that to be religious is a matter of morality, that human wrongdoing can be dealt with by sincere repentance, and that future rewards and punishments will be based on merit.[6] The distinctive features of the Christian faith, such as the deity of Christ and the doctrine of the Trinity, were therefore marginalized or totally discounted. But opposition to the doctrine of the Trinity also came from a biblicism that argued that the doctrine was not to be found in Holy Scripture. This led to a pervading belief that the doctrine of the Trinity was invented by the Fathers and really stemmed not from Scripture but from Greek metaphysics.

It was against that background that the two major influences on nineteenth-century theology, Schleiermacher and Hegel, proposed recasting the doctrine. Schleiermacher's project was to rebuild the whole of Christian theology on the religious experience common to all humanity, but he did not get so far as to propose exactly how the doctrine of the Trinity should be recast. Hegel reinterpreted the doctrine as a pictorial representation of his own philosophical speculation—that *der Geist*, the absolute Spirit or Mind, created a world which, as finite spirit and matter, was totally other than itself, but that it then embraced that which was not itself, overcoming the difference in a greater unity. This was the famous Hegelian dialect of thesis (*der Geist*), antithesis (the world), and synthesis (*der Geist* realizing itself in the history of the world), and this was what

5. For a recent fuller critical account and analysis see Holmes, *The Holy Trinity*.

6. Holmes traces these back to the Deist, Lord Herbert of Cherbury. Holmes, *Trinity*, 177.

was pictorially represented for the unsophisticated in the doctrine of the Trinity. But notice carefully what this implied. The incarnation was not a once-for-all-event in which God became a particular human being, but was a process of world history in which God realized or actualized himself in becoming incarnated in the created order. What Kierkegaard called "the infinite qualitative difference" between God and creation was thus eliminated.

By the end of the nineteenth century, Hegelianism was going out of fashion, and it was the tradition of Schleiermacher, now represented by the Ritschlian school, that was popular. As expressed by Adolf von Harnack in his famous lectures at the University of Berlin in 1900, this was altogether simpler. Jesus was a man whose supreme consciousness of God was all that was meant by his "divinity." He had preached the universal fatherhood of God: all could become children of God in the same sense that he was the son of God. At the same time, conservative Christianity of various kinds adhered to the deity of Christ and the doctrine of the Trinity, but trinitarian doctrine seemed to be quite unconnected with the life of faith. It was simply an abstract piece of complicated and puzzling information about God to which one had to assent in order to be orthodox.

It was in this context, in which the doctrine of the Trinity was generally thought to be a dead letter, that Karl Barth launched his astonishing re-assertion of the doctrine. His originality was in re-expressing it in terms of God's self-revelation. Christian faith was not based on the common notions of Enlightenment Deism, but upon the revelation of God, and that revelation was inherently trinitarian. God revealed himself, and he revealed himself through himself. That was what was meant by the Father, the Son, and the Holy Spirit—the Revealed, the Revealer, and the resulting Revelation. But Barth's later recasting of the Reformed doctrine of election led to a development in his thought. God had elected in eternity to be united to humanity in the Word-made-flesh and therefore there is no longer any place for the pre-incarnate Logos, the *logos asarkos*. By his own election, God was thus united to creation in such a way that it could seem as if the act of creation was swallowed up in the infinitely greater act of incarnation.

A little later than Barth, the Roman Catholic theologian, Karl Rahner, published a significant little book in which he argued that the problem with the doctrine of the Trinity was that the doctrine of God as the eternal Trinity (the "Immanent" or "Ontological" Trinity) had become wrongly separated from the revelation of God as Triune in the history of salvation (the "Economic" Trinity). What became known as "Rahner's rule" stated that: "The 'Economic' Trinity is the 'Immanent' Trinity and the 'Immanent' Trinity is the 'Economic' Trinity."[7] As Barth's later doctrine seemed to bridge the gulf between God and creation, so Rahner's rule seemed to do the same. It was not entirely clear, however, whether the identification of the Immanent Trinity with the Economic Trinity was just epistemological, so that we can only *know* God as Immanent Trinity through the economy, or whether it was ontological, in which case it could be that the Immanent Trinity was reduced to the Economic Trinity. Did this again compromise the transcendence of God?

Both Barth and Rahner also had a strong emphasis on the unity of the Triune God. Barth refused to speak of three "Persons" since that in modern ears implied three individuals, and spoke instead of three eternal "modes of being." God was one individual, "the one God in threefold repetition." Any idea of three distinct individuals, distinct centers of consciousness with distinct minds and wills, was to be rejected as tritheistic.

In contrast to this strong emphasis on the unity of God as a single subject by both Barth and Rahner, another school of thought has become increasingly prominent over the last few decades. This "social trinitarianism" seems to lay great stress on distinguishing the three Persons, almost to the point where it is suspected of tritheism. Here we may group (among others) Leonard Hodgson, Jürgen Moltmann, John Zizioulas, Robert Jenson, and, among philosophical theologians, Cornelius Plantinga and Richard Swinburne. We shall investigate Zizioulas particularly later in the chapter, but just to complete our preliminary survey of the debates, we need to note that social trinitarianism has come in for severe criticism from philosophical theologians such as Michael C. Rae and Brian Leftow. In the current climate, opinion appears to be polarized between those who focus on the *unity* of the Trinity and those who focus on the *distinct Persons* of the Trinity; that is, those who focus on the *One* and those who focus on the *Three*.[8]

b) The Wesleyan Tradition and the Trinity

Before trying to think theologically about how we might understand the doctrine of Christian "perfection" to be based on the doctrine of the

7. Rahner, *Trinity*, 10f.

8. See the analysis of the current debate in McCall, *Which Trinity? Whose Monotheism?*

eternal or Immanent Trinity, there is one other preliminary task. That is to note briefly the role of the doctrine of the Trinity in the thinking of the Wesleys and their successors.

At first sight, that may not seem to be very promising territory. John Wesley was not a systematic but a pastoral theologian. He did not compose a *summa* or expound the whole of Christian theology, but concentrated on those elements that were vital for the revival of the church in his day, "repentance, faith, and holiness." In the primary official source for his theology, the Sermons, there is only one sermon on the Trinity, written rather late in his ministry. But over against that, there are two considerations, the trinitarian hymns of Charles Wesley, which John fully endorsed, and what Elmer Colyer calls the "deep structure" of their shared theology, evident in John's writings.

The trinitarian hymns of Charles Wesley have been the subject of a number of recent scholarly articles. They are mainly to be found in *Hymns on the Trinity*, published in 1767. The background to the book was the debate between Samuel Clarke, whose views on the Trinity subordinated the Son and Spirit to the Father, and Daniel Waterland, who defended the orthodox doctrine of the Athanasian Creed and criticized Clarke, along with Arians, Socinians, and Deists. This was followed by a book by William Jones, Principal of Jesus College, Oxford, *The Catholic Doctrine of a Trinity*, published in 1756. The Wesleys were familiar with the debate, and Charles's *Hymns on the Trinity*, published eleven years later, took the structure of Jones's book as a blueprint. The first part of the collection adopted Jones's headings: Hymns on the Divinity of Christ, The Divinity of the Holy Ghost, The Plurality and Trinity of Persons, and the Trinity in Unity. The second part was entitled "Hymns and Prayers to the Trinity."

Jason Vickers has argued that Wesley's hymns to the Trinity, together with his earlier *Hymns on the Nativity of our Lord* (1745) must be taken into account against the general assumption that the doctrine of the Trinity had become a dead letter in eighteenth-century Protestant theology. While the systematic theologians had reduced it to a mere abstract statement that had to be defended intellectually against charges of incoherence, the hymns demonstrate that in the pastoral theology of the Wesleys, trinitarian doctrine and spiritual life were intimately connected.[9] The Trinity is made known to us in the economy: "The Father sent the Son, / His Spirit sent him too, / The everlasting Spirit filled, / And Jesus our salva-

9. Vickers, *Invocation and Assent.* See also Vickers, "And We the Life of God Shall Know," and Kimbrough, *Lyrical Theology.*

tion sealed." But that results in doxology: "Senders and Sent we praise, / With equal thanks approve / The economy of grace, / The Triune God of Love . . ."[10] But that knowledge of God, which becomes ours through the economy, results in praise of the eternal Trinity:

> Three Persons equally Divine
> We magnify and love:
> And both the quires erelong shall join
> To sing thy praise above:
> Hail holy, holy, holy Lord,
> (Our heavenly song shall be)
> Supreme, Essential One ador'd
> In co-eternal Three.[11]

The hymns of course carried "enormous theological freight" (according to David Tripp).[12] Barry E. Bryant called them "metrical theology,"[13] and the Wesley brothers explicitly intended them to be didactic. It is highly significant then that (according to Tripp), almost 25 percent of the hymns in the *Collection of Hymns for the Use of the People Called Methodists*, are "explicitly Trinitarian" in the sense that "all three Persons are unmistakably indicated." These are by no means abstract treatises, but pulsate with assurance and faith in the Triune God. Perhaps no better example can be given than the note of assurance that floods through, "Arise, my soul, arise," a hymn on the heavenly intercession of the crucified and ascended Christ. It becomes explicitly trinitarian in the final stanza:

> The Father hears him pray,
> His dear anointed One;
> He cannot turn away
> The presence of his Son:
> His Spirit answers to the blood,
> And tells me I am born of God.

Not only the hymns of Charles, but the writings of John also make clear that the doctrine of the Trinity was the deep underlying structure

---

10. Wesley, *Hymns on the Trinity*, 65f. Elmer Colyer comments on the "fascinating theological idea" in this verse that the Spirit also sends the Son, indicating that Charles did not think of the *monarchia* as restricted to the Father alone and seems to hint at "perichoretic co-activity." See Colyer, "Towards a Trinitarian Evangelical Wesleyan Theology."

11. Wesley, *Hymns on the Trinity*, 70.

12. Tripp, "Trinitarian Hymnody."

13. Bryant, "Trinity and Hymnody."

of their thought. At the beginning of the revival they were both intent on preaching salvation by faith and proclaiming the new birth, and evangelistic preaching along with the conserving of the fruit in the Methodist societies always remained their primary goal and task. To some extent therefore, intending to found, *not* a denomination, but a society for spiritual renewal within the national church, they took for granted to some extent (as evangelical Protestants generally do) the church's underlying trinitarian structure of Christian theology. But there were occasions when this deep structure became clear in John's writings. In the 1775 sermon, "On the Trinity," already mentioned, Wesley disavows in a strongly apophatic way the attempt to explain the mystery intellectually. We may understand the *fact*, but cannot comprehend the *manner*, and he instances many things that the ordinary person believes but does not comprehend.[14] But in manner reminiscent of Gregory of Nazianzus, he asserts that the spiritual experience of even the newest Christian is inherently trinitarian:

> The knowledge of the Three-One God is interwoven with all true Christian faith, with all vital religion. . . . I know not how anyone can be a Christian believer till "he hath" (as St John speaks) "the witness in himself" [1 John 5:10]; till "the Spirit of God witnesses with his spirit that he is a child of God" [Rom 8:16]—that is, in effect, till God the Holy Ghost witnesses that God the Father has accepted him through the merits of God the Son—and having this witness he honours the Son and the blessed Spirit "even as he honours the Father" [John 5:24].[15]

In the sermon, "Spiritual Worship," preached five years later, he presents a trinitarian hermeneutic for one of his favorite epistles, 1 John. And in his Letter to a Roman Catholic, he gives an exposition of the Nicene Creed in which he integrates dogmatics and spirituality. His doctrine of the Christian life is seen to be beautifully melded with the underlying doctrine of the Trinity. As a Protestant he believes: "That this one God is the Father of all things, especially of angels and men; that he is in a peculiar manner the Father of those whom he regenerates by his Spirit, whom he adopts in his Son, as co-heirs with him, and crowns with an eternal inheritance."

14. Sermon 55, *Works* (BE) 2:373–86.

15. Sermon 55, 385. Nazianzen frequently asserts that Christian faith is faith in the Holy Trinity. See, e.g., *Or.* 40, "On Holy Baptism," 16 (*NPNF*, 365: PG 36, 380B): "As long as you are a catechumen, you are but in the porch of religion; you must come inside, and cross the court, and examine the holy things, and look into the Holy of Holies, and be in company with the Trinity."

Similarly in expounding the second article of the creed, he adds the threefold office of Christ as prophet, revealing the whole will of God, as priest, giving himself as a sacrifice for sin and even now interceding for us, and as king who has all power in heaven and earth. In expounding the third article, he similarly adds to the creed the specific ministry of the Holy Spirit in the lives of Christians: "I believe in the infinite and eternal Spirit of God, equal with the Father and the Son, to be perfectly holy in himself, but the immediate cause of all holiness in us: enlightening our understandings, rectifying our wills and affections; uniting our persons to Christ, assuring us of the adoption of sons, leading us in our actions; purifying and sanctifying our souls and bodies, to a full and eternal enjoyment of God."[16]

Geoffrey Wainwright sees this passage as particularly important for its integration of trinitarian theology and Wesley's understanding of the *ordo salutis*, laid out most clearly in Sermon 43, "The Scripture Way of Salvation,"[17] and summarized in an often quoted passage from Sermon 85, "On Working Out Our Own Salvation."[18] That the Holy Spirit is "the immediate cause of all holiness in us" is seen in his work "enlightening our understandings," which may be taken as referring to "preventing [prevenient] grace." "Rectifying our wills and affections" is the operation of "convincing grace" or "repentance." "Renewing our natures" and "uniting our persons to Christ" may be seen as initial sanctification simultaneous with justification. "Assuring us of the adoption of sons" is another aspect of regeneration; and in the continuing work of "purifying and sanctifying our souls and bodies," the Spirit is leading us on to entire sanctification.[19]

The Christian pilgrimage will reach its climax in "The New Creation," when, "to crown all, there will be a deep, an intimate, and uninterrupted union with God; a constant communion with the Father and his Son Jesus Christ, through the Spirit; a continual enjoyment of the Three-One God, and of all the creatures in him!"[20]

It is possible to see too a trinitarian structure to Wesley's arrangement of his sermons for publication. It is not the usual structure of a systematic theology, beginning with God the Father in creation, going on to God the Son in salvation, and concluding with God the Holy Spirit at

---

16. *Works* (Jackson) 10:82.
17. *Works* (BE) 2:153–69.
18. *Works* (BE) 3:199–209, esp. 203f.
19. Wainwright, "Trinitarian Theology and Wesleyan Holiness."
20. *Works* (BE) 2:510.

work in the church and the believer. Rather Wesley's sermons focus first on justification in connection with Christ and the atonement, then on the Holy Spirit in the new birth and in assurance and sanctification, while all the time assuming the "sufficient, sovereign grace" of the Father "whose mercy is over all his works."[21] Nor is the way Wesley arranges his sermons just a surface matter. It reflects the "deep structure" of his theology. In an article rich in evidence, William Ury declares, "The Persons of the Trinity form the matrix of his pastoral theology."[22]

Elmer Colyer traces the sad decline of nineteenth-century Methodist theology, particularly in America, so that, "Towards the end of the nineteenth century in American Methodism, it is possible to be 'Wesleyan' and not be 'evangelical,' something unthinkable for early Methodists in England and America."[23] In theologians such as Daniel Whedon, "the Trinity simply fades into the background, as the philosophical anthropology and the doctrine of the one God they develop move into the foreground of theological construction."[24] In Borden Parker Bowne, "the marginalization of the Trinity is even more profound" since he "replaces the Trinitarian deep-structure of Wesleyan theology with a Personalist God-world relation." With John Cobb in the twentieth century, the deviation from the trinitarian faith continues: "The doctrine of the Trinity as affirmed by Wesley is not the deep-structure of Cobb's theology, rather it is the process panentheist God-world relation, and it plays a crucial defining role in the other theological loci."[25] In the systematic or doctrinal theologians, as in the philosophical theologians, Colyer sees a marginalization of the doctrine of the Trinity. This begins with Richard Watson who adopts a scholastic method foreign to Wesley. He attempts to deduce the doctrine of the Trinity from Scripture and thus he and his successors "consistently uproot the doctrine of the Trinity from its soteriological, evangelical and doxological matrix."[26] Even the rediscovery of Wesley as a theologian in the twentieth century has not given the doctrine of the Trinity its vital and key role in his thought. Colyer concludes:

> Here in Wesley I find an unashamed evangelical focus on the gospel, a broad catholic sensitivity and sensibility, and evidence

21. See Noble, "Wesley as a Theologian."
22. Ury, "A Wesleyan Concept of 'Person,'" 52.
23. Colyer, "Towards a Trinitarian Evangelical Wesleyan Theology," 182.
24. Ibid., 184.
25. Ibid., 186.
26. Ibid., 189.

for a deeply Trinitarian theology. More and more I have come to see latent in the work of the Wesley brothers a fully Trinitarian evangelical Wesleyan theology yet to be given comprehensive and architectonically rigorous expression, something John Wesley never attempted himself, and something American Methodism has generally neglected because of its foundational appeal to philosophical first principles and borrowing of theological form from outside the tradition, both of which have marginalized or eclipsed the Trinitarian insights of the Wesley brothers.[27]

Not only in American Methodism, but around the world, the Wesleyan tradition needs to rediscover its deep roots in the trinitarian faith that shaped the Wesleys as presbyters of the Church of England. Over a decade ago in Australia, Glen O'Brien examined what was perceived to be a polarization of the Wesleyan holiness movement into two positions, stressing either christological or pneumatological aspects of the doctrine of Christian holiness, and called in a comprehensive article for "A Trinitarian Revisioning of the Wesleyan Doctrine of Christian Perfection."[28] It is in that project that we are now engaged.

Having surveyed the contemporary debates on the doctrine of the Trinity and looked in this section at trinitarian theology in the Wesleys and their successors, we must now come to the question of how the doctrine of the Immanent Trinity, that God is eternally the Triune God, shapes our doctrine of Christian holiness, and particularly, Christian "perfecting." In this next section we shall think about how the lack of a trinitarian perspective in a would-be Christian monotheism can result in the distortion of the theology of Christian perfecting. Then we shall begin to think in the final section about how the recovery of a fully trinitarian doctrine could help to put our understanding of Christian perfecting on a sounder theological basis.

c) The Monotheistic Model: Holiness as Separation

Christians have always recognized that God alone is holy. Any holiness in creatures is derived from God, and can only be a pale shadow of the burning holiness of the God who is a consuming fire (Deut 4:24). Very often, therefore, the procedure in studying Christian holiness has been to begin with the holiness of God as first revealed in the Pentateuch. When word

27. Ibid., 192.

28. O'Brien, "Trinitarian Revisioning"

studies were a standard method of biblical theology, it was seen as significant that the root meaning of the word group *qds* (adjective *qadosh*, noun *qadesh*), translated as "holy" or "holiness," was "separate" or "set apart." An appeal was sometimes made to phenomenology of religion, particularly to Rudolf Otto's definition of "the Holy" as *mysterium tremendum et fascinans*.[29]

John Webster, in a book he describes as "a Trinitarian dogmatics of holiness," rejects the appeal to phenomenology: "Holiness is not simply Otto's famous *mysterium tremendum* or 'the quality of that which concerns man ultimately' (Tillich), or Derrida's 'unscathed which is safe and sound.' For a holy theology, abstractions like 'the holy' are best avoided, for what there is is the Holy One, the One known by the holy name, the One who has bared his holy arm. And for the knowledge of this One, what is required is exegesis of Holy Scripture."[30]

But even if we begin from Holy Scripture, it is possible to interpret it with a historian's hermeneutic or a literary hermeneutic, rather than a Christian theological hermeneutic. Such studies are of course relevant, and the study of the history of the concept from Old Testament times is valuable and indeed indispensable. But when we fail to read the Old Testament through the lens of the gospel it gives rise to two linked problems in our understanding of holiness and of God.

The first of these is that when the "holy" is contrasted with the "profane," and linked to the contrast between "pure" and "defiled" or "sinful," a rather negative understanding of holiness can result. It is true that in the history of the language, the root meaning of *quadosh* is the idea of separation. But when our understanding stops at this point and holiness is defined only in this way, as "separation," the danger is that, since it is regarded as out of the ordinary or exceptional, sinful existence then appears to be the normal, even the norm. When this was transferred into Hellenistic culture, imbued with Platonism, it tended to strengthen the idea of holiness as "other-worldly," ascetic, and world-denying. It was "spiritual" in the Hellenistic or Gnostic sense of devaluing and even despising physical life, particularly the life of the body. In this way, the opposition between the holy and the profane can come to be understood in a way quite contrary to the Old Testament emphasis on God's physical creation as "very good" (Gen 1:31).

---

29. Otto, *Holy.*
30. Webster, *Holiness.*

The second problem is the tendency to think that the doctrine of God is fully settled in the Old Testament, and to interpret it as a form of abstract monotheism, ignoring the doctrine of the Trinity. That God was the Triune God appeared to be irrelevant.[31] But while the Old Testament is essential to the Christian doctrine of God, it does not give a *fully* Christian doctrine of God, and it therefore cannot give a fully Christian understanding of holiness. Of course, the *Shema*, endorsed by Jesus himself, is an essential part of the Christian doctrine of God: "Hear, O Israel! The Lord our God is One" (Deut 6:4; Mark 12:29). Faced with the stubborn tendency for human religion to revert to some form of polytheism, it was only to be expected that Christians would stress monotheism, and even interpret the Old Testament as monotheistic. But in fact, much of the Old Testament promotes *monolatry* rather than monotheism. That is to say that Moses and the prophets are concerned that Israel should worship (*latreuō*) and serve one God, rather than with the abstract metaphysical question of interest to the Greeks as to whether more than one God existed.

Strong monotheism in reaction to pagan polytheism may also be seen to lie behind the tendency in some Christian traditions to give a higher priority to proclaiming that God is One than to proclaiming that God is Three. This is particularly a charge made against Western Christianity, whether Roman or Protestant. It is a charge particularly leveled by Karl Rahner against Thomas Aquinas, that in the structure of his *Summa Theologiae* he dealt first with *De Deo Uno*, On the One God, and only subsequently with *De Deo Trino*, On the Triune God.

The problem may be traced further back to Augustine, whose trinitarian theology certainly launched out in a new direction. He believed in the doctrine of the Trinity on the authority of the Holy Scriptures as interpreted by the church, and particularly received the doctrine of the Trinity through Ambrose from the Cappadocians. But whereas the theologians of the East had based their doctrine on God's action in the "economy" (*oikonomia*), that is, the gospel story of the Father's sending of the Son and the Spirit, Augustine looked around for an analogy to help him conceptualize the Trinity. On the basis of the teaching that the human being was in the image of God, he eventually hit on the analogy of the human mind or rational soul. Within the mind he found a trinity of memory, understanding, and will. The *memoria* is our latent reservoir of knowledge,

31. This approach to the holiness of God, beginning with the Old Testament and ignoring the doctrine of the Trinity was standard among Wesleyan theologians. See Atkinson, *Beauty*; Metz, *Biblical Holiness*; Purkiser, *Biblical Foundations*; Taylor, *Theological Formation*; and Oswalt, *Called*.

and *intelligentia* is that articulation of our knowledge of spiritual truth, particularly self-knowledge, which results when the will (*voluntas*) turns our attention in love (*amor*) to articulate what is already in the *memoria*.[32] This concept of the mind or "rational soul" as knowing itself and loving itself and therefore as a trinity of being, knowing, and loving, which was developed from Augustine's Platonist assumptions, gave him the model he was looking for. But subsequent Western theology became so fascinated by this "psychological analogy" and its implications for metaphysics, epistemology, and ethics, that it tended to displace the *oikonomia*, the story of salvation, as the root of the doctrine of the Trinity.

All this made the Western doctrine of the Trinity more abstruse and irrelevant, and it may also be seen as the root of Western rationalistic individualism. Nothing could be more individualistic than the Platonist view that the human being is essentially an eternal soul, which has always existed, will exist, and is inherently immortal because, being "spiritual," it shares the same substance as "the divine." Augustine discarded the Platonist view of the soul as eternal from eternity past, but he did tend to regard it as immortal, and by seeing the "rational soul" or mind as the definitive image of God, his trinitarian doctrine tended to conceive of God as one "Person" rather than as three.

Given this doctrine of God, in which the guiding model for thinking of God as Trinity is the rational soul of the individual, it is understandable that Christian holiness should be understood in individualistic terms. To be holy, the individual Christian had to *separate* herself from the world and focus introspectively upon her internal "spiritual" thought-life. The implication of this self-absorbed interiority was that the better she understood and loved herself, the better she understood and loved God. Conversely the deeper her knowledge and love of God, the deeper her self-knowledge and her self-love. The result could be a negative and even judgmental attitude towards "the world" along with a spirituality of withdrawal and individual introspection.[33] Strong transcendent monotheism could thus result in a spirituality that was in the image of an individualistic God of separation.

---

32. Augustine, *On the Trinity* (*De Trinitate*), X, 11 (17) (*NPNF*[1] 2:142). See Nash, *Light of the Mind* and Williams, "*De Trinitate.*"

33. See Jenson, *Gravity of Sin*, 38–46, on this curious tension in the Augustinian tradition in which sinfulness is self-centered desire and yet at the same time, the way to find God was through a spirituality of inwardness.

d) The Trinitarian Model:
Holiness as a Communion of Love

How then will our understanding of Christian holiness be affected if we shape our idea of the holy not from the concept of God as an isolated and solitary individual who keeps himself separate from the world, but as God the Holy Trinity?

In the great revival of trinitarian theology over the last seventy years or so, the prime movers, Barth and Rahner,[34] did not employ Augustine's psychological analogy. But they still thought of God as one single subject. But although Barth is to be given the credit for putting the doctrine of the Trinity back at the top of the theological agenda, it was his contemporary, Leonard Hodgson, Regius Professor of Divinity at Oxford, following the pioneering work of C. C. J. Webb and Lionel Thornton, who put forward a different analogy to Augustine's. This has become known as the "social analogy." Hodgson argued that the doctrine of the Trinity arose from the Christian experience of "adoptive sonship," our sharing by the gift of the Spirit in Jesus' intimate communion with the God he called "Father." The life of Christ was "a life of self-giving in response to the Father's love, through the Spirit. The doctrine of the Trinity is the projection into eternity of this essential relationship, the assertion that eternally the divine life is a life of mutual self-giving to one another of Father and Son through the Spirit who is the *vinculum* or bond of love between them."[35] Hodgson maintained, therefore, that Father, Son, and Holy Spirit must be Persons in the fullest sense (which he did not define), and that the life of God was therefore a "divine society."[36] Charles W. Lowry, an American Episcopal rector and professor, also argued that the doctrine of the Trinity arises from the Christian experience of *worship*, and went beyond Hodgson in speaking of the Persons of the Trinity as three "centers of consciousness."[37]

Jürgen Moltmann became one of the most explicit and prominent advocates of the social analogy towards the end of the twentieth century, going so far as to repudiate the term "monotheism" as insufficiently Christian![38] John T. Zizioulas, Metropolitan of Pergamon, similarly op-

---

34. This final section is a summary of part of the argument of Noble, "East and West."

35. Hodgson, *Trinity*, 68.

36. Welch, *This Name*, 140.

37. Lowry, *Trinity*, 26.

38. Moltmann, *Trinity*.

posed the tendency of Western theology to make the unity of God prior to the tri-unity. According to Zizioulas, the significant point of the doctrine of the Trinity held by the Cappadocians was that they did not see the *ousia* or "being" of God as the guarantee of unity, as if the *ousia* were some fourth entity ontologically superior to the three Persons (*hypostases*). That was the problem with the trinitarian thinking of Tertullian and the Latin West, according to Zizioulas, and it would have brought the church back to the Greek ontology, the supremacy of impersonal *ousia* and therefore of necessary processes which denied personal freedom. Rather, for the Cappadocians, the guarantee of the unity of the Trinity was the Father, who was the *archē*, the "origin" or "source," of the Son and the Spirit. This point is absolutely crucial, says Zizioulas:

> Thus when we say that God "is," we do not bind the personal freedom of God—the being of God is not an ontological "necessity" . . . but we ascribe the being of God to his personal freedom. . . . God as Father and not as substance, perpetually confirms through "being" his *free* will to exist. And it is precisely his Trinitarian existence that constitutes this confirmation: the Father out of love—that is, freely—begets the Son, and brings forth the Spirit. Thus God as Person—as the hypostasis of the Father—makes the one divine substance to be what it is: the one God.[39]

Both Moltmann and Zizioulas and the other theologians who have advocated some kind of social analogy for the Trinity need to be subjected to some acute questions. Moltmann appears to be coming very close to some form of Tritheism, his panentheism also appears to depart from the aseity and transcendence of God, and on some points his egalitarian political and social views, rather than the revelation of God in Christ, seem to be determining his doctrine. On the other hand, Zizioulas's doctrine of the Father seems to call in question the equality of the Persons of the Trinity and he seems to be operating with the assumption that the word "person" means the same when referring to God as when referring to humanity.[40] Further, T. F. Torrance has pointed out that the *ousia* or Being of God can never be thought of as "impersonal": "The Being of God is the personal, living and active Being, fellowship-seeking and communion-constituting Being, but if it is fellowship-seeking and communion-con-

---

39. Zizioulas, *Being as Communion*, 41.

40. See McCall, *Which Trinity?*, and Holmes, *Holy Trinity*, for recent critique of the "social Trinity."

stituting towards his human children, it is the fruit among men of the ever-living and productive Communion which God's being is *ad intra*."[41] But the essential point that we are concerned with stands: that it is because God is Tri-personal that he is the source of all personhood and all sentient, intelligent, personal, relational life.

Much that is said by Hodgson, Moltmann, and Zizioulas will ring bells with Wesleyan theologians, particularly perhaps the emphases on personhood and human freedom. But, despite Zizioulas's claim for the Cappadocians, there is one concept essential to the idea of the "social Trinity" that is oddly missing from their trinitarian theology. It is a word or concept that is fully biblical, and that is highly significant in the views of the "social Trinity" in Hodgson, Zizioulas, and Moltmann. But it is just not present in the trinitarian theology of the Cappadocians, nor for that matter, in the trinitarian thought of Athanasius or Clement and Origen. It is the concept of *love*. Clearly the idea of love is vitally important to the modern concept of personhood and to any Christian idea of true community. More than that, from a Wesleyan perspective, this is a vital element, indeed the *central* element in Wesley's concept of Christian "perfection." Indeed, in this, Wesleyan spiritual theology accurately reflects the spiritual theology of the Eastern Fathers who all characterize the highest stages of spiritual advancement as perfection in love. So, if the "social Trinity" is to provide a trinitarian understanding of what it is to be truly personal or a trinitarian understanding of Christian perfection, this must be an element. Yet a brief scanning of the Eastern Fathers reveals that while love is present in their doctrine of the Christian life, it is scarcely present at all in their doctrine of the Trinity. We search in vain for any significant appearance of the concept of love.

So where did it come from? Who made love a significant concept, not just the love of God for humanity or humanity for God, but in the articulation of the doctrine of the Trinity? The answer is evident in the quotation from Leonard Hodgson about the mutual self-giving of the Father and the Son through the Holy Spirit who is the *vinculum*, the bond of love between them. The source of such language is beyond dispute Augustine. Augustine is the great theologian of love. Perhaps, as in other things, the seed of his thought is to be found in the Cappadocians (at least in Gregory of Nyssa). But Augustine is the one who develops this line of thought so

---

41. Torrance, *Theological Science*, 132 (*ad intra* may be taken to mean "internally"). Torrance's Trinitarian theology holds out the best hope of combining the concerns for divine Unity with the concerns of the social Trinitarians.

that not only is the doctrine of the Trinity the key to the spiritual life of love, but our understanding of love becomes the key to the doctrine of the Trinity.[42]

Love was a key theme for Augustine long before he became the great theologian of grace. Already in *De Moribus Ecclesiae Catholicae* (*On the Ethics of the Catholic Church*),[43] written the year after his baptism, the focus of his eudaemonistic ethics is on love. But the concept of love is not only the key to Augustine's ethics: as we have seen, it also becomes the key to his psychology, and particularly his model of human motivation. John Burnaby, in his classic work, *Amor Dei* (sub-titled *A Study of Augustine's Teaching on the Love of God as the Motive of the Christian Life*), comments that at this early point in his career represented by the *De Moribus*, Augustine's concept of love is almost pure *erōs*.[44] Yet already we see him linking love in the Christian with the Persons of the Trinity. But it is in his great work, *On the Trinity*, that Augustine develops the idea of love as vital to our understanding of our Trinitarian God.

In the final book of *On the Trinity*, Book XV, Augustine recalls that in an earlier book, Book VIII, "when we came to treat of love, which in the Holy Scriptures is called 'God' (1 John 4:10), then a trinity began to dawn on us a little, that is, one that loves, that which is loved, and love." He ruminates at length on this and on his trinity of memory, understanding, and will. He will not allow that the Father alone is to be understood as *memoria*, the Son alone as *intelligentia*, or the Spirit alone as *voluntas* or *amor*. All three are One. And yet, he links the concept of love particularly (though not exclusively) with the Holy Spirit: "And the Holy Spirit, according to the Holy Scriptures, is neither of the Father alone, nor of the Son alone, but of both, and so intimates to us a mutual love wherewith the Father and Son reciprocally love one another." This is of course the origin of the famous *filioque* phrase, which the Western church later added to the creed without getting the approval of an ecumenical council: that the Holy Spirit "proceeds from the Father (*ex patre*) and the Son (*filioque*)." But the key point for us to note here is that this is the outworking of the vision of the Holy Trinity as a communion (*koinōnia*) of love. Augustine here makes unprecedented use of the doctrine of God's love in 1 John

---

42. That Augustine is the one who speaks of love among the Three, surely a necessary element in a "social" analogy for the Trinity, should make us hesitate to take a too simplistic version of the de Régnon thesis that the West began with the One while the East began with the Three.

43. *NPNF*[1] 4:411–63.

44. Burnaby, *Amor*, 89.

particularly to articulate his doctrine of the Trinity. We are to think of the Holy Trinity not just in categories of ontological relations of origin, as the Cappadocians did—being (*ousia*), origin (*archē*), cause (*aitia*), begetting (*genēsia*) and procession (*ekporeusis*), substance or subsistence (*hypostasis*), and nature (*physis*)—but by using the category of interpersonal relationship, love. And since, for the Platonist Augustine, love is a substance, this is also ontological.

John Zizioulas, as an Orthodox bishop, rejects the *filioque*, of course, but he takes up the idea of the Holy Trinity as a communion in his influential book, *Being as Communion*.[45] And although he is not a Platonist, like Augustine he sees this as ontological. He argues that the old pagan Greek philosophical categories of being, *ousia*, and *hypostasis*, were categories of an impersonal ontology. For Greek philosophy, only the impersonal was real. The impression that persons were real and could change the course of events was illusory. He sees that as the underlying theme of ancient Greek drama. Each role or character in the drama wore a *prosōpon*, a "face" or "mask" (in Latin, a *persona*). The hero acted to change the course of events, but failed. The Fates had already determined the future and therefore the idea that living persons were real and could really alter the course of history was false. The tragedy was that the admirable hero therefore perished when he tried. But a revolution in the history of thought was brought about, according to Zizioulas, when Greek Christian theology distinguished between *ousia* (translated strictly as "being," but sometimes confusingly as "substance") and *hypostasis* (substance or subsistence) in the doctrine of the Trinity, and equated the latter with *prosōpon* or *persona*. Where the Latin West spoke of three "Persons" in one "substance," the Greek East spoke of three *hypostases* in one *ousia*. That implied that Persons (*prosōpa* or *personae*) had real substance (*hypostasis*) or being. This development in the doctrine of the Trinity had consequences in anthropology, for it implied that human persons were real, could really act freely, and were responsible for their actions.

Our modern concept of the "person," which we assume applies primarily to human beings, actually originated then in trinitarian theology. It is because we came to speak of the Father, the Son, and the Holy Spirit as "Persons" that we began to conceive what it means for human beings to be regarded as "persons." Unfortunately however, partly because of Boethius's definition of a "person" as "an individual substance of rational nature," we came to equate being a person with being a self-contained, self-existent,

45. Zizioulas, *Being as Communion*.

self-sufficient, separate "individual" who is able to think and feel and will. But, in fact, the key point about the Christian doctrine of the Trinity was the assertion that these three Persons are *one*. They have no being or existence except in their *interpersonal relations*. There was no substratum of impersonal being (*ousia*), conceived of as some kind of material or stuff, which united the Persons as one. What unites them is their *koinōnia*, their communion. However, that is to be seen as an *ontological* statement. The communion *is* their being (*ousia*). One cannot separate their being from their interpersonal relations. They do not first exist and *then* relate to each other. They exist (or better "subsist") *in* their relationship to each other. The words "begotten" or "proceed" are not to be understood impersonally, materially, or semi-physically. Rather they are to be understood as meaning that the three Persons have their very Being as they are from, to, and in each other in a fully *personal* way. They do not exist independently as separate monads or "individuals" for whom personal relationships are optional or added characteristics. They have their very Being in mutual indwelling (*perichōrēsis*), for as the One God they are indivisible (*indivisa*). God is three *Persons*, but not three individuals. In fact, we have to say that God is three Persons, but one Individual. God is an indivisible Unity of three Persons who have their very Being from and to and in each other.[46]

This brings us then to the question of why we speak of the *Holy* Trinity. What constitutes the holiness of God? Is the Triune God "holy" because he is separate from sin and sinners? Surely the reverse has to be the truth. He is separate from sinners because he is holy. If we ask the question, "Is God eternally holy?" the Christian has to answer yes. But if then God was holy "before the foundation of the world" (John 17:5, AV)—that is to say, before there were any sinners or any sin to be separate from—then we need some more positive understanding of what holiness is. The doctrine of the Trinity suggests that the eternal holiness of God consists in the fact that he is a communion of interpersonal love. The fullest possible understanding of what it means to say, "God is holy," is to say "God is love" (1 John 4:8).

But we must take a further step. Love implies grace, which means *gift*. In love the Father and the Son *give* themselves to each other in the unity of the Holy Spirit. And such is the rich power of that interpersonal *self-giving* love that the love between them, the "bond of love," has to be viewed as the mysterious, but truly third, Person who is (as Tom Smail has

---

46. See T. F. Torrance, *Theological Science*, 168–202, a chapter entitled, "Trinity in Unity and Unity in Trinity."

put it) "the Giving Gift."[47] What is more, such is the power and creativity of that divine love of the Holy Trinity that the Triune God freely chooses to create a world with creatures who will reflect the love shared among the divine Persons in such a way that the creatures become, not merely impersonal lumps of mud or clay formed by the potter, but, miraculously, fully *personal* human beings, reflecting the free interpersonal love of the Father, the Son, and the Holy Spirit. It is sin, not holiness, that is then seen to be exceptional and negative in that it is divisive and destructive. But the appearance of sin calls forth love and compassion in the form of the One who is the greatest Love of all, the Love Incarnate who is "Love divine, all loves excelling."

In the light then of creation and redemption, we cannot speak of God as a self-contained fellowship of love. Without compromising God's *aseity*, or self-sufficiency, we have to speak of the Triune God under the only conditions we have known or can know him, because he has included us "in Christ" within the circle of Triune love and fellowship. John Webster puts the point like this: "Holiness, because it is the holiness of the God and Father of our Lord Jesus Christ now present in the Spirit's power, is pure majesty in relation. . . . Majesty and relation are not opposed moments in God's holiness; they are simply different articulations of the self-same reality." He sums up the point: "In short: the holiness manifest in the works of the majestic triune God is manifest as *personal, moral relation*, as relation between the Persons of the Holy Trinity and the creatures whom God summons into holy fellowship with himself."[48]

Only then within the church—which is the fellowship (*koinōnia*) of the Father and the Son in the Holy Spirit and within which the Spirit *includes* us by uniting us to Christ—can we articulate what the holiness of God is. We can only speak truly of the holiness of God within that fellowship that is the reflection of, and the participation by the Spirit in, the fellowship of the Holy Trinity. The church corporately (rather than merely the individual Christian) is the image of God that reflects God's holiness.

e) The Church as the Image of the Holy Trinity

What then, in the light of such an understanding of the Holy Trinity as a communion of love, must "Christian holiness" look like? Zizioulas and Miroslav Volf have both suggested that the church is to be seen as the

47. Smail, *Giving Gift*.
48. Webster, *Holiness*, 41–43.

image of the Holy Trinity, but then each of them finds in the doctrine of the Trinity (perhaps somewhat suspiciously) a basis for his own preferred ecclesiology! Zizioulas finds that the episcopal structure of the Orthodox Church mirrors the Trinity, while Volf finds the same for the Congregationalist or Independent doctrine of the church.[49] We evidently need to take the greatest care that we do not read into the doctrine of the Trinity what we want to see reflected in the human sphere. But perhaps two points may be briefly noted about Christian holiness as a reflection of the Holy Trinity that may open up new areas for exploration.

First, we cannot think of Christian holiness in a merely individualistic way. That has perhaps been one of the major failings, not just of Wesleyan thinking, but of all evangelical Protestant thinking. We have succumbed to the spirit of the age in concentrating sometimes almost exclusively on the journey of salvation, the *ordo* or *via salutis*, of the individual. Correspondingly, we have largely neglected our doctrine of the church. We further succumbed to typically "modern" ways of thinking in conceiving of the church as simply a "collection" of individuals. But this way of thinking of human beings *collectively* is the same kind of "modern" rationalist thinking we see in Marxism or various forms of political liberalism where individuals are treated as part of "collectives," classes of people segregated economically as "consumers," or "workers," or politically as voters or elites, or socially according to age groups or social class. This collectivism and its accompanying commercialism infiltrate the church when we apply techniques of mass production to conversions, or shape churches primarily to be "seeker-friendly," giving that greater priority than being reflections of the missional Trinity.[50] Rather than thinking of the basic unit of humanity as the *individual* so that individuals have to be herded into *collectives*, we need to learn to think instead more biblically of the basic unit of humanity as the family, the *corporate* body within which true *personhood* is brought to birth and so to maturity.

The doctrine of the Trinity as a community of interpersonal love suggests then that we are going to have to think of the church as *corporate*, modeled on the family, rather than as a "collective" modeled on the business organization or the state. Only in such a context can we think of human beings as "persons" rather than as "individuals." The communion or fellowship (*koinōnia*) of the church is then understood *to be* in fact the communion or fellowship of the Holy Trinity. It is by the Spirit that

49. Zizioulas, *Being as Communion*, and Volf, *Our Likeness*.

50. See Drane, *McDonaldization*.

we are able to say, "Our fellowship is with the Father and with his Son Jesus Christ" (1 John 1:3). And it is only within the loving fellowship of the church that "perfect love," that is to say, mature, whole-hearted, self-denying love, becomes a possibility. Young Christians can never mature to the point where they love God with all their hearts, unless they are nurtured within a church community that has just that quality of love from those who are mature in the faith. Sanctified people are nurtured within genuinely holy, that is, *loving*, church fellowships. It is worth remembering that Paul's great prayer that the Christians at Thessalonica be sanctified "wholly" or "entirely" (1 Thess 5:23) is not addressed to individuals within that church but in the plural to the Thessalonian church as a whole. Similarly the great prayer of Ephesians 3 and the call to Christian maturity in Ephesians 4 are both addressed to the church as a body.

Perhaps we may plead that, despite the individualistic focus of much of our traditional preaching about sanctification, in fact our practice has been better than our preaching. Even Wesley's preaching on Christian holiness concentrates on the individual, but it was the warm *fellowship* of what were significantly called Methodist "Societies" that were the matrix of holy love which produced genuine Methodist saints. And his revival of the ancient "love feast" (the *agapē*), along with his strong emphasis on the importance of the Lord's Supper, which is after all not just a "Eucharist" (Thanksgiving), but "Holy Communion" (*hagia koinōnia*), was at the heart of his creative organization of the Methodist Societies. Too many of Wesley's heirs have lost that focus, being influenced by a "low church" suspicion of liturgy, but a recovery of the church as the matrix for Christian holiness will necessarily include a rediscovery of the centrality of the sacraments.[51]

But secondly, to reflect the Holy Trinity, the church must not be wrapped up in itself. Such was the power of love, one might say the "ferment" of love, within the Holy Trinity, that the Triune God freely created a world which was other than God. Creation was therefore an act of grace in which the Holy Trinity willed not only to create a material universe in all its vast splendor, but to create within that a race who could be given personhood and interpersonal life, truly reflecting the interpersonal love and communion of the Father, the Son, and the Holy Spirit. What is more, given the scandal and disgrace and disruption of human sin and rebellion, that holy love of God, while it took the form of the grieving wrath and

51. Among significant works on the sacraments by Wesleyan theologians, see Wainwright, *Eucharist*, and Staples, *Outward Sign*.

wrathful grief of a wronged parent or spouse, was moved simultaneously to a powerfully self-sacrificing compassion. To reflect that, Christian holiness must not only take a corporate form in loving fellowships within which persons are nurtured, but it must also take the form of mission, centered in evangelism, the preaching and embodying of the gospel, the good news of the compassionate Savior. Faced with the appalling evil and suffering of the world, such corporate Christian holiness, while reacting often with God's grieving wrath at injustice, abuse, and exploitation, must be redemptive rather than judgmental. Only within a church whose holiness reflects in that way the holiness of the Triune God can genuinely holy people who are deeply committed to mission be nurtured.

And yet we must not think that mission is the *ultimate* purpose of the church of Jesus Christ: it is only its *penultimate* purpose. Even when we realize that the mission of the church is not its own mission, but God's, the *missio Dei*:

> The *missio Dei* is not the End. Or to put that another way, the End will end the mission. Continuing the *missio Dei* is not the ultimate purpose of God and so mission is not the ultimate purpose of the church. At the End, the *eschaton*, the end of "the present evil age" (Galatians 1:4), the mission will be completed . . . at "the End of the Age," the *missio Dei* will end. It will be completed. That is vitally important because it means that while mission is an integral and essential part of the nature of the church in this age, it is not what ultimately makes the church to be the church. The church will still be the church, the body of Christ, in the age to come. The salvation of the world through the *missio Dei* is therefore the *penultimate* purpose of the church, but the *ultimate* purpose of the church is *the glory of God*.[52]

That implies then that the ultimate purpose of the church—the one, holy, catholic, apostolic church—is the worship of the Triune God. That will be the life of the church in the age to come, and that is the heart of the *raison d'être* of the church today.[53]

Alan J. Torrance, in arguing that Barth was wrong to try to dispense with the term "Person" in the doctrine of the Trinity, comes to the conclusion that the "revelation model" he proposed, helpful though it is, has to

---

52. Noble, "The Mission," 83.

53. See Wainwright, *Doxology*, for a Christian Theology worked out from Christian worship.

give way to the "doxological model."[54] According to that model, worship or doxology must not be understood as a task, something *we* must *do*. That is a Pelagian view of worship. We could call it a commercial view. Rather, worship has to be understood as *gift*. It is Christ, our great high priest, who is the true worshipper, the truly human Human who leads us in our worship. Worship is participating by the Spirit in the Son's joyous communion with the Father. When we join in that worship, it is by grace (*charis*). It is the gift (*charisma*) of being allowed to participate in the Incarnate Son's worshipping response to the love of the Father in the fellowship of the Holy Spirit.[55] It is done not to gain anything, or achieve anything, or win anything, or produce anything. It is simply the sheer joy of participating in the loving relationship between the Persons of the Holy Trinity, knowing that in doing so, we are united with all the human persons redeemed to be part of that eternal joyous fellowship.[56] "Worthship" is recognizing that it is these three Persons who are of supreme worth. Loving and enjoying the three Persons for their own sakes, and *therefore* loving and enjoying human persons for their own sakes, is what holiness is all about. That is the communion of perfect love to which the God and Father of our Lord Jesus Christ has destined us (Eph 1:3–10).

No wonder Charles Wesley could engage in ecstatic trinitarian worship:

> Father of everlasting grace,
> Thy goodness and Thy truth we praise;
> Thy goodness and Thy truth we prove;
> Thou hast, in honour of Thy Son,
> The gift unspeakable sent down,
> The Spirit of life, and power, and love.
>
> Send us the Spirit of Thy Son,
> To make the depths of Godhead known,
> To make us share the life divine;
> Send Him the sprinkled blood to apply,
> Send him our souls to sanctify,
> And show and seal us ever Thine.

54. Torrance, *Persons in Communion*, 307ff.

55. This was presented by Torrance's father, James B. Torrance, in his Didsbury Lectures: see J. B. Torrance, *Worship*.

56. See Dawn, *Royal "Waste."*

Holy Trinity: Holy People

So shall we pray, and never cease,
So shall we thankfully confess,
Thy wisdom, truth, and power, and love;
With joy unspeakable adore,
And bless and praise Thee evermore,
And serve Thee with Thy hosts above.

Till, added to that heavenly choir,
We raise our songs of triumph higher,
And praise Thee in a bolder strain,
Out-soar the first-born seraph's flight,
And sing, with all our friends in light,
Thy everlasting love to man.

Bibliography

Abraham, William J. *Aldersgate and Athens: John Wesley and the Foundations of Christian Belief.* Waco, TX: Baylor, 2010.

———. "Christian Perfection." In *The Oxford Handbook of Methodist Studies,* edited by William J. Abraham and James E. Kirby, 587–601. Oxford: Oxford University Press, 2009.

———. "What Should United Methodists Do with the Quadrilateral?" *Quarterly Review* 22 (2002) 85–88.

Alexander, Donald L., editor. *Christian Spirituality: Five Views of Sanctification.* Downers Grove, IL: InterVarsity, 1988.

Anselm of Canterbury. *Why God Became Man.* Translated by Joseph M. Colleran. Albany, NY: Magi, 1969.

Ashwin-Siejkowski, Piotr. *Clement of Alexandria: A Project of Christian Perfection.* London: T. & T. Clark, 2008.

Atkinson, J. Baines. *The Beauty of Holiness.* London: Epworth, 1953.

Aulén, Gustaf. *Christus Victor.* London: SPCK, 1931.

Bachmann, E. Theodore, editor. *Luther's Works* (American Edition). Vol. 35. Philadelphia: Muilenberg, 1960.

Barr, James. "Abba, Father." *Theology* 91 (1988) 173–79.

———. *The Semantics of Biblical Language.* Oxford: Oxford University Press, 1961.

Barton, Stephen C. *Holiness Past and Present.* London: T. & T. Clark, 2003.

Bassett, Paul M., and William M. Greathouse. *The Historical Development.* Vol. 2 of *Exploring Christian Holiness.* Kansas City: Beacon Hill, 1985.

Bauckham, Richard, and Benjamin Drewery. *Scripture, Tradition and Reason: A Study in the Criteria of Christian Doctrine.* Edinburgh: T. & T. Clark, 1988.

Bauckham, Richard. "The Holiness of Jesus and His Disciples in the Gospel of John." In *Holiness and Ecclesiology in the New Testament,* edited by Kent E. Brower and Andy Johnson, 95–113. Grand Rapids: Eerdmans, 2007.

———. "The Origins and Growth of Western Mariology." In *Chosen by God: Mary in Evangelical Perspective,* edited by David F. Wright, 141–60. London: Marshall Pickering, 1989.

Berger, Teresa. *Theology in Hymns?* Nashville, TN: Kingswood, 1995.

Bettenson, Henry. *The Early Christian Fathers.* Oxford: Oxford University Press, 1956.

Boersma, Hans. *Violence, Hospitality and the Cross.* Grand Rapids: Baker, 2004.

Borg, Marcus J. *Conflict, Holiness, and Politics in the Teachings of Jesus.* Harrisburg, PA: Trinity, 1984.

Braaten, Carl E. and Robert W. Jenson, editors. *Union with Christ: The New Finnish Interpretation of Luther.* Grand Rapids: Eerdmans, 1998.

Bray, Gerald L. *Holiness and the Will of God: Perspectives on the Theology of Tertullian.* London: Marshall, Morgan and Scott, 1979.

Brower, Kent E. *Holiness in the Gospels.* Kansas City: Beacon Hill, 2005.

———. *Living as God's Holy People: Holiness and Community in Paul.* The Didsbury Lectures Series. Milton Keynes, UK: Paternoster, 2010.

Brower, Kent E., and Andy Johnson, editors. *Holiness and Ecclesiology in the New Testament.* Grand Rapids: Eerdmans, 2007.

Brown, Warren S., Nancey Murphy, and H. Newton Maloney, editors. *Whatever Happened to the Soul? Scientific and Theological Portraits of Human Nature.* Minneapolis: Fortress, 1998.

Brownlie, John. *Hymns of the Early Church.* London: Morgan & Scott, 1913.

Brueggemann, Walter. *Theology of the Old Testament: Testimony, Dispute, Advocacy.* Minneapolis: Fortress, 1997.

Bryant, Barry E. "Trinity and Hymnody: The Doctrine of the Trinity in the Hymns of Charles Wesley." *Wesleyan Theological Journal* 25 (1990) 64–73.

Bullen, Donald A. *A Man of One Book?: John Wesley's Interpretation and Use of the Bible.* Studies in Christian History and Thought. Milton Keynes, UK: Paternoster, 2007.

Burnaby, John. *Amor Dei: A Study of Augustine's Teaching on the Love of God as the Motive of the Christian Life.* [1938]. New edition with an introduction by Oliver O'Donovan. Norwich, UK: Canterbury, 1990.

Burton-Christie, Douglas. "The Place of the Heart: Geography and Spirituality in the *Life of Antony.*" In *Purity of Heart in Early Ascetic and Monastic Literature*, edited by Harriet A. Luckman and Linda Kulzer, 45–65. Collegeville, MN: Liturgical, 1999.

Calvin, John. *Institutes of the Christian Religion.* Translated by Henry Beveridge. Peabody, MA: Hendrickson, 2008

Campbell, Ted A. "The Interpretive Role of Tradition." In *Wesley and the Quadrilateral: Renewing the Conversation*, edited by Stephen W. Gunter et al., 63–75. Nashville, TN: Abingdon, 1997.

———. *John Wesley and Christian Antiquity: Religious Vision and Cultural Change.* Nashville, TN: Kingswood, 1991.

———. *Wesleyan Beliefs: Formal and Popular Expressions of the Core Beliefs of Wesleyan Communities.* Nashville, TN: Kingswood, 2010.

Cell, George Croft. *The Rediscovery of John Wesley.* New York: Holt, 1935.

Cheatle, Andrew J. *W. E. Sangster: Herald of Holiness.* Milton Keynes, UK: Paternoster, 2010.

Christensen, Michael J., and Jeffery A. Wittung, editors. *Partakers of the Divine Nature: The Development of Deification in the Christian Traditions.* Grand Rapids: Baker, 2007.

Christensen, Michael J. "John Wesley: Christian Perfection as Faith Filled with the Energy of Love." In *Partakers of the Divine Nature: The Development of Deification in the Christian Traditions*, edited by Christensen and Wittung, 219–29. Grand Rapids: Baker, 2007.

Clapper, Gregory S. *John Wesley on Religious Affections.* Metuchen, NJ: Scarecrow, 1989.

Coakley, Sarah. *Powers and Submissions: Spirituality, Philosophy and Gender.* Oxford: Blackwell, 2002.

————. *Sacrifice Regained*. Cambridge: CUP, 2009.

Collins, Kenneth J., editor. *Exploring Christian Spirituality: An Ecumenical Reader.* Grand Rapids: Baker, 2000.

————. *The Theology of John Wesley: Holy Love and the Shape of Grace*. Nashville, TN: Abingdon, 2007.

Collins, Kenneth J., and John H. Tyson, editors. *Conversion in the Wesleyan Tradition.* Nashville, TN: Abingdon, 2001.

Colón-Emeric, Edgardo. *Wesley, Aquinas and Christian Perfection: An Ecumenical Dialogue*. Waco, TX: Baylor, 2009.

Colyer, Elmer M. "Towards a Trinitarian Evangelical Wesleyan Theology." In *Alister E. McGrath and Evangelical Theology: A Dynamic Engagement*, edited by Sung Wook Chung, 165–94. Carlisle, UK: Paternoster, 2003.

Congregational Praise. London: Independent, 1951.

Coppedge, Allan. *The God Who Is Triune*. Downers Grove, IL: InterVarsity, 2007.

Cunningham, Joseph. "Perceptible Inspiration: A Model for John Wesley's Pneumatology." PhD thesis, University of Manchester, 2010.

Daniélou, Jean. *From Glory to Glory: Texts from Gregory of Nyssa's Mystical Writings.* Crestwood, NY: St Vladimir's, 1961.

Dawn, Marva J. *A Royal "Waste" of Time: The Splendour of Worshipping God and Being Church for the World*. Grand Rapids: Eerdmans, 1999.

Dayton, Donald W. "Asa Mahan and the Development of the American Holiness Theology." *Wesleyan Theological Journal* 9 (1974) 60–67.

————. "The Doctrine of the Baptism of the Holy Spirit: Its Emergence and Significance." *Wesleyan Theological Journal* 13 (1978) 114–26.

Deasley, A. R. G. "Entire Sanctification and the Baptism with the Holy Spirit: Perspectives on the Biblical View of the Relationship." *Wesleyan Theological Journal* 14 (1979) 27–44.

Dreuille, Mayeul de. *Seeking the Absolute Love: The Founders of Christian Monasticism.* Leominster, UK: Gracewing, 1999.

Denney, James. *The Death of Christ*. 1902. Reprint. London: Tyndale, 1951.

Descartes, René. *Discourse on Method*. Translated by Arthur Wollaston. Harmondsworth, UK: Penguin, 1960.

Dix, Gregory, and Henry Chadwick, editors. *The Treatise on the Apostolic Tradition of St Hippolytus of Rome*. New York: Routledge, 1992.

Dorries, David W. *Edward Irving's Incarnational Christology*. Fairfax, VA: Xulon, 2002.

Drane, John. *The McDonaldization of the Church: Spirituality, Creativity, and the Future of the Church*. London: Darton, Longman & Todd, 2000.

Dunning, H. Ray. *Reflecting the Divine Image: Christian Ethics in Wesleyan Perspective.* Downers Grove, IL: InterVarsity, 1998.

Earle, Ralph H., Jr, and Mark R. Laaser. *The Pornography Trap: Setting Pastors and Laypersons Free from Sexual Addiction*. Kansas City: Beacon Hill, 2002.

Eugenio, Dick Osita. "Communion with God: The Trinitarian Soteriology of T. F. Torrance." PhD thesis, University of Manchester, 2011.

Evans, G. R. *Bernard of Clairvaux: Selected Works*. New York: Paulist, 1987.

Fairweather, Eugene R., editor. *A Scholastic Miscellany: Anselm to Ockham*. Library of Christian Classics, Vol. 10. London: SCM, 1956.

Finlan, Stephen, and Vladimir Kharlamov, editors. *Theōsis: Deification in Christian Theology*. 2 vols. Eugene, OR: Pickwick, 2006, 2011.

Flemming, Dean. "'On Earth as It Is in Heaven': Holiness and the People of God in Revelation." In *Holiness and Ecclesiology in the New Testament*, edited by Kent E. Brower and Andy Johnson, 343–62. Grand Rapids: Eerdmans, 2007.

Flew, Robert Newton. *The Idea of Perfection in Christian Theology: An Historical Study of the Christian Ideal for the Present Life*. Oxford: Clarendon, 1934.

Forsyth, P. T. *The Cruciality of the Cross*. London: Independent Press, 1909.

———. *The Work of Christ*. London: Hodder & Stoughton, 1910.

Foss, Martin. *The Idea of Perfection in the Western World*. Princeton, NJ: Princeton University Press, 1946.

Gadamer, H. G. *Truth and Method*. [1965]. Translated by Joel Weinsheimer and Donald G. Marshall. London: Sheed and Ward, 1975.

Gammie, John T. *Holiness in Israel*. Minneapolis: Fortress, 1989.

Gilby, Thomas. *St Thomas Aquinas: Theological Texts*. 1955. Reprint. Durham, NC: Labyrinth, 1982.

Gillette, Gertrude. "Purity of Heart in St Augustine." In *Purity of Heart in Early Ascetic and Monastic Literature*, edited by Harriet A. Luckman and Linda Kulzer, 175–95. Collegeville, MN: Liturgical, 1999.

Golitizin, Alexander. "Temple and Throne of the Divine Glory: 'Pseudo-Macarius and Purity of Heart, Together with Some Remarks on the Limitations and Usefulness of Scholarship.'" In *Purity of Heart in Early Ascetic and Monastic Literature*, edited by Harriet A. Luckman and Linda Kulzer, 107–29. Collegeville, MN: Liturgical, 1999.

Gorman, Michael J. "'You Shall Be Cruciform for I Am Cruciform': Paul's Trinitarian Reconstruction of Holiness." In *Holiness and Ecclesiology in the New Testament*, edited by Kent E. Brower and Andy Johnson, 148–66. Grand Rapids: Eerdmans, 2007.

Grass, Tim. *The Lord's Watchman: A Life of Edward Irving* (1792–1834). Eugene, OR: Wipf and Stock, 2012.

Greathouse, William M. *Romans 1–8: A Commentary in the Wesleyan Tradition*. Kansas City: Beacon Hill Press, 2008.

———. "Sanctification and the *Christus Victor* Motif in Wesleyan Theology." *Wesleyan Theological Journal* 7 (1972) 47–59. Edited version reprinted in *Wesleyan Theological Journal* 38 (2003) 217–29.

———. *Wholeness in Christ: Toward a Biblical Theology of Holiness*. Kansas City: Beacon Hill, 1998.

Green, Joel B. *Body, Soul and Human Life: The Nature of Humanity in the Bible*. Milton Keynes, UK: Paternoster, 2008.

———. "Living as Exiles: The Church in the Diaspora in I Peter." In *Holiness and Ecclesiology in the New Testament*, edited by Kent E. Brower and Andy Johnson, 311–25. Grand Rapids: Eerdmans, 2007.

———. *What About the Soul? Neuroscience and Christian Anthropology*. Nashville, TN: Abingdon, 2004.

Gundry, Stanley N., editor. *Five Views on Sanctification*. Grand Rapids, Zondervan, 1987.

Gunter, W. Stephen. *The Limits of "Love Divine."* Nashville, TN: Kingswood, 1989.

———. "Personal and Spiritual Knowledge: Kindred Spirits in Polanyian and Wesleyan Epistemology." *Wesleyan Theological Journal* 35 (2000) 130–48.

Gunter, W. Stephen, et al. *Wesley and the Quadrilateral: Renewing the Conversation.* Nashville, TN: Abingdon, 1997.

Gunton, Colin E. *The Actuality of the Atonement: A Study of Metaphor, Rationality and the Christian Tradition.* Edinburgh: T. & T. Clark, 1988.

Hägg, Henny Fiskå. *Clement of Alexandria and the Beginnings of Christian Apophaticism.* Oxford: Oxford University Press, 2006.

Hagner, Donald A. "Holiness and Ecclesiology: The Church in Matthew." In *Holiness and Ecclesiology in the New Testament,* edited by Kent E. Brower and Andy Johnson, 40–56. Grand Rapids: Eerdmans, 2007.

Hampson, Daphne. "The Challenge of Feminism to Christianity." *Theology* 88 (1985) 341–50.

———. *Theology and Feminism.* Oxford: Blackwell, 1990.

Hanson, R. P. C. *The Attractiveness of God: Essays in Christian Doctrine.* London: SPCK, 1973.

Hardy, Edward R., editor. *Christology of the Later Fathers.* Philadelphia: Westminster, 1954.

Hauerwas, Stanley. *Character and the Christian Life: A Study in Theological Ethics.* San Antonio, TX: Trinity University Press, 1975.

———. *Sanctify Them in the Truth: Holiness Exemplified.* Nashville, TN: Abingdon, 1998.

Heath, Elaine A. *Naked Faith: The Mystical Theology of Phoebe Palmer.* Eugene, OR: Pickwick, 2009.

Hegre, T. A. *The Cross and Sanctification.* Minneapolis: Bethany Fellowship, 1960.

Hilton, Walter. *The Ladder of Perfection.* Translated by Leo Shirley-Price. London: Penguin, 1957.

Hodgson, Leonard. *The Doctrine of the Trinity.* 1943. Reprint. New York: Scribners, 1944.

Hoffmann, Bengt. *The Theologia Germanica of Martin Luther.* New York: Paulist, 1980.

Holmes, Michael W. *The Apostolic Fathers: Greek Texts and English Translations.* 3d ed. Grand Rapids: Baker, 2007.

Holmes, Stephen. *The Holy Trinity: Understanding God's Life.* Milton Keynes, UK: Paternoster, 2012.

Howard, Dick. *So Who's Perfect? A Candid Look at Our Humanness.* Kansas City: Beacon Hill, 1985.

Howard, Richard E. *Newness of Life: A Study in the Thought of Paul.* Kansas City: Beacon Hill, 1975.

Hyde, Michael J. *Perfection: Coming to Terms with Being Human.* Waco, TX: Baylor University Press, 2010.

Isaacs, Marie. *The Concept of Spirit.* London: Heythrop Monographs, 1976.

Jansen, John Frederick. *Calvin's Doctrine of the Work of Christ.* London: Clark, 1956.

Jenson, Matt. *The Gravity of Sin: Augustine, Luther and Barth on* homo incurvatus in se. London: T. & T. Clark, 2006.

Jeremias, Joachim. *The Prayers of Jesus,* London: SCM, 1967.

Jones, Scott J. *John Wesley's Conception and Use of Scripture.* Nashville, TN: Kingswood, 1995.

———. "The Rule of Scripture." In *Wesley and the Quadrilateral: Renewing the Conversation,* edited by Stephen W. Gunter et al., 39–61. Nashville, TN: Abingdon, 1997.

Kärkäinen, Veli-Matti. *One with God: Salvation and Deification and Justification.* Collegeville, MN: Unitas, 2004.

Keck, Leander E. "What Makes Romans Tick?" In *Pauline Theology III, Romans,* edited by David M. Hay and E. Elizabeth Johnson, 3–29. Minneapolis: Fortress, 1995.

Keen, Craig. "The Transgression of the Integrity of God." In *The Transgression of the Integrity of God: Essays and Addresses,* 3–32. Eugene, OR: Cascade, 2012.

Kelly, J. N. D. *Early Christian Doctrines.* 4th ed. London: Black, 1968.

Kierkegaard, Søren. *Purity of Heart is to Will One Thing.* London: Fontana, 1961.

Kimborough, S. T., Jr. *Charles Wesley: Poet and Theologian.* Nashville, TN: Kingswood, 1992.

———. *The Lyrical Theology of Charles Wesley.* A Reader. Eugene, Or: Wipf and Stock, 2011.

Knight, Henry H. *The Presence of God in the Christian Life: John Wesley and the Means of Grace.* Metuchen, NJ: Scarecrow, 1992.

———. "The Transformation of the Heart: The Place of Conversion in John Wesley's Theology." In *Conversion in the Wesleyan Tradition,* edited by Kenneth J. Collins and John H. Tyson, 43–55. Nashville, TN: Abingdon, 2001.

LaCugna, Catherine Mowry. *God For Us: The Trinity and Christian Life.* San Francisco: HarperCollins, 1973.

Lamont, Daniel. *Christ and the World of Thought.* Edinburgh: T. & T. Clark, 1934.

Lane, Anthony N. S. *The Unseen World: Christian Reflections on Angels, Demons and the Heavenly Realm.* Grand Rapids: Baker, 1996.

Langford, Thomas. *Practical Divinity: Theology in the Wesleyan Tradition.* 2 vols. Nashville, TN: Abingdon, 1983, 1988.

Leclerc, Diane. *Discovering Christian Holiness: The Heart of Wesleyan-Holiness Theology.* Kansas City: Beacon Hill, 2010.

———. *Singleness of Heart: Gender, Sin and Holiness in Historical Perspective.* Metuchen, NJ: Scarecrow, 2001.

Leclercq, Jean, OSB. "Introduction." In *Bernard of Clairvaux: Selected Works,* edited by G. R. Evans, 13–57. New York: Paulist, 1987.

Lee, Hoo-Jung, "Experiencing the Spirit in Wesley and Macarius." In *Rethinking Wesley's Theology for Contemporary Methodism,* edited by Randy L. Maddox, 197–212. Nashville: Abingdon, 1998.

Leupp, Roderick T. *Knowing the Name of God: A Trinitarian Tapestry of Grace, Faith and Community.* Downers Grove, IL: InterVarsity, 1996.

———. *The Renewal of Trinitarian Theology: Themes, Patterns and Explorations.* Downers Grove, IL: InterVarsity, 2008.

Lewis, C. S. *The Four Loves.* London: Bles, 1960.

Lindström, Harald. *Wesley and Sanctification.* London: Epworth, 1950.

Lloyd, Gareth. *Charles Wesley and the Struggle for Methodist Identity.* Oxford: Oxford University Press. 2007.

Long, D. Stephen. *John Wesley's Moral Theology.* Nashville, TN: Kingswood, 2005.

Lowery, Kevin Twain. *Salvaging Wesley's Agenda: A New Paradigm for Wesleyan Virtue Ethics.* Eugene, OR: Pickwick, 2008.

Lowry, C. *The Trinity and Christian Devotion.* New York: Harper, 1946.

Luckman, Harriet A. "Basil of Caesarea and Purity of Heart." In *Purity of Heart in Early Ascetic and Monastic Literature,* edited by Harriet A. Luckman and Linda Kulzer, 89–106. Collegeville, MN: Liturgical, 1999.

Macmurray, John. *Persons in Relation.* London: Faber & Faber, 1961.

———. *The Self as Agent.* London: Faber & Faber, 1957.

Maddox, Randy, editor. *Aldersgate Reconsidered.* Nashville, TN: Kingswood, 1990.

———. "The Enriching Role of Experience." In *Wesley and the Quadrilateral: Renewing the Conversation,* edited by Stephen W. Gunter et al., 107–27. Nashville, TN: Abingdon, 1997.

———. *Responsible Grace: John Wesley's Practical Theology.* Nashville, TN: Kingswood, 1994.

———. *Rethinking Wesley's Theology for Contemporary Methodism.* Nashville: Abingdon, 1998.

Maloney, George. "Introduction to Pseudo-Macarius." *The Fifty Spiritual Homilies and the Great Letter.* Classics of Western Spirituality. New York: Paulist, 1992.

Mannermaa, Tuomo. "Why is Luther so Fascinating? Modern Finnish Luther Research." In *Union with Christ: The New Finnish Interpretation of Luther,* edited by Carl E. Braaten and Robert W. Jenson, 1–20. Grand Rapids: Eerdmans, 1998.

Marshall, I. Howard. "Holiness in the Book of Acts." *Holiness and Ecclesiology in the New Testament,* edited by Kent E. Brower and Andy Johnson, 114–28. Grand Rapids: Eerdmans, 2007.

May, Gerald G. *Addiction and Grace: Love and Spirituality in the Healing of Addictions.* San Francisco: HarperCollins, 1988.

McCall, Thomas H. *Which Trinity? Whose Monotheism? Philosophical and Systematic Theologians on the Metaphysics of Trinitarian Theology.* Grand Rapids: Eerdmans, 2010.

McCormick, Kelly Steve. "John Wesley's Use of John Chrysostom on the Christian Life: Faith Filled with the Energy of Love." PhD thesis, Drew University, 1983.

McEwan, David B. *Wesley as a Pastoral Theologian.* Studies in Evangelical History and Thought. Milton Keynes, UK: Paternoster, 2011.

McFadyen, Alistair. *Bound to Sin: Abuse, Holocaust and the Christian Doctrine of Sin.* Cambridge: Cambridge University Press, 2000.

McFarlane, Graham. *Christ and the Spirit: The Doctrine of the Incarnation according to Edward Irving.* Carlisle, UK: Paternoster, 1996.

McGonigle, Herbert B. *Scriptural Holiness: The Wesleyan Distinctive.* Ilkeston, UK: The Flame Trust, 1995.

———. *Sufficient Saving Grace: John Wesley's Evangelical Arminianism.* Studies in Evangelical History and Thought. Carlisle, UK: Paternoster, 2001.

McGrath, Alister. *Christianity's Dangerous Idea.* New York: HarperCollins, 2007.

———. "The Moral Theory of the Atonement: An Historical and Theological Critique." *Scottish Journal of Theology* 38 (1985) 205–20.

McGuckin, John. *Saint Cyril of Alexandria and the Christological Controversy.* Crestwood, NY: St Vladimir's, 2004.

———. "The Strategic Adaptation of Deification in the Cappadocians." In *Partakers of the Divine Nature: The History and Development of Deification in the Christian Tradition,* edited by Michael J. Christensen and Jeffery A. Wittung, 95–114. Grand Rapids: Baker, 2007.

McIntyre, John. *The Shape of Soteriology.* Edinburgh: T. & T. Clark, 1992.

McLeod Campbell, John. *The Nature of the Atonement.* [1856]. Reprint, with a new introduction by J. B. Torrance. Edinburgh: Handsel, 1996.

Meeks, Douglas. *Trinity, Community and Power: Mapping Trajectories in Wesleyan Theology.* Nashville, TN: Kingswood, 2000.

Metz, Donald S. *Studies in Biblical Holiness.* Kansas City: Beacon Hill, 1971.

Miles, Rebekah. "The Instrumental Role of Reason." In *Wesley and the Quadrilateral: Renewing the Conversation,* edited by Stephen W. Gunter et al., 77–106. Nashville, TN: Abingdon, 1997.

Moltmann, Jürgen. *The Trinity and the Kingdom of God.* [1980]. Translated by Margaret Kohl. London SCM, 1981.

Murphy, Nancey. *Bodies and Souls, or Spirited Bodies?* Cambridge: Cambridge University Press, 2006.

Nash, R. H. *The Light of the Mind: St Augustine's Theory of Knowledge.* Lexington, KY: University of Kentucky Press, 1969.

Niebuhr, Reinhold. *The Nature and Destiny of Man.* 2 vols. London: Nisbet: 1941, 1943.

Niesel, Wilhelm. *The Theology of Calvin.* Translated by Harold Knight. London: Lutterworth, 1956.

Noble, Thomas A. "The Doctrine of Original Sin in the Evangelical Reformers." *European Explorations in Christian Holiness* 2 (2002) 70–87.

———. "East and West in the Theology of John Wesley." *Bulletin of the John Rylands University Library of Manchester* 85.2 & 3 (2003) 359–72.

———. "Eschatology in the Church Fathers." In *What Are We Waiting For? Christian Hope and Contemporary Culture,* edited by Russell Hook and Steve Holmes, 63–74. Milton Keynes, UK: Paternoster, 2008.

———. "John Wesley as a Theologian: An Introduction." *Evangelical Quarterly* 82 (2010) 238–57.

———. "The Mission of the Holy Trinity." In *Missio Dei: A Wesleyan Understanding,* edited by Keith Schwanz and Joseph Coleson, 77–84. Kansas City: Beacon Hill, 2011.

———. "Original Sin and the Fall: Definitions and a Proposal." In *Darwin, Creation and the Fall: Theological Challenges,* edited by R. J. Berry and T. A. Noble, 99–129. Nottingham, UK: InterVarsity, 2009.

———. "Our Knowledge of God according to John Calvin." *Evangelical Quarterly* 54 (1982) 2–13.

———. "*Prolegomena* for a Conference on Original Sin." *European Explorations in Christian Holiness* 2 (2001) 6–18.

———. "Scripture and Experience," *A Pathway into the Holy Scripture,* edited by Philip E. Satterthwaite and David F. Wright, 277–96. Grand Rapids: Eerdmans, 1994.

———. "'To Serve the Present Age': Authentic Wesleyan Theology Today." *Wesleyan Theological Journal* 46 (2011) 73–89.

Nolen-Hoeksema, Susan, et al.. *Atkinson & Hilgard's Introduction to Psychology.* 15th ed. Andover, UK: Cengage Learning EMEA, 2009.

Nygren, Anders. *Agape and Eros: A Study of the Christian Idea of Love.* 3 vols. Translated by A. G. Hebert. London: SPCK, 1932, 1938, 1939.

Oakes, Peter. "Made Holy by the Holy Spirit: Holiness and Ecclesiology in Romans." In *Holiness and Ecclesiology in the New Testament,* edited by Kent E. Brower and Andy Johnson, 167–83. Grand Rapids: Eerdmans, 2007.

O'Brien, Glen. "A Trinitarian Revisioning of the Wesleyan Doctrine of Christian Perfection." *Aldersgate Papers* 2 (2001) 17–68.

Oord, Thomas Jay, and Michael Lodahl. *Relational Holiness: Responding to the Call of Love*. Kansas City: Beacon Hill, 2005.

Orr, James. *The Progress of Dogma*. London: Hodder and Stoughton, 1908.

Osborne, Grant R. *The Hermeneutical Spiral: A Comprehensive Introduction to Biblical Interpretation*. Downers Grove, IL: InterVarsity, 1991.

Oswalt, John N. *Called to Be Holy: A Biblical Perspective*. Nappanee, IN: Evangel, 1999.

Otis, Brooks. "The Throne and the Mountain: An Essay on St Gregory Nazianzus [sic]." *Classical Journal* 56 (1961) 146–64.

Otto, Rudolf. *The Idea of the Holy*. [1917]. Translated by John W. Harvey. Oxford: Oxford University Press, 1923.

Outler, Albert C. *John Wesley*. Oxford: Oxford University Press, 1964.

———. "The Wesleyan Quadrilateral in John Wesley." *Wesleyan Theological Journal* 20 (1985) 7–18.

Overduin, Jacob, *Searching for Holiness: A Comparison of Holiness in the Dutch Reformation and the Wesleyan Experience*, private circulation, 2012.

Packer, J. I. *A Passion for Holiness/Rediscovering Holiness*. Ann Arbor, MI: Servant, 1992.

Passmore, John. *The Perfectibility of Man*. 3d ed. Indianapolis: Liberty Fund, 2000.

Perkins, Harold William. *The Doctrine of Christian or Evangelical Perfection*. London: Epworth, 1927.

Peterson, David. *Possessed by God: A New Testament Theology of Sanctification and Holiness*. Leicester, UK: Apollos, 1995

Phillips, J. B. *Your God is Too Small*. London: Epworth, 1952.

Polanyi, Michael. *Personal Knowledge: Towards a Post-Critical Philosophy*. London: Routledge & Kegan Paul, 1958.

Pope, William Burt. *A Compendium of Christian Theology*. 3 vols. London: Wesleyan Conference Office, 1879.

Powell, Samuel M. *Participating in God: Creation and Trinity*. Minneapolis: Augsburg Fortress, 2003.

———. *A Theology of Christian Spirituality*. Nashville, TN: Abingdon, 2005.

———. *The Trinity in German Thought*. Cambridge: Cambridge University Press, 2001.

Przywara, Eric. *An Augustine Synthesis*. London: Sheed and Ward, 1936.

Purkiser, W. T. *The Biblical Foundations*. Vol. 1 of *Exploring Christian Holiness*. Kansas City: Beacon Hill, 1983.

Rack, Henry. *Reasonable Enthusiast: John Wesley and the Rise of Methodism*. Philadelphia: Trinity, 1989.

Rahner, Karl. *The Trinity*. London: Burns and Oates, 1970.

Rainey, David. "John Wesley's Doctrine of Salvation in Relation to His Doctrine of God." PhD thesis, King's College London, 2006.

Rashdall, Hastings. *The Idea of Atonement in Christian Theology*. London: Macmillan, 1919.

Redemption Hymnal. 2d ed. Eastbourne, UK: Victory, 1954.

Robinson, Armitage, translator. *Irenaeus: Demonstration of the Apostolic Preaching*. London: SPCK, 1920.

Rodes, Stanley J. "'From Faith to Faith': An Examination of the Servant-Son Metaphor in John Wesley's Theological Thought." PhD thesis, University of Manchester, 2011.

————. *From Faith to Faith: John Wesley's Covenant Theology and the Way of Salvation.* Eugene, OR: Wipf and Stock, 2013.

Rossall, Judith A. "God's Activity and the Believer's Experience in the Theology of John Calvin." PhD thesis, Durham University, 1991.

Rousseau, Philip. *Basil of Caesarea.* Berkeley: University of California Press, 1994.

Rowell, Geoffrey, Kenneth Stevenson, and Rowan Williams. *Love's Redeeming Work: The Anglican Quest for Holiness.* Oxford: Oxford University Press, 2001.

Rupp, Gordon. *Principalities and Powers.* London: Epworth, 1952.

————. *The Righteousness of God.* London: Hodder & Stoughton, 1953.

Russell, Norman. *Cyril of Alexandria.* New York: Routledge, 2000.

Ryle, J. C. *Holiness.* London: Clarke, 1877.

Sanders, E. P. *Judaism: Practice and Belief 63BCE–66CE.* London: SCM, 1992.

Sangster, W. E. *The Path to Perfection.* 1943. Reprint. London: Epworth, 1957.

————. *The Pure in Heart.* Epworth, 1954.

Schaff, Philip. *The Creeds of Christendom.* Revised by David S. Schaff. Grand Rapids: Baker, 1993.

Schweitzer, E. "σάρξ." In *TDNT* 7:98–151.

Sellers, R. V. *Two Ancient Christologies.* London: SPCK, 1940.

Siddals, Ruth M. "Logic and Christology in Cyril of Alexandria." *Journal of Theological Studies* 38 (1987) 341–67.

Smail, Tom. *The Giving Gift: The Holy Spirit in Person.* London: Hodder and Stoughton, 1988.

Smith, Timothy L., "John Wesley and the Wholeness of Scripture." *Preacher's Magazine*, June/July/August 1986, 12–15.

Srawley, J. H. "St. Gregory of Nyssa on the Sinlessness of Christ." *Journal of Theological Studies* 7 (1906) 434–41.

Staples, Rob L. *Outward Sign and Inward Grace: The Place of the Sacraments in Wesleyan Spirituality.* Kansas City: Beacon Hill, 1991.

Steele, Richard B. *"Gracious Affection" and "True Virtue" according to Jonathan Edwards and John Wesley.* Metuchen, NJ: Scarecrow, 1994.

Stuhlmacher, Peter. *Paul's Letter to the Romans: A Commentary.* Louisville, KY: Westminster/ John Knox, 1994.

Sunberg, Carla. "The Cappadocian Mothers: Deification Exemplified in the Writings of Basil, Gregory and Gregory." PhD thesis, University of Manchester, 2012.

Taylor, Richard S. *A Right Conception of Sin.* Kansas City: Beacon Hill, 1945.

————. *The Theological Formation.* Vol. 3 of *Exploring Christian Holiness.* Kansas City: Beacon Hill, 1985.

Telford, John, editor. *The Letters of John Wesley.* Vol. 4. London: Epworth, 1931.

Thiselton, Anthony C. "Flesh." In *NIDNTT* 1:671–82.

————. *The Two Horizons.* Exeter, UK: Paternoster, 1980.

Thomas, Gordon J. "The Perfection of Christ and the Perfecting of Believers in Hebrews." In *Holiness and Ecclesiology in the New Testament*, edited by Kent E. Brower and Andy Johnson, 293–310. Grand Rapids: Eerdmans, 2007.

Thompson, Andrew C. "Outler's Quadrilateral, Moral Psychology, and Theological Reflection in the Wesleyan Tradition." *Wesleyan Theological Journal* 46 (2011) 49–72.

Thomson, Robert W, translator. *Athanasius, Contra Gentes and De Incarnatione.* Oxford: Clarendon, 1971.

Tidball, Derek. *The Message of Holiness*. Nottingham, UK: Inter-Varsity, 2010.

Toon, Peter. *Justification and Sanctification*. London: Marshall, Morgan and Scott, 1983.

Torrance, Alan J. *Persons in Communion: An Essay on Trinitarian Description and Human Participation*. Edinburgh: T. & T. Clark, 1996.

Torrance, James B. *Worship, Community, and the Triune God of Grace*. Carlisle, UK: Paternoster, 1996.

Torrance, T. F. *Atonement*. Milton Keynes, 2009.

———. *The Christian Doctrine of God*. Edinburgh: T. & T. Clark, 1996.

———. *God and Rationality*. London: Oxford University Press, 1971.

———. *The Hermeneutics of John Calvin*. Edinburgh: Scottish Academic Press, 1988.

———. *Incarnation*. Milton Keynes, 2008.

———. *The Mediation of Christ*. Edinburgh, 1992.

———. *Theological Science*. 1969. Reprint. Oxford: Oxford University Press, 1996.

Tripp, David. "Methodism's Trinitarian Hymnody: A Sampling, 1780 and 1989, and Some Questions." *Quarterly Review* 14 (1994) 359–85.

Truesdale, Al. "Reification of the Experience of Entire Sanctification in the American Holiness Movement." *Wesleyan Theological Journal* 31 (1996) 95–119.

Tyson, John H. *Charles Wesley on Sanctification*. Grand Rapids: Asbury, 1986.

———. "John Wesley's Conversion at Aldersgate." In *Conversion in the Wesleyan Tradition*, edited by Kenneth J. Collins and John H. Tyson, 27–42. Nashville, TN: Abingdon, 2001.

Ury, M. William. "A Wesleyan Concept of 'Person.'" *Wesleyan Theological Journal* 38:2 (2003) 30–56.

Vickers, Jason E. "'And We the Life of God Shall Know': Incarnation and the Trinity in Charles Wesley's Hymns." *Anglican Theological Review* 90 (2008) 329–44.

———. *Invocation and Assent: The Making and Remaking of Trinitarian Theology*. Grand Rapids: Eerdmans, 2008.

Volf, Miroslav. *After Our Likeness: The Church as the Image of the Trinity*. Grand Rapids: Eerdmans, 1998.

Wainwright, Geoffrey. *Doxology: The Praise of God in Worship, Doctrine, and Life*. London, Epworth, 1980.

———. *Eucharist and Eschatology*. London: Epworth, 1971.

———. "Trinitarian Theology and Wesleyan Holiness." In *Orthodox and Wesleyan Spirituality*, edited by S. T. Kimborough, 59–80. Crestwood, NY: St Vladimir's, 2002.

———. "Why Wesley was a Trinitarian." *The Drew Gateway* 59.2 (1990) 26–43.

Wallace, R. S. *Calvin's Doctrine of the Christian Life*. Edinburgh: Oliver and Boyd, 1959.

Walters, John Robert. "Perfection in New Testament Theology." PhD thesis, Oxford, 1985.

———. *Perfection in New Testament Theology: Theology, Ethics and Eschatology in Relational Dynamic*. Oxford: Oxford University Press, 1986.

Watson, Philip. *Let God be God!: An Interpretation of the Theology of Martin Luther*. London: Epworth, 1947.

Webster, John. *Holiness*. London: SCM, 2003.

Weinandy, Thomas G. "Cyril and the Mystery of the Incarnation." In *The Theology of Cyril of Alexandria: A Critical Appreciation*, edited by Thomas G. Weinandy and Daniel A. Keating, 23–54. London: T. & T. Clark, 2003.

———. *In the Likeness of Sinful Flesh: An Essay on the Humanity of Christ*. Edinburgh: T. & T. Clark, 1993.

Welch, Claude. *In This Name: The Doctrine of the Trinity in Contemporary Theology.* New York: Scribners, 1952.

Wesley, Charles. *Hymns for the Nativity of Our Lord*. Madison, NJ: The Charles Wesley Society, 1991.

———. *Hymns on the Trinity*. Madison, NJ: The Charles Wesley Society, 1998

———. *Short Hymns on Select Passages of the Holy Scriptures*. London: printed by G. Paramore, 1794.

Wesley, John. *Letters*, Vol. IV. Edited by Thomas Telford. London: Epworth, 1931.

Wiley, H. Orton. *Christian Theology*. 3 vols. Kansas City: Beacon Hill, 1940–43.

Williams, N. P. *The Ideas of the Fall and of Original Sin*. London: Longmans, 1927.

Williams, Rowan. "*De Trinitate*." In *Augustine through the Ages: An Encyclopedia*, edited by Allan D. Fitzgerald, 845–51. Grand Rapids: Eerdmans, 1999.

Wink, Walter. *Engaging the Powers*. Philadelphia: Fortress, 1992.

———. *Naming the Powers*. Philadelphia: Fortress, 1984.

———. *Unmasking the Powers*. Philadelphia: Fortress, 1986.

Winslow, D. F. *The Dynamics of Salvation: A Study in Gregory of Nazianzus*. Cambridge, MA: Philadelphia Patristic Foundation: 1979.

Wolff, Hans Walter. *Anthropology of the Old Testament*. London: SCM, 1974.

Wood, Laurence W. *The Meaning of Pentecost in Early Methodism: Rediscovering John Fletcher as John Wesley's Vindicator and Designated Successor*. Lanham, MD: Scarecrow, 2002.

Wood, A. Skevington. *Love Excluding Sin: Wesley's Doctrine of Sanctification*. Stoke-on-Trent, UK: The Wesley Fellowship, 1986.

Wright, N. T. *The Resurrection of the Son of God*. Minneapolis: Fortress, 2003.

———. "Romans and the Theology of Paul." In *Pauline Theology III, Romans*, edited by David M. Hay and E. Elizabeth Johnson, 30–67. Minneapolis: Fortress, 1995.

Wynkoop, Mildred Bangs. *A Theology of Love: The Dynamic of Wesleyanism*. Kansas City: Beacon Hill, 1972.

Zizioulas, John T. *Being as Communion: Studies in Personhood and the Church*. Crestwood, NY: St Vladimir's, 1985.

Index of Names

CPSIA information can be obtained at www.ICGtesting.com
Printed in the USA
LVOW05s2358260514

387206LV00004B/4/P